Expatriate Managers

T0383129

This book reveals important insights into the complexities and realities of the lives and works of international managers and their families. Based on rigorous academic research, it provides a "close-up and personal" picture of the realities of managing in a global world.

—Susanne Tietze, *University of Keele, UK*

Since the 1990s, economic and cultural globalization has propelled the transnational mobility of managers and fueled cross-border careers. Some scholars have argued for the emergence of a new global business elite with cosmopolitan mindsets and homogeneous lifestyles, whereas others have highlighted their disconnection from the local surroundings and their everyday life within national expatriate 'bubbles.' Thus the question of whether today's mobile professionals can be described as interculturally open and competent cosmopolitans, or as pronounced anti-cosmopolitans, is still unanswered.

Expatriate Managers: The Paradoxes of Living and Working Abroad considers a core protagonist of economic globalization and the management of multinational corporations (MNCs) through the lens of a practice-based theoretical approach while seeking to address this question. It builds on intensive ethnographic case studies of expatriate managers, most of them high-ranking executives, from two comparatively different home countries, the U.S. and Germany. These managers, together with their families, have been assigned to China, Germany, or the U.S. to perform demanding coordination tasks within their MNCs. Based on detailed accounts of expatriate managers' experiences and everyday practices, the book reveals the multiple and sometimes paradoxical ways in which they deal with cultural differences as they build up new forms of working, belonging, and dwelling.

The findings suggest that the newly emerging mindsets and lifestyles of expatriate managers transcend the polarized images of mobile elites as either cosmopolitan 'global managers' or parochial anti-cosmopolitans. *Expatriate Managers: The Paradoxes of Living and Working Abroad* examines the global elite from an everyday perspective, showing that understanding the dynamics of a global economy requires probing into the lifeworlds, agency, and everyday arrangements of the social actors who are putting globalization into practice.

Ursula Mense-Petermann is a Professor at Bielefeld University, Germany.

Anna Spiegel is a Postdoctoral Researcher at Bielefeld University, Germany.

Bastian Bredenkötter is a Doctoral Researcher at Bielefeld University, Germany.

Routledge Studies in International Business and the World Economy

For a full list of titles in this series, visit www.routledge.com/Routledge-Studies-in-International-Business-and-the-World-Economy/book-series/SE0358

62 **The Nature of the Firm in the Oil Industry**
International Oil Companies in Global Business
Basak Beyazay-Odemis

63 **Sustainable Management Development in Africa**
Building Capabilities to Serve African Organizations
Edited by Hamid H. Kazeroony, Yvonne du Plessis, and Bill Buenar Puplampu

64 **Global Mindsets**
Exploration and Perspectives
Edited by John Kuada

65 **Management and Organizations in Transitional China**
Yanlong Zhang and Lisa A. Keister

66 **Global Advertising Practice in a Borderless World**
Edited by Linda Brennan and Robert Crawford

67 **Social and Solidarity Economy**
The World's Economy with a Social Face
Sara Calvo, Andres Morales, Video Edited by Yanni Zikidis

68 **Managing Culture and Interspace in Cross-border Investments**
Building a Global Company
Edited by Martina Fuchs, Sebastian Henn, Martin Franz, and Ram Mudambi

69 **Venture Capital and Firm Performance**
The Korean Experience in a Global Perspective
Jaeho Lee

70 **Expatriate Managers**
The Paradoxes of Living and Working Abroad
Anna Spiegel, Ursula Mense-Petermann, and Bastian Bredenkötter

Expatriate Managers
The Paradoxes of Living
and Working Abroad

Anna Spiegel, Ursula Mense-Petermann,
and Bastian Bredenkötter

Routledge
Taylor & Francis Group

LONDON AND NEW YORK

First published 2018
by Routledge

2 Park Square, Milton Park, Abingdon, Oxfordshire OX14 4RN
52 Vanderbilt Avenue, New York, NY 10017

Routledge is an imprint of the Taylor & Francis Group, an informa business

First issued in paperback 2019

Library of Congress Cataloging-in-Publication Data
Names: Spiegel, Anna, author. | Mense-Petermann, Ursula, author. |
     Bredenkèotter, Bastian, author.
Title: Expatriate managers : the paradoxes of living and working
     abroad / by Anna Spiegel, Ursula Mense-Petermann, and Bastian
     Bredenkèotter.
Description: New York : Routledge, 2017. | Includes index.
Identifiers: LCCN 2017020232 | ISBN 9781138190214 (hardback) |
     ISBN 9781315641218 (ebook)
Subjects: LCSH: Employment in foreign countries. | Executives—
     Employment—Foreign countries.
Classification: LCC HF5382.55 .S65 2017 | DDC 658.4/095—dc23
LC record available at https://lccn.loc.gov/2017020232

ISBN: 978-1-138-19021-4 (hbk)
ISBN: 978-0-367-87673-9 (pbk)

Typeset in Sabon
by Apex CoVantage, LLC

Contents

Acknowledgments   vii

1 Introduction   1
ANNA SPIEGEL AND URSULA MENSE-PETERMANN

PART I
Embedding the Expatriate Manager   17

2 Working in Transnational Social Spaces: Expatriate Managers in
  Transnationally Integrated MNCs   19
URSULA MENSE-PETERMANN

3 Expatriate Managers as Boundary Spanners in MNCs   41
BASTIAN BREDENKÖTTER

4 Cosmopolitans or Parochial Anti-Cosmopolitans? Expatriate
  Managers' Resources, Social Positions, and Orientations   55
ANNA SPIEGEL AND URSULA MENSE-PETERMANN

PART II
Negotiating Difference in the Private Sphere   83

5 Difference, Spatiality, and Sociability in the Everyday Life of
  Expatriate Managers   85
ANNA SPIEGEL

6 Gendered Mobilities, Gendered Cosmopolitanism:
  Male and Female Expatriate Managers and Their
  Accompanying Spouses   105
ANNA SPIEGEL

PART III
Negotiating Difference in the Professional Sphere   135

 7 Role-Taking and Role-Making: Expatriates as Creative
    Organizational Boundary Spanners in MNCs   137
    BASTIAN BREDENKÖTTER

 8 Expatriate Managers as Cosmopolitan Professionals? Dealing
    with Difference at the Workplace   159
    ANNA SPIEGEL

PART IV
Comparative Perspectives and Conclusion   179

 9 Host Country Effects? How Host Locality Properties
    Impact Practiced Cosmopolitanism   181
    URSULA MENSE-PETERMANN

10 Conclusion: The Paradoxes of Practiced
    Elite Cosmopolitanism   215
    ANNA SPIEGEL

    Appendix   235
    Index   237

Acknowledgments

This book is the result of intensive ethnographic research into the lifeworlds of expatriate managers during their assignments on three continents. It is also the result of intensive teamwork over a period of four years, and it would not have been possible without the dedication and commitment of all the team members and institutions supporting our research.

The book builds on research carried out in the project "Expatriate Managers: A New Cosmopolitan Elite? Habitus, Everyday Practices and Networks" (ME 2008/5–1). We thank the German Research Foundation for funding our research project and the Institute for World Society Studies of the Faculty of Sociology at Bielefeld University for hosting it.

We want to thank our colleagues Junchen Yan, Kathleen M. Park, and Dellvin Williams, who participated in fieldwork as members of 'mixed researcher teams' and to whom we owe important observations and insights into the phenomena under investigation, as well as our cooperation partners Ruth Ayaß and Gert Schmidt for inspiring project discussions. We are especially grateful to Tomke König, Irene Skovgaard Smith, Julia Büchele, and Johanna Stadlbauer, who engaged us in inspiring and eye-opening debates during joint workshops.

We are also very much obliged to thank those who supported us in processing and putting together all our data, thoughts, and initial texts into one coherent book. We thank Franziska Richter, Leonie Buschkamp, and Annette Heinze, who supported our work by transcribing interview records and field protocols. Special thanks go to Florian Poppen, who edited the book chapters and streamlined the whole manuscript with admirable precision, speed, and reliability, and to Holly Patch, who imaginatively translated the interview passages quoted in this book in a way that kept the 'tone' of what had originally been said, rigorously proofread the whole book manuscript, and helped us to make our English less German.

But most importantly, we have to thank our research participants, who trusted us and welcomed us into their lives, their homes, and their companies. Without them, the research would not have been possible.

And last but not least, we want to thank our beloved partners and families, who were unwavering in their support. Their patience and optimism provided the foundation for this book.

Bielefeld, April 2017
Anna Spiegel, Ursula Mense-Petermann,
and Bastian Bredenkötter

1 Introduction

Anna Spiegel and Ursula Mense-Petermann

This book puts a social figure center stage who has increasingly become an object of attention whenever questions of economic globalization, increasing transnational mobility, and questions of elite formation at a global scale are discussed: *the expatriate manager.*

Expatriate managers are assigned to foreign subsidiaries of multinational corporations (MNCs) for a limited period of time.[1] Hence, they are transnationally mobile professionals, and they display transnational careers. Instead of only being interested in the mobility and career patterns of expatriates, however, scholars from different disciplinary backgrounds have ascribed a primary role to expatriates in economic globalization, discussing them as protagonists of the fluid, flexible, and mobile modernity. They are considered to be the core connectors and integrators of the transnational networks of modern MNCs, to feature paradigmatic forms of (hyper)mobility, and to form a transnational elite class 'in-itself' and 'for-itself.' Hence, the expatriate manager emerges as *the* actor who puts globalization into practice.

As such eminent actors, expatriate managers have been addressed from a series of different perspectives and portray the 'star role' in different bodies of literature. In the dominant part of the expatriate literature—namely, the International Business (IB) and management literature—the expatriate manager emerges as an interculturally knowledgeable "boundary spanner" (Au and Fukuda 2002; Mense-Petermann 2006; Park and Mense-Petermann 2014) and "culture carrier" (Björkman and Lu 2001). Expatriates are said to play an important part in implementing global programs, distributing best practices, bringing into line the organizational cultures of headquarters and their globally spread subsidiaries, and, thus, in furthering the global integration of MNCs (Black, Gregersen, and Mendenhall 1992; Kanter 1995). Moreover, expatriates are expected to acquire a wide and deep range of knowledge which can help organizations to better understand and manage culturally diverse and changing conditions in a world that requires both global awareness and local sensitivity (Berthoin 2001, 62). They are described as being able to meet these expectations because they are cosmopolitans who are "comfortable in many places and able to understand and bridge the differences among them" (Kanter 1995, 23). The image that is invoked by such contributions from the IB and management literature, however, tends to be that of a heroic manager—even though the same literature asserts a high rate of failure and premature returns by expatriates.

Yet the literature has not only addressed expatriate managers in their role as boundary spanners and culture carriers in MNCs but also as protagonists of a newly emerging global elite: a "transnational capitalist class" (Sklair 2001; Robinson 2012; McKenna, Ravishankar, and Weir 2015) or "world class" (Kanter 1995; see also Frank 2007; Rothkopf 2009). Hence, expatriate managers are not only considered important actors for the management of MNCs but also—in a wider politico-economic perspective—as the main actors propelling economic globalization at large and the emergence of a transnationally integrated elite class on a global scale. And as a class 'in-itself' and 'for-itself,' they are also said to be connected with one another by transnational networks, to share homogeneous lifestyles, and to have common mindsets and orientations—namely, cosmopolitan ones.

Hence, both of these strands of literature explicitly or implicitly stress *cosmopolitanism* as a prime characteristic of expatriates helping them to successfully act as "global integrators" (Kanter 1995) and to build up powerful transnational networks. Thus, far from only formulating cosmopolitanism as a necessary management prerequisite, this perspective depicts cosmopolitanism as an already achieved quality of globally active managers.

In yet another body of literature, studies with a sociological, social anthropological, or social geographical background, a completely different picture of the expatriate is painted: These studies—mainly investigating the nonprofessional lifeworlds and everyday practices of expatriates—claim that expatriates have strong anti-cosmopolitan orientations, which are perpetuated in nationally homogeneous 'expat bubbles' (Fechter 2007). Here, the view is held that elite forms of mobility and dwelling strongly advance parochial, home country–bound orientations. This view, however, leaves open the question of how expatriate managers, as parochial anti-cosmopolitans, manage to play their role as boundary spanners in MNCs successfully. Thus, the question of whether today's mobile managers can be described as interculturally open and competent cosmopolitans or as pronounced anti-cosmopolitans remains unanswered.

How is it possible that such contradictory images regarding expatriates' cosmopolitanism emerge? We suggest that this is a result of three main shortcomings of the existing body of expatriate literature.[2]

First of all, the mentioned strands of literature only focus on one side of expatriate life: Whereas the IB, management, and global business elite literature concentrates on the professional sphere and discusses expatriates' tasks, resources, privileges, and networks as being intrinsic to their professional positions and jobs, the sociological, social anthropological, and social geographic literature mainly focuses on the non-work sphere of expatriate life and investigates residential decisions and dwelling practices, leisure spaces, urban spaces, urban mobility practices, and the private sociabilities emerging in these spaces. These bodies of literature thereby systematically neglect the ways in which professional performance and working practices, on the one hand, and everyday life in the non-work environment, on the other, are related to one another. We argue, however, that professional and nonprofessional lifeworlds of expatriate managers are deeply entangled and any understanding of expatriate managers' working practices and professional dispositions inevitably needs to take into account these multifaceted and, in part, paradoxical entanglements. Second, these strands of literature implicitly suggest that transnational mobility and a privileged position in the global economy automatically induce the development of either cosmopolitan or parochial dispositions. What is missing here is an analysis of the processes through which the disposal over privileges, material and symbolic resources, and mobile lifestyles translate into specific orientations and practices. And last but not least, most of the literature referred to above is prescriptive in character and is built on "thin descriptions" (Geertz, 1973), only. In our study, we have therefore applied an ethnographic approach to expatriates' lifeworlds, orientations, and practices.

Against this background, the aims of this book are as follows:

- to deliver "thick descriptions" (ibid.) of and in-depth insights into expatriate managers' lifeworlds and orientations;
- to theorize emerging orientations and practices of expatriate managers that transcend the polarized images of mobile elites as cosmopolitan 'global managers,' on the one hand, and as parochial anti-cosmopolitans living in hermetically sealed 'bubbles,' on the other;
- to highlight the paradoxical character of expatriate managers' cosmopolitanism.

In order to do so, this book builds on empirical research carried out by the authors along with other colleagues[3] during the past four years. It is based on intensive ethnographic case studies of expatriate managers. The ethnographic case studies not only took expatriates' agency at work into account but also shed light on their social positions and self-positioning and their everyday life within the societal context of their host localities.

In the remainder of this introduction, we will elaborate on our main theoretical concepts: practiced cosmopolitanism, MNCs as transnational social spaces, and social practices. We will also inform the reader on the ethnographic approach applied in our study and give an overview of the structure of the book.

Theorizing Corporate Expatriate Cosmopolitanism

In this subchapter, we introduce our theoretical approach to accounting for and understanding expatriate cosmopolitanism and anti-cosmopolitanism, respectively. Although we position our own approach within the debate by discussing the relevant literature more extensively in Part I of this book, we will now provide a brief introduction of the core theoretical categories informing our analysis.

Practiced Cosmopolitanism

This book is about *practiced cosmopolitanism* (Nowicka and Rovisco 2009a) of corporate expatriates. We build on an understanding of cosmopolitanism as a specific mode of managing meaning (Hannerz 1990, 247) characterized by a general openness and curiosity toward the cultural Other[4] as well as respect and enjoyment of cultural differences (Szerszynski and Urry 2002; Beck 2009; Kendall, Woodward, and Skrbiš 2009). This understanding of cosmopolitanism is mainly inspired by the work of the anthropologist Ulf Hannerz, who defined cosmopolitanism as "an orientation, a willingness to engage with the other" and as "an intellectual and aesthetic openness toward divergent cultural experiences, a search for contrast rather than uniformity" (Hannerz 1990, 239). What we emphasize with the term "practiced cosmopolitanism" is that it is not enough to solely focus on cosmopolitanism as a "cultural disposition" (Szerszynski and Urry 2002, 468), a "subjective outlook" (Kendall, Woodward, and Skrbiš 2009, 13), an orientation, or a "mindset" (Tan, Ng, and Ang 2011), but that it is always necessary to take into account *how* such dispositions, orientations, mindsets, and outlooks are enacted and put into practice in everyday life. Hannerz already emphasized that cosmopolitanism needs to be put into 'practice' at the everyday level by integrating and combining different culturally rooted practices and meanings. He also emphasized that the way this integration and combination would most likely be acquired would be through participating rather than through sheer observational modes of action (Hannerz 1990, 241). Still, his initial concept of cosmopolitanism as a general openness to the cultural Other seems too vague and not tangible enough empirically (see Vertovec and Cohen 2002; Nowicka and Rovisco 2009a, 2011b). There have been various attempts to sharpen the concept of cosmopolitanism and to integrate the level of social practices. Three of these attempts to develop a more focused concept of cosmopolitanism were constitutive for writing this book.

First, it is necessary to complement the aesthetic dimension of cosmopolitanism with the dimension of social relations. This idea has been formulated most convincingly by Glick Schiller and colleagues, who understand cosmopolitanism solely in terms of interactions, participation, and shared "*sociabilities*" (Glick Schiller, Darieva, and Gruner-Domic 2011). They suggest understanding cosmopolitanism as a specific pattern of "sociability practices"—namely, practices establishing "social relations of inclusiveness and openness to the world" (ibid., 402). Cosmopolitanism is, then, a specific way of conceiving of and at the same time constructing cultural Otherness and of interacting with the Other. Second, several studies researched cosmopolitanism with a focus on the *spatiality* of everyday life and everyday practices related to these spaces. For example, in her study on construction workers in London, Datta analyzes "cosmopolitanism as spatial—where forms and degrees of openness to others are shaped by localized spatial contexts where encounters with others take place" (Datta 2009, 355). Rovisco and Nowicka have emphasized the need to research lived cosmopolitanism "in the micro-scale of everyday life interactions in concrete settings and places" (Rovisco and Nowicka 2011a, 2). Cosmopolitanism is then related to specific spatial practices of dealing with Others. Third, we argue, cosmopolitanism needs to be understood as a specific form of *belonging* that is the process of establishing emotionally charged attachments to social or spatial locations (Lovell 1998; Yuval-Davis 2006; Pfaff-Czarnecka 2011, 2012). Cosmopolitanism is then related to forms of multiple belonging with fragmented, multilayered, and malleable relations and attachments toward multiple objects, places, and cultural practices.

These three shifts reinforce Beck's perspective on cosmopolitanism as being related to a "new kind of space-time experience and of human sociability" (Beck 2002, 30). Seeing cosmopolitanism as a specific form of sociability being enacted in concrete spatial practices—be it local or translocal—and related to specific forms of multiple and flexible belonging links it to the sphere of everyday life, highlights the possible junctures and disjunctures between orientations and practices, and thus opens up the concept for empirical research.

MNCs as Transnational Social Spaces

In this book, we concentrate on *corporate* expatriates for whom the MNC constitutes the main institution shaping their working and living abroad. At the same time, the MNC is the organizational context in which expatriate managers' dealing with difference in the professional sphere takes place. We conceive of MNCs as *transnational social spaces* (Morgan 2001a, 2001b; Dörrenbächer 2007). What is new about this way of thinking about MNCs is, first, a conceptualization of MNCs as *social spaces*.[5] Being rooted in the framework of social constructivism (Berger and Luckmann 1967), the concept of social space (Bourdieu 1985; Massey 1994; McDowell 1999; Lachenmann 2010) highlights that all structures and meaning are products of continuous interactions among social agents who simultaneously create and rely on structures. Being constituted by human agency, social space is thus inherently dynamic, relational, and process-like in character, and intimately linked to actors' identity politics and sense-making. Applying the social space approach to the study of organizations in general and MNCs in particular is to conceive of organizational processes and structures as the result of agency and everyday practices of various actors within an organization and thus to emphasize the negotiated character of power relations and organizational structures, identities, and cultures within the MNC (Geppert and Clark 2003; Dörrenbächer 2007). The social space approach also takes social practices within MNCs to be intimately linked to actors' identity politics, material arrangements, and interpretive schemes (Dörrenbächer 2007).

Moreover, our approach offers a *transnational* perspective on MNCs (Pries 2001b, 2001a; Geppert and Clark 2003; Dörrenbächer 2007). It emphasizes the specific spatiality and socio-cultural dynamics that social spaces take under conditions of increased global connectivity. Developed in the context of migration and globalization studies, the notion of transnational social spaces highlights the fact that under conditions of heightened mobility and connectivity, the lived experiences, networks, and identities of people transcend the physical borders of the nation state. And it argues that these transnational experiences, networks, and identities are not ephemeral and transitory, but that they create relatively permanent social formations beyond the clearly demarcated territories of single nation states (Glick Schiller 1992; Glick Schiller, Basch, and Blanc-Szanton 1992; Pries 2001a, 2001b). This implies that social practices not only need to be analyzed within the immediate territory of their occurrence but also within the wider spatial frames of their social relevance. Seeing MNCs as transnational social spaces posits that "MNCs are basically understood as plurilocal entities formed by multiple and complex social relationships" and that these entities are created "through continued and structured interaction between actors that belong to different organizational units" (Dörrenbächer 2007, 322).

However, what is specific about MNCs is that they need to be conceived of as both organizational transnational social spaces themselves and as creating other related transnational social spaces in the sphere of the everyday life—namely, expatriate communities. To sum up, the analysis of MNCs as *transnational social spaces* allows for investigating the everyday practices of specific actors within these spaces and of *how* globalization and boundary spanning is 'done' at the interactional level by these actors. We consider expatriate managers to be key actors in these processes.

Social Practices and Agency

Both our ways of thinking about cosmopolitanism as 'practiced cosmopolitanism' and of MNCs as transnational social spaces are based on the fundamentals of sociological social practice theories, such as structuration theory (Giddens 1984), the concept of habitus (Bourdieu 1985), and theories of the social construction of reality (Berger and Luckmann 1967). Social practice theories emanate from the idea that the social is fundamentally constituted by routinized practices by individual social actors and, thus, put human agency at the center of their attention. However, they go beyond individualist approaches, as they highlight the entanglement of structures and agency. Instead of conceiving of social actors in isolation, social practice theories see actors as embedded in symbolic and material contexts and as involved in constant negotiations with other actors. They, therefore, see agency and practices as produced by social structure but at the same time as creatively producing the latter. Giddens posits,

> The basic domain of study of the social sciences, according to the theory of structuration, is neither the experience of the individual actor, nor the existence of any form of societal totality, but social practices ordered across space and time.
>
> (Giddens 1984, 2)

Following this practice theoretical approach and its idea of structured and structuring agency, regarding expatriate managers' agency in the professional sphere, we focus on how individual agency derives from specific organizational settings on the one hand, and how on the other hand, it reconfigures the organization through the actions of key actors to "impose, negotiate, resist, accept or oppose certain rules of the game" (Dörrenbächer and Geppert 2006). Additionally, with regard to their agency in the non-work sphere, we ask how expatriate managers make use of the resources and privileges they have at their disposal thanks to MNCs' 'expatriate packages' (see Chapter 4), what kind of agency they develop, and how they negotiate their institutionally framed elite position on an everyday level. With this focus on the everyday lifeworlds of expatriate managers, we go beyond the analysis of how the elite status of expatriate managers is institutionally constituted and highlight the ambivalent interplay of institutional formation of elite positions and the everyday negotiations of such social positions. We thus see practiced cosmopolitanism as negotiated in these complex interplays of structure and agency.

An Ethnographic Approach to Corporate Expatriates' Lifeworlds

At the methodological level, the aim of this book is to contribute to the endeavor of further theorizing the concept of cosmopolitanism with ethnographically inspired research, as has been demanded by a diversity of authors (Kendall, Woodward, and Skrbiš 2009; Nowicka and Rovisco 2009b; Glick Schiller, Darieva, and Gruner-Domic 2011; Rovisco and Nowicka 2011a). As Kendall et al. put it, "Our understanding of cosmopolitanism should not be constructed from a series of imaginary, utopian or ideal types; the fluidity and complexity of cosmopolitanism is only likely to be revealed by the study of mundane reality" (2009, 17).

For studying the mundane reality of corporate expatriates, we applied an ethnographic approach (Marcus 1998; Hammersley and Atkinson 2007). Ethnography is a relatively new approach in the study on expatriates, specifically on their professional practices as boundary spanners, as most qualitative research available today about expatriates on assignments is based almost exclusively on interview research (see, however, Yagi and Kleinberg 2011; Ybema and Byun 2011). Interview research, however, is always focused on specific topics and is based on the representation provided by the interviewees themselves. Contrastingly, a constitutive factor of ethnography is the differentiation between explicit knowledge, which can be accessed through discourse, and tacit knowledge, which cannot be explicated and only becomes manifest in the form of acquired intuition, trust, and practical knowledge. Consequently, ethnography assumes that the knowledge of social actors is visible in their practices and in their skills of implementing rules, or as Bettina Heintz puts it, "We know more than we know to express" (Heintz 2000, 175). A main aim of ethnography is, thus, to generate deep insights into the actors' lifeworlds—that is, to probe into their individual horizons of meaning and interpretation from an 'inside' perspective *and* to (re)construct practices within their specific social contexts (Yin 1984; Hollstein 2011).

Our specific ethnographic approach to the (hyper)mobile professional and private lifeworlds of expatriate managers has been inspired by what has been coined "multi-sited ethnography" (Marcus 1995; Falzon 2009), "globography" (Hendry 2003), "mobile methods" (Büscher and Urry 2009; Büscher, Urry, and Witchger 2011), or "focused ethnography" (Knoblauch 2005). Our focused ethnography concentrated on a particular, pre-defined section of the lifeworlds under observation (Knoblauch 2001, 125)—namely, the corporate expatriates' *sociabilities*, *spatialities*, and forms of *belonging*, as developed in the preceding subchapter. The periods we spent in the field were shorter than is typically the case for classical ethnographic research. The visits to the expatriates in our sample usually lasted two to five days. The research was data-intensive and analysis-intensive (rather than experience-intensive, as is the case with conventional ethnography). We applied complex methods (Lachenmann 2008), oscillating between proximity and distance, between communication and observation. First, we applied methods that focused rather on the explicit knowledge stocks of the corporate managers. We carried out semi-structured interviews with the managers, and if possible with their partners, about their professional and nonprofessional everyday life on their assignments. Visualizations of their social networks, which research participants created and explained during the interview, played an important role (Hollstein 2011; Scheibelhofer 2011). Second, we applied methods that aimed to discover tacit knowledge. In the professional spaces, we carried out 'job shadowings' (Czarniawska-Joerges 2007; Jirón 2008);[6] we followed and observed the managers for a couple of days, joining meetings and sitting next to the managers while they were doing office work. And third, we applied methods that combined observation and communication. On everyday "go-alongs" (Kusenbach 2003), the researchers accompanied research participants while they were engaged in leisure activities, such as shopping, going to parties, exercising, and dining. During the job shadowings and go-alongs, the researchers also conducted theoretically informed everyday conversations with the expatriates, with colleagues and subordinates, and with families and friends whenever possible.

The research was conducted by 'mixed research teams' in terms of the nationality of the researchers. A mixed team consisted of one researcher originating from the same home country as the expatriate and one researcher originating from the host country.[7] This mixed team approach played a major role in strengthening the validity of our findings (Erickson and Stull 1998; Burawoy et al. 2000; Gerstl-Pepin and Gunzenhauser 2002; Lachenmann 2008; Matsutake Worlds Research Group 2009).

Interviews and conversations were, when possible, recorded with the consent of the research participants; when this was not possible, they were objectified in the form of memory protocols. Observations were recorded in detailed field notes and observation protocols. For analysis, the audio files were transcribed, and all materials were later coded with the help of ATLAS.ti. Elements of Grounded Theory were used to analyze the data (Strauss and Corbin 1990; Charmaz 2006). On the basis of data analysis, we developed ideal-typical cases (Weber 1949; Kelle and Kluge 2010) for presenting modes of dealing with difference. The emphasis of this ethnographic approach was thus not on representativeness backed up by a huge number of cases, but on *theoretical generalization* on the basis of a detailed extrapolation of typical logics and rationalities in our in-depth case studies.[8]

In total, we carried out 29 case studies. Most of the expatriate managers in our sample were high-ranking executives. They held positions ranging from lower and middle management positions as group or department heads in the regional headquarters of large MNCs to higher management positions as general managers of MNC production units and top management positions sitting on boards of large Chinese or U.S. subsidiaries of the MNCs. Following a comparative research design, we included expatriate managers from two different home countries—German managers and U.S.-American managers—who were assigned to three different host countries—China, Germany, and the U.S.—in our sample. The host countries where chosen based on the idea that they significantly differed in the everyday discourses on cultural differences between home country and host country.[9] In addition to these case studies, we carried out seven expert interviews with members of the global mobility divisions either at the headquarters or at the local subsidiary of the expatriates' employer MNCs.

Structure of the Book

This book aims at exploring expatriate managers' practiced cosmopolitanism in the professional and in the non-work spheres, and at highlighting the paradoxical character of their cosmopolitanism. To develop our main arguments, the book is divided into four parts.

In Part I, we set the scene for our empirical analyses of expatriate managers' professional and everyday lifeworlds by critically discussing several bodies of literature, each of which focuses on a specific aspect of expatriates' working and living abroad. Building on this discussion, we develop our analytical framework for the empirical reconstructions presented in Parts II and III.

The chapters of Part II are dedicated to the empirically grounded analysis of expatriates' everyday life and dealing with difference *in the non-work sphere*. Drawing on our ethnographic case studies, we focus on the question of how expatriate managers negotiate difference in their private everyday spaces, the urban space, and their homes. Part II, thus, offers a differentiated, empirically grounded picture of the emerging paradoxes of the orientations and everyday practices of expatriate managers and their families in the private sphere.

Part III analyzes how expatriates negotiate difference *in the professional sphere* by focusing on everyday management practices within the MNC. The chapters of this part explore expatriates' role-making as boundary spanners and reconstruct their dealing with differences at the workplace.

Finally, Part IV summarizes the empirical findings in a comparative and synthesizing perspective. In a first step, we systematically investigate and compare the impact of different host countries and host localities on expatriates' modes of dealing with difference. Finally, we conclude by proposing a typology of 'paradoxical cosmopolitanisms'—a concept that highlights the ambivalent and self-contradictory quality of expatriate managers' practiced cosmopolitanism in the varying spheres of their professional and everyday lives.

Notes

1 In this book, we concentrate on corporate expatriates—i.e., we focus on managers who have been assigned by headquarters to foreign subsidiaries. However, due to idiosyncrasies in sampling, some managers in our sample are not expatriates in this narrow sense, but 'impatriates', i.e., managers employed in a foreign subsidiary of an MNC who have been delegated to headquarters for a limited period of time, or so-called local hires, i.e., managers with the MNC home-country nationality, who, however, have already lived in the host country for a longer period of time and had been hired there by the subsidiary. See the appendix for more details on the expatriates in our sample.

2 We will give a detailed discussion of the relevant literature in Part I of this book.

3 In addition to the three authors of this book, the research team consisted of Ruth Ayaß, Kathleen M. Park, Gert Schmidt, Dellvin Williams, and Junchen Yan.

4 The Other and the related concept of Othering are basic concepts for highlighting the importance of binary identity constructions within processes of defining collective identities. They are specifically used by post-colonial theorists to describe the symbolic and material processes by which the West has defined non-Western peoples as different and inferior to the West and thus legitimized Western dominance over non-Western peoples (Said 2003).

5 The concept of social space had been introduced in sociology as an alternative to the long-established concept of 'society', which had been criticized for being too

static and unable to grasp social change and for its methodological nationalism (for detailed critiques on methodological nationalism, see Pries 2005; Amelina et al. 2012).

6 In searching for an adequate term that would resonate with the rationality of our specific field, we translated the term 'ethnography' or 'participant observation' into the term 'job shadowing', a term that is used for describing a specific training technique for new employees by observing an experienced employee.

7 In addition to the authors, Kathleen M. Park, Dellvin Williams, and Junchen Yan participated in fieldwork as part of these mixed teams.

8 Such qualitative studies working with smaller samples and focused on in-depth case studies can be the basis for theoretical advancement. This position of developing empirically grounded contributions to theoretical debates has been scrutinized very prominently within the framework of Grounded Theory (Glaser and Strauss 1967; Charmaz 2001, 2006). The method of constant comparison of cases, codes, and prior studies constitutes the basis for the development of theses and arguments, which are generalizable on a theoretical level beyond the individual case. Such ethnographic case studies are able to deliver 'thick' knowledge on global processes, actors, and themes, and on the micro-dynamics of 'doing globalization'. In that sense, our book is a 'global ethnography' (Burawoy et al. 2000) on the lifeworlds of mobile professionals, focusing on their lived experiences of globalization to which "the ethnographer has a privileged insight" (Burawoy 2000, 4).

9 For further details regarding our sample, see the appendix.

Bibliography

Amelina, Anna, Devrimsel Nergiz, Thomas Faist, and Nina Glick Schiller, eds. 2012. *Beyond Methodological Nationalism: Research Methodologies for Cross-Border Studies*. London: Routledge.

Au, Kevin Y., and John Fukuda. 2002. "Boundary Spanning Behaviors of Expatriates." *Journal of World Business* 37 (4): 285–96. doi:10.1016/S1090-9516(02)00095-0.

Beck, Ulrich. 2002. "The Cosmopolitan Society and Its Enemies." *Theory, Culture & Society* 19 (1–2): 17–44. doi:10.1177/0263276402019001.01.

Beck, Ulrich. 2009. "Mobility and the Cosmopolitan Perspective." In *Tracing Mobilities: Towards a Cosmopolitan Perspective*, edited by Weert Canzler, Vincent Kaufmann, and Sven Kesselring, 25–35. Farnham, Burlington: Ashgate.

Berger, Peter L., and Thomas Luckmann. 1967. *The Social Construction of Reality: A Treatise in the Sociology of Knowledge*. Garden City, New York: Doubleday.

Berthoin, Ariane. 2001. "Expatriates' Contributions to Organizational Learning." *Journal of General Management* 26 (4): 62–84. doi: 10.1177/030630700102600405

Björkman, Ingmar, and Yuan Lu. 2001. "Institutionalization and Bargaining Power Explanations of HRM Practices in International Joint Ventures: The Case of Chinese-Western Joint Ventures." *Organization Studies* 22 (3): 491–512. doi:10.1177/0170840601223005.

Black, J. Stewart, Hal B. Gregersen, and Mark E. Mendenhall. 1992. *Global Assignments: Successfully Expatriating and Repatriating International Managers*. San Francisco: Jossey-Bass.

Bourdieu, Pierre. 1985. "The Social Space and the Genesis of Groups." *Theory and Society* 14 (6): 723–44. doi:10.1177/053901885024002001

Burawoy, Michael. 2000. "Introduction: Reaching for the Global." In *Global Ethnography: Forces Connections and Imaginations in a Postmodern World*, edited by Michael Burawoy, Joseph A. Blum, Sheba George, Lynne Haney, Maren

Klawiter, Stephen H. Lopez, Seán Ó Riain, and Millie Thayer, 1–40. Berkeley: University of California Press.

Burawoy, Michael, Joseph A. Blum, Sheba George, Lynne Haney, Maren Klawiter, Stephen H. Lopez, Seán Ó Riain, and Millie Thayer, eds. 2000. *Global Ethnography: Forces Connections and Imaginations in a Postmodern World*. Berkeley: University of California Press.

Büscher, Monika, and John Urry. 2009. "Mobile Methods and the Empirical." *European Journal of Social Theory* 12 (1): 99–116. doi:10.1177/1368431008099642.

Büscher, Monika, John Urry, and Katian Witchger. 2011. *Mobile Methods*. London and New York: Routledge.

Charmaz, Kathy. 2001. "Grounded Theory." In *Contemporary Field Research: Perspectives and Formulations*, edited by Robert M. Emerson, 335–52. Prospect Heights, IL: Waveland Press.

Charmaz, Kathy. 2006. *Constructing Grounded Theory: A Practical Guide Through Qualitative Analysis*. London: Sage.

Czarniawska-Joerges, Barbara. 2007. *Shadowing: And Other Techniques for Doing Fieldwork in Modern Societies*. Malmö, Copenhagen: Liber/CBS Press

Datta, Ayona. 2009. "Places of Everyday Cosmopolitanisms: East European Construction Workers in London." *Environment and Planning A* 41 (2): 353–70. doi:10.1068/a40211.

Dörrenbächer, Christoph. 2007. "Inside the Transnational Social Space: Cross-Border Management and Owner Relationship in a German Subsidiary in Hungary." *Journal for East European Management Studies* 12 (4): 318–39. doi:10.1688/1862-0019_jeems_2007_04_doerrenbaecher

Dörrenbächer, Christoph, and Mike Geppert. 2006. "Micro-Politics and Conflicts in Multinational Corporations: Current Debates, Re-Framing, and Contributions of This Special Issue." *Journal of International Management* 12 (3): 251–65. doi:10.1016/j.intman.2006.07.001.

Erickson, Ken C., and Donald D. Stull. 1998. *Doing Team Ethnography: Warnings and Advice*. Thousand Oaks: Sage.

Falzon, Mark-Anthony, ed. 2009. *Multi-Sited Ethnography: Theory, Praxis and Locality in Contemporary Research*. Farnham, Burlington: Ashgate.

Fechter, Anne-Meike. 2007. *Transnational Lives: Expatriates in Indonesia*. Aldershot, Burlington: Ashgate.

Frank, Robert L. 2007. *Richistan: A Journey Through the 21st Century Wealth Boom and the Lives of the New Rich*. London: Piatkus.

Geertz, Clifford. 1973. *The Interpretation of Cultures: Selected Essays*. New York: Basic Books.

Geppert, Mike, and Ed Clark. 2003. "Knowledge and Learning in Transnational Ventures: An Actor-Centred Approach." *Management Decision* 41 (5): 433–42. doi:10.1108/00251740310479287.

Gerstl-Pepin, Cynthia I., and Michael G. Gunzenhauser. 2002. "Collaborative Team Ethnography and the Paradoxes of Interpretation." *International Journal of Qualitative Studies in Education* 15 (2): 137–54. doi:10.1080/09518390110111884.

Giddens, Anthony. 1984. *The Constitution of Society: Introduction of the Theory of Structuration*. Berkeley: University of California Press.

Glaser, Barney G., and Anselm L. Strauss. 1967. *The Discovery of Grounded Theory: Strategies for Qualitative Research*. Chicago: Aldine Pub. Co.

Glick Schiller, Nina, ed. 1992. *Towards a Transnational Perspective on Migration: Race, Class, Ethnicity, and Nationalism Reconsidered.* New York: New York Academy of Sciences.

Glick Schiller, Nina, Linda Basch, and Cristina Blanc-Szanton. 1992. "Transnationalism: A New Analytic Framework for Understanding Migration." *Annals of the New York Academy of Sciences* 645 (1): 1–24. doi:10.1111/j.1749-6632.1992.tb33484.x.

Glick Schiller, Nina, Tsypylma Darieva, and Sandra Gruner-Domic. 2011. "Defining Cosmopolitan Sociability in a Transnational Age: An Introduction." *Ethnic and Racial Studies* 34 (3): 399–418. doi:10.1080/01419870.2011.533781.

Hammersley, Martyn, and Paul Atkinson. 2007. *Ethnography: Principles in Practice,* London: Routledge.

Hannerz, Ulf. 1990. "Cosmopolitans and Locals in World Culture." In *Global Culture: Nationalism, Globalization and Modernity: A Theory, Culture & Society Special Issue,* edited by Mike Featherstone, 237–51. London, Newbury Park, and New Delhi: Sage.

Heintz, Bettina. 2000. *Die Innenwelt der Mathematik: Zur Kultur und Praxis einer beweisenden Disziplin.* Wien, New York: Springer.

Hendry, Joy. 2003. "An Ethnographer in the Global Arena: Globography Perhaps?" *Global Networks* 3 (4): 497–512. doi:10.1111/1471-0374.00074.

Hollstein, Betina. 2011. "Qualitative Approaches." In *Sage Handbook of Social Network Analysis,* edited by John Scott and Peter J. Carrington, 404–17. London and New Delhi: Sage.

Jirón, Paola. 2011. "On becoming 'la sombra/the shadow'." In *Mobile Methods,* edited by Monika Büscher, John Urry, and Katian Witchger, 36–53. London and New York: Routledge.

Kanter, Rosabeth M. 1995. *World Class: Thriving Locally in the Global Economy.* New York: Simon & Schuster.

Kelle, Udo, and Susann Kluge. 2010. *Vom Einzelfall zum Typus: Fallvergleich und Fallkontrastierung in der qualitativen Sozialforschung.* Wiesbaden: VS Verlag für Sozialwissenschaften.

Kendall, Gavin, Ian Woodward, and Zlatko Skrbiš. 2009. *The Sociology of Cosmopolitanism: Globalization, Identity, Culture and Government.* London: Palgrave Macmillan UK.

Knoblauch, Hubert. 2001. "Fokussierte Ethnographie: Soziologie, Ethnologie und die neue Welle der Ethnographie." *Sozialer Sinn* 2001 (1): 123–41.

Knoblauch, Hubert. 2005. "Focused Ethnography." Forum Qualitative sozialforschung/Forum: Qualitative Social Research 6 (3): 1–14. Art. 44

Kusenbach, Margarethe. 2003. "Street Phenomenology: The Go-Along as Ethnographic Research Tool." *Ethnography* 4 (3): 455–85. doi:10.1177/146613810343007.

Lachenmann, Gudrun. 2008. "Researching Translocal Gendered Spaces: Methodological Challenges." In *Negotiating Development in Muslim Societies: Gendered Spaces and Translocal Connections,* edited by Gudrun Lachenmann and Petra Dannecker. Lanham: Lexington Books.

Lachenmann, Gudrun. 2010. "Globalisation in the Making: Translocal Gendered Spaces in Muslim Societies." In *Translocality: The Study of Globalising Processes from a Southern Perspective,* edited by Ulrike Freitag and Achim von Oppen, 335–67. Leiden: Brill.

Lovell, Nadia, ed. 1998. *Locality and Belonging*. London: Routledge.

Marcus, George E. 1995. "Ethnography in/of the World System: The Emergence of Multi-Sited Ethnography." *Annual Review of Anthropology* 24: 95. doi: 10.1146/annurev.an.24.100195.000523

Marcus, George E. 1998. *Ethnography Through Thick and Thin*. Princeton: Princeton University Press.

Massey, Doreen. 1994. *Space, Place and Gender*. Cambridge: Polity Press.

Matsutake Worlds Research Group. 2009. "Strong Collaboration as a Method for Multi-Sited Ethnography." In *Multi-Sited Ethnography: Theory, Praxis and Locality in Contemporary Research*, edited by Mark-Anthony Falzon, 197–214. Farnham, Burlington: Ashgate.

McDowell, Linda. 1999. *Gender, Identity & Place: Understanding Feminist Geographies*. Minneapolis: University of Minnesota Press.

McKenna, Steve, Mayasandra-Nagaraja Ravishankar, and David Weir. 2015. "Critical Perspectives on the Globally Mobile Professional and Managerial Class." *Critical Perspectives on International Business* 11 (2): 118–21. doi:10.1108/cpoib-10-2014-0043.

Mense-Petermann, Ursula. 2006. "Transnationalisierung als glokale Restrukturation von Organisationsgrenzen." In *Transnationale Konzerne: Ein neuer Organisationstyp?* edited by Ursula Mense-Petermann and Gabriele Wagner, 63–84. Wiesbaden: VS Verlag für Sozialwissenschaften.

Morgan, Glenn. 2001a. "The Multinational Firm: Organizing Across Institutional and National Divides." In *The Multinational Firm: Organizing Across Institutional and National Divides*, edited by Glenn Morgan, Peer H. Kristensen, and Richard Whitley, 1–24. Oxford: Oxford University Press.

Morgan, Glenn. 2001b. "Transnational Communities and Business Systems." *Global Networks* 1 (2): 113–30. doi:10.1111/1471-0374.00008.

Nowicka, Magdalena, and Maria Rovisco, eds. 2009a. *Cosmopolitanism in Practice*. Aldershot, Burlington: Ashgate.

Nowicka, Magdalena, and Maria Rovisco. 2009b. "Introduction: Making Sense of Cosmopolitanism." In *Cosmopolitanism in Practice*, edited by Magdalena Nowicka and Maria Rovisco, 1–16. Aldershot, Burlington: Ashgate.

Park, Kathleen, and Ursula Mense-Petermann. 2014. "Managing Across Borders: Global Integration and Knowledge Exchange in MNCs." *Competition & Change* 18 (3): 265–79. doi:10.1179/1024529414Z.00000000060.

Pfaff-Czarnecka, Joanna. 2011. "From 'Identity' to 'Belonging' in Social Research: Plurality, Social Boundaries, and the Politics of the Self." Working Paper No. 368. Bielefeld: Faculty of Sociology, Bielefeld University.

Pfaff-Czarnecka, Joanna. 2012. *Zugehörigkeit in der mobilen Welt: Politiken der Verortung*. Göttingen: Wallstein.

Pries, Ludger, ed. 2001a. *New Transnational Social Spaces: International Migration and Transnational Companies in the Early Twenty-First Century*. London: Routledge.

Pries, Ludger. 2001b. "The Approach of Transnational Social Spaces: Responding to New Configurations of the Social and the Spatial." In *New Transnational Social Spaces: International Migration and Transnational Companies in the Early Twenty-First Century*, edited by Ludger Pries, 3–33. London: Routledge.

Pries, Ludger. 2005. "Configurations of Geographic and Societal Spaces: A Sociological Proposal Between 'Methodological Nationalism' and the 'Spaces of Flows.'" *Global Networks* 5 (2): 167–90. doi:10.1111/j.1471-0374.2005.00113.x

Robinson, William I. 2012. "Global Capitalism Theory and the Emergence of Transnational Elites." *Critical Sociology* 38 (3): 349–63. doi:10.1177/0896920511411592.

Rothkopf, David J. 2009. *Superclass: The Global Power Elite and the World They Are Making*. New York: Farrar Straus and Giroux.

Rovisco, Maria, and Magdalena Nowicka. 2011a. "Introduction." In *The Ashgate Research Companion to Cosmopolitanism*, edited by Maria Rovisco and Magdalena Nowicka, 1–14. Farnham, Burlington: Ashgate.

Rovisco, Maria, and Magdalena Nowicka, eds. 2011b. *The Ashgate Research Companion to Cosmopolitanism*. Farnham, Burlington: Ashgate.

Said, Edward W. 2003. *Orientalism*. London: Penguin Books.

Scheibelhofer, Elisabeth. 2011. "Potential of Qualitative Network Analysis in Migration Studies: Reflections Based on an Empirical Analysis of Young Researchers' Mobility Aspirations." *Migration Letters* 8 (2): 111–20.

Sklair, Leslie. 2001. *The Transnational Capitalist Class*. Oxford: Blackwell.

Strauss, Anselm, and Juliet Corbin. 1990. *Basics of Qualitative Research: Grounded Theory Procedures and Techniques*. Newbury Park: Sage.

Szerszynski, Bronislaw, and John Urry. 2002. "Cultures of Cosmopolitanism." *Sociological Review* 50 (4): 461–82. doi:10.1111/1467-954X.00394

Tan, Mei L., Kok-Yee Ng, and Soon Ang. 2011. "Global Cultural Capital and Cosmopolitan Human Capital: The Effects of Global Mindset and Organizational Routines on Cultural Intelligence and International Experience." In *The Oxford Handbook of Human Capital*, edited by Alan Burton-Jones, 96–119. Oxford: Oxford University Press.

Vertovec, Steven, and Robin Cohen, eds. 2002. *Conceiving Cosmopolitanism: Theory, Context, and Practice*. Oxford: Oxford University Press.

Weber, Max. 1949. *On the Methodology of the Social Sciences*. Translated and edited by Edward A. Shils and Henry A. Finch. Glencoe: Free Press.

Yagi, Noriko, and Jill Kleinberg. 2011. "Boundary Work: An Interpretive Ethnographic Perspective on Negotiating and Leveraging Cross-Cultural Identity." *Journal of International Business Studies* 42 (5): 629–53. doi:10.1057/jibs.2011.10

Ybema, Sierk, and Hyunghae Byun. 2011. "Unequal Power Relations, Identity Discourse, and Cultural Distinction Drawing in MNCs." In *Politics and Power in the Multinational Corporation: The Role of Institutions, Interests and Identities*, edited by Christoph Dörrenbächer and Mike Geppert, 315–79. Cambridge: Cambridge University Press.

Yin, Robert K. 1984. *Case Study Research: Design and Methods*. Beverly Hills and London: Sage.

Yuval-Davis, Nira. 2006. "Belonging and the Politics of Belonging." *Patterns of Prejudice* 40 (3): 197–214. doi:10.1080/00313220600769331.

Part I

Embedding the Expatriate Manager

In Part I, we set the scene for our empirical investigation into expatriate managers' professional and everyday lifeworlds by critically discussing a set of relevant bodies of literature—namely, the MNC literature, the literature on organizational boundary spanning, and the transnational elite literature.

Drawing upon the international and strategic management literature, as well as on institutionalist and micropolitical approaches to the analysis of MNCs, Chapter 2 analyzes the strategic and organizational challenges with which MNCs are confronted, and the role of expatriate managers within MNCs. We develop an understanding of the MNC as a transnational social space embracing different sorts of actors and their (potentially conflictual) interactions. In this view, expatriate managers emerge as a key sort of actors when it comes to dealing with the fundamental tensions and conflicts characterizing transnationally integrated MNCs.

Chapter 3 takes stock of the expatriate literature and especially focuses on those studies that have discussed the boundary-spanning role and capacities of expatriates. Drawing on this literature, we develop our own theoretical perspective on expatriate managers' working and management practices.

Chapter 4 critically discusses the pointed thesis of the emergence of a transnational and cosmopolitan class of "global managers" (Kanter 1995) by confronting it with a contradicting strand of the literature—namely, contributions that focus on mobile professionals as members of 'expatriate communities'—and point to parochial, ethnicity-, and nationality-based orientations and forms of belonging. A special focus is put on the global mobility policies of MNCs that shape expatriate managers' lifestyles and everyday practices to a vast extent, and constitute expatriate managers as a transitory elite oriented toward 'expatriate communities.'

Hence, Part I offers an in-depth discussion of the relevant literature, and—building on this discussion—develops our analytical framework for the case studybased empirical reconstructions presented in Parts II and III.

Bibliography

Kanter, Rosabeth M. 1995. *World class: Thriving locally in the global economy.* New York: Simon & Schuster.

2 Working in Transnational Social Spaces

Expatriate Managers in Transnationally Integrated MNCs

Ursula Mense-Petermann

Since the end of the 1980s, the numbers of MNCs, their foreign affiliates, employees, and value added have been steadily rising. In 2010, according to UNCTAD's World Investment Report (UNCTAD 2013), a number of 103,786 MNCs (2005: 77,000, UNCTAD 2007) with 892,114 foreign affiliates and 63 million employees reached a value added of $5.735 trillion U.S. dollars. The number of employees of MNCs in 2014 was estimated to have risen to 75 million, and the value added to an estimated $7.9 trillion U.S. dollars (UNCTAD, 2015).[1] Therefore, Collinson and Morgan (2009) stress that the

> rationale for their existence, their impact on societies and environments, their role in transferring technologies, people, skills and wealth across national boundaries, and their involvement in political debates places them in the centre of our experience of the modern world.
>
> (Collinson and Morgan 2009, 1)

Hence, the societal impact of MNCs and their role in economic globalization cannot be overestimated.

Besides the general societal importance of the MNC, it is also of highest importance to and has a huge impact on expatriate managers' working and living abroad. As will be elaborated on in the chapters that follow, it shapes the working conditions and spaces, the material and power resources, as well as the living conditions and dwelling spaces of expatriate managers to a vast extent. MNC structures and strategies explain if, to what extent, and for which tasks expatriate managers are employed. The existing literature on expatriation, however, has mostly "failed to analyze the relationship that exists between expatriation policies and the international strategy of the company" (Bonache, Brewster, and Suutari 2001). This is why we start our analysis of expatriate managers' experiences of working and living abroad with an analysis of the modern MNC to specify the formal and informal functions and roles that expatriate managers play within them.

Expatriate managers are assigned to a vast variety of different functional and hierarchical positions and charged with different tasks and projects on their posts. Therefore, expatriates cannot be defined by their concrete, specific functions or positions. Yet understanding how expatriate managers work and live takes more than just defining them by the fact that they have been assigned to a foreign subsidiary of their 'home' organization for a definite period of time (i.e., by contractual features). Instead, what we contend and are going to show in Part I of this book is that expatriates—no matter what functions or positions they occupy—must be understood as 'boundary spanners'; their main (latent) function is to deal with and *balance* the multidimensional *tensions* and *contradictions* that are characteristic of the modern MNC.

In this chapter, we shed light on these different sorts of tensions and contradictions confronting expatriate managers. We conceive of the modern MNC as a "transnational social space" (Morgan 2001c, 2001b)—i.e., as a structured arena in which different sorts of actors meet and negotiate order on an everyday basis. The modern MNC is structured as a differentiated network (Nohria and Ghoshal 1997) and characterized by conflicting institutional pulls due to multiple and multilayered societal embeddedness (Westney 1993; Kostova 1999; Kostova and Zaheer 1999; Kostova and Roth 2002). It is also characterized by micropolitics and conflicts occurring when different interpretive schemes, rationalities, interests, and identities meet (Dörrenbächer and Geppert 2006). Hence, in our understanding, MNCs are characterized by *"fundamental tensions* in the nature of the MNE itself" (Collinson and Morgan 2009, 13; emphasis added; see also Westney 1993). The main proposition that we put forward in this chapter is that expatriate managers are key actors when it comes to dealing with these multidimensional *tensions* and negotiating the conflicting rationalities, identities, and interests of groups of actors.

In this chapter, we reconstruct the different tensions on the basis of the theories of the MNC developed in the IB and management literature and in more sociologically oriented approaches to MNCs throughout the past decades. Drawing upon seminal contributions from a contingency-approach perspective (Bartlett and Ghoshal 1989; Nohria and Ghoshal 1997), an institutionalist perspective (Westney 1993; Kostova 1999; Kostova and Zaheer 1999; Kostova and Roth 2002), a micropolitical perspective (Forsgren, Holm, and Johanson 2005; Dörrenbächer and Geppert 2006; Geppert, Matten, and Walgenbach 2006; Geppert and Dörrenbächer 2014); and a 'transnational social space' perspective (Morgan 2001c, 2001b), we identify four different lines of tension or contradiction expatriate managers are expected to balance: (1) the *strategic* contradiction between local responsiveness and global integration of MNCs, (2) the *socio-political* tensions caused by contradicting institutional pulls, (3) *the micropolitical* conflicts caused by different interests of different sorts of managers, and (4) the tensions resulting from everyday processes of negotiating order within MNCs embracing different sorts of actors with differing *allegiance patterns, interpretive schemes, and interests.*

Expatriate managers, we argue, are at the core of these multidimensional tensions, and their main function—beyond the many different functional tasks assigned to them—is to balance these tensions.

Tensions and Contradictions in MNCs

Research on MNCs from different disciplines and strands of debate, although adopting quite different theoretical perspectives, converge in making very clear that the modern MNC cannot be conceived of as a hierarchically integrated, smoothly working, unitary organization, but is instead characterized by built-in tensions and contradictions. All of these strands maintain that it is exactly these tensions and contradictions which are key in explaining MNCs structures and strategies. Yet the different strands of MNC-related research diverge in the sorts of tensions they posit to be fundamental for the modern MNC. In the following subchapters we will discuss four different theoretical approaches to the modern MNC, each of which focuses on a specific kind of tension.

We argue that all of these approaches have their merits in stressing one specific sort of tension, but that only the "transnational social space" approach to MNCs (Morgan 2001c, 2001b) is able to grasp the multidimensional character of MNC-internal tensions, and is, thus, best suited to cater to the enormous challenges confronting expatriate managers, being the actors whose main task it is to balance those tensions.

Balancing Contradicting Strategic Goals in Transnationally Integrated MNCs

Theorizing the structures and strategies of MNCs in IB and management research dates back to the 1960s (Aharoni 1966) and 1970s (Johanson and Vahlne 1977) and has delivered a series of models explaining why, where, and how enterprises start to go international (see also Dunning 1988).[2] One of the most influential theories of the modern MNC, however, was developed in the late 1980s on the basis of the contingency approach to organizations (Bartlett and Ghoshal 1989). This approach[3] explicitly focused on context variables as determinants of MNCs structures and strategies. Christopher Bartlett and Sumantra Ghoshal (1989) argued that, until well into the 1980s, MNCs were successful when they employed a strategy that fit their respective product and industry environment and concentrated on *either* global efficiency *or* local responsiveness *or* MNC-internal knowledge transfer. Each of these alternative strategies, as long as employed consistently and fitting the respective context conditions, was able to assure success. Thus, the authors identified three different strategies and respective cross-border organizational coordination patterns: First, the *international* enterprise sets out to transfer products and capabilities that have been developed at its home base and that have proved successful in its home market to its foreign subsidiaries. Product and process innovations are implemented and established in the home country where the international enterprise has a strong market position. The know-how generated in this process is to then be transferred to the foreign sites in order to realize economies of scale. Second, the *multinational* enterprise is strategically oriented toward adapting as much as possible to the local markets and conditions of the different countries where its subsidiaries are located, and, hence, local responsiveness. To achieve this, it grants its foreign subsidiaries a high degree of autonomy with regard to its product, production, sourcing, and sales policies. In favor of the best possible acceptance in the different national markets, it neglects the advantages of global integration. Third, the *global* enterprise, to the contrary, is strategically oriented toward global integration. It produces and sells 'world products' and aims at realizing economies of scale on a global scale. For the sake of global competitiveness, it neglects local responsiveness.

Bartlett and Ghoshal (1989) posit that each of these types of coordinating border-crossing activities 'fitted' specific market and industry context conditions to a specific historical phase and was thus able to secure success. Toward the end of the 1980s, however, due to increasing global competition in all industries, context conditions changed fundamentally—and with them, the conditions for success for MNCs. This transformation lead, the authors argue, to an erosion of the one-dimensional industry-specific strategies that had dominated until then. Since then, the authors maintain, MNCs have no longer been able to rely on just one strategic alternative but have had to instead simultaneously seek to achieve global efficiency, local responsiveness, and innovative strength through transnational learning. Enterprises that employ such a multidimensional strategy are termed "transnational enterprises" (ibid.) or "differentiated networks" (Nohria and Ghoshal 1997).

The subunits of the *transnational enterprise* are not differentiated according to country-specific markets—as in the case of the multinational enterprise—or with regard to production costs—as in the case of the global enterprise. Instead, they are differentiated according to their different functions:

> The transnational centralizes some resources at home, some abroad, and distributes yet others among its many national operations. The result is a complex configuration of assets and capabilities that are distributed, yet specialized. Furthermore, the company integrates the dispersed resources through strong interdependencies.
>
> (Bartlett and Ghoshal 1989, 60)

To sum up, the *transnational* enterprise can be described as a geographically and functionally "differentiated network" (Nohria and Ghoshal 1997) without a hierarchical or geographical center. Hedlund (1986) has coined the term "heterarchy" for this organizational form.

Bartlett and Ghoshal's study of changing environmental conditions and organizational reactions comes together, however, with an evolutionary proposition that posits the transnational enterprise as a *"transnational solution"* without alternative (i.e., as the *one best way* to organize border-crossing activities today). From this perspective, the transnational enterprise no longer represents one out of several alternative coordination strategies, but instead, in a prescriptive sense, represents the solution to the competitive problems that MNCs face in the process of ongoing globalization and increasing integration of the world economy (Bartlett and Ghoshal 1989, 64). The authors, thus, neglect the difference between empirically observable changes in the strategies of MNCs and normative prescriptions for management. This is the reason why the contribution of Bartlett and Ghoshal has been discussed very critically in more sociologically oriented organization studies (see Geppert, Matten, and Walgenbach 2006; Collinson and Morgan 2009). Besides "methodological weaknesses" (Collinson and Morgan 2009, 11), they have been criticized for underlying assumptions representing an economic view of the world and neglecting "the social determinants of organizational structures, the political nature of decision-making, the irrationality of organizations, and the social construction of markets" (Morgan 2001b, 9).

Moreover, the idea of the transnational enterprise as a polycentric network or heterarchy is to be seen critically. Drawing on empirical research on restructuring processes of MNCs in the 1990s that aimed at a functional differentiation and transnational integration of the globally dispersed subsidiaries, it becomes clear that such restructuring by no means have led to polycentric network or heterachic organization, but instead in many cases meant centralization of decision making and power (Mense-Petermann 2005). This is because formerly widely autonomous subsidiaries that were oriented toward local responsiveness (as in the multinational enterprise) when integrated into a transnational network of functionally differentiated units have to meet global standards—e.g., regarding product quality (Mense-Petermann 2006). Hence, the functional differentiation and transnational integration of MNCs' globally dispersed operations go well together with strong headquarters and "ethnocentric" staffing practices of management posts in the foreign subsidiaries (Perlmutter and Heenan 1974).

These criticisms notwithstanding, Bartlett and Ghoshal's contingency-approach-based theory of the MNC is asserted to have advanced our understanding of the modern MNC, its dynamics, and especially the impact for management considerably.[4] Collinson and Morgan (2009, 11) emphasize Bartlett and Ghoshal's contribution of identifying

the potential innovative capabilities of the MNE as lying in its very internal diversity. They recognized, that this potential was difficult to achieve and could result in a breakdown of the firm into competing units. So there had to be some delicate balancing between centralization and decentralization, between integration and responsiveness. Although organization structures played a part in this, they also emphasized the importance of creating a global management culture that kept the senior management of the transnational working together and coordinating the different parts of the firm.

The merits of Bartlett and Ghoshal's contribution, hence, lie in having high-lighted the built-in contradicting rationalities and conflicting goals that are characteristic of modern MNCs. The mentioned criticisms notwithstanding, we therefore refer to this type of organization as *transnationally integrated MNCs*. By this term, we aim at stressing the tensions resulting from trans-national integration without, however, implying that transnationally inte-grated MNCs are heterarchies or polycentric networks without hierarchical center.

According to Bartlett and Ghoshal the challenge of integrating the "dif-ferentiated network" (Nohria and Ghoshal 1997) can be met by a strong corporate culture. The most important task for transnational management, therefore, is to develop a shared vision that can guide and integrate the actions of the staff (Bartlett and Ghoshal 1989, 66). This is why Bartlett and Ghoshal (1987, 52) posit that what is critical

> is not just the structure, but also the mentality of those who constitute the structure. The common thread that holds together the diverse tasks we have described is a managerial mindset that understands the need for multiple strategic capabilities, that is able to view problems from both local and global perspectives, and that accepts the importance of a flexible approach.

However, they maintain: "There is no single model for the global man-ager" (Bartlett and Ghoshal 2003, 108). Rather, they differentiate between four separate groups of managers who are equally important for the trans-national integration of MNCs: business managers, country managers, func-tional managers, and, last but not least, the top executives at corporate headquarters, "the leaders who manage the complex interactions between the three" (ibid., 102).

First, *global business or product-division managers* are responsible for furthering global-scale efficiency and competitiveness (ibid.). Second, *coun-try managers* (i.e., the heads of the national subsidiaries) have to be sen-sitive and responsive to the local market. And, what is more important, "this manager has the difficult task of conveying the importance of such intelligence to people higher up, especially those whose perceptions may be dimmed by distance or even ethnocentric bias" (ibid., 105). Hence, in trans-national enterprises, country managers cannot act as "king of the country," but are expected to translate the needs and possible contributions of their subsidiary and communicate them effectively to the parent company (ibid.).

Third, the role of *functional managers* is to "scan for specialized information worldwide, 'cross-pollinate' leading—edge knowledge and best practice, and champion innovations that may offer transnational opportunities and applications" (ibid., 107). Hence, worldwide learning is the province of the functional manager.

Thus, each of these three types of managers represents one of the three strategic capabilities Bartlett and Ghoshal (2003, 102) argue assure success in a globalizing economy: "global-scale efficiency and competitiveness; national-level responsiveness and flexibility; and cross-market capacity to leverage learning on a worldwide basis." Yet in transnational enterprises, differing and potentially conflicting perspectives of these types of managers have to be negotiated and balanced; no one perspective or type of manager is to be dominant. According to the authors, such conflicts can be resolved in negotiations (ibid., 104). Hence, fourth, it is the main task of *corporate top management* to balance "the negotiations between the three" (ibid., 108).

Note, however, that the *expatriate manager* as a specific sort of manager does not appear in the typology of Bartlett and Ghoshal. Although some of the empirical cases of functional managers Bartlett and Ghoshal refer to point to the transnational mobility of such managers, questions of cultural difference that come about with expatriation and cross-border collaboration of managers from different origins are completely neglected by the authors. Collinson and Morgan (2009, 11), therefore, criticize Bartlett and Ghoshal's approach to the management of transnational MNCs as being more "wishful thinking" than a convincing empirical assessment of observable structures and processes.

Even though Bartlett and Ghoshal do not offer a convincing answer to the question of how to meet the challenge of balancing the contradicting strategic goals within transnationally integrated MNCs, what can be derived from the 'transnational' or 'differentiated network' approach is the identification of the problem and the resulting management demands regarding coordination and integration of transnationally integrated MNCs.

Balancing Contradicting Institutional Pulls

As we have seen, the IB literature focuses on contradicting strategic goals resulting from globalized economic environments as the main features of the modern MNC. This has been criticized by scholars from the institutionalist organization studies camp as representing a simplistic "economic view of the world" (Morgan 2001b, 8) and for neglecting the societal embeddedness of MNCs.[5] Institutionalist theories of the modern MNC also point out that MNCs are characterized by built-in tensions, yet they stress a different kind of tension postulated to be characteristic of MNCs. The perspective of institutionalist organization scholars does not consider primarily *markets*, but mainly the *institutional context* of organizations to be the decisive variable in explaining MNCs' structures and strategies.[6] We share the institutionalist critique of the economistic and prescriptive character of the IB approach. In addition to the strategic contradictions discussed earlier, we deem the tensions resulting from conflicting "institutional pulls," as elaborated on by institutionalist scholars, to be a core second sort of tension characterizing MNCs.

Westney (1993) has developed such a theory of the modern MNC based on the so-called New Institutionalism in Organizational Analysis (Powell and DiMaggio 1991) that emphasizes the multiple and multilayered embeddedness of MNCs. The specifics of MNCs in comparison with enterprises that restrict their operations to their home country, from her perspective, lie in the fact that they, first, are embedded in a multiplicity of organizational fields,[7] second, change organizational fields, and third, are, therefore, subject to a plurality of and contradictory "isomorphic pulls."[8]

Most MNCs cross both national borders as well as sectoral boundaries. Their subsidiaries, therefore, are embedded in different local organizational fields. Part of these local organizational fields are political organizations (like local, regional, and national governments), professions and their organizations, and other relevant organizations in the host country, like suppliers, customers, competitors, banks, consulting firms, schools, and vocational training institutions. With an increasing number of foreign subsidiaries, the embeddedness of MNCs in different and potentially contradicting organizational fields increases, too. Thus, "Westney was able to transcend the notion that integration or responsiveness were managerial strategies and instead to locate them as *fundamental tensions* in the nature of the MNE itself" (Collinson and Morgan 2009, 13; emphasis added).

However, besides this multiple embeddedness in different local organizational fields, MNCs can also change organizational fields by stretching their boundaries; they can contribute to construct a 'global industry' in which they compete with MNCs from other home countries on a global scale, in which they employ consulting firms that are global players themselves,[9] in which they hire employees who have graduated from globalized MBA-programs,[10] and in which their operations are regulated by transnational regulating agencies (Morgan 2001a). In such a 'global industry,' the formal structures and strategies of MNCs are subject to isomorphic pulls by transnational actors and agents. Consequently, MNCs are characterized by—potentially conflictual—multiple and multilayered embeddedness in institutionalized environments.

By the same token, Kostova, along with colleagues (Kostova 1999; Kostova and Zaheer 1999; Kostova and Roth 2002), argues that MNC subsidiaries are subject to "institutional duality" (Kostova and Zaheer 1999); subsidiaries, on the one hand, are "pressurized by the headquarters to adopt a particular set of practices derived from the home base of the firm; on the other hand, the subsidiary is pressurized by its host context to follow local practices" (Collinson and Morgan 2009, 13). Hence, the studies of Kostova and colleagues as well as that of Westney (1993) teach us that the multiple and multilayered embeddedness of MNCs results in internal organizational tensions and contradictions.

The institutionalist approach to MNCs, thus, makes clear that MNCs must be able to balance both contradicting strategic goals *and* contradictory institutional pulls. How can they deal with this challenge?

In their seminal article "Formal Structure as Myth and Ceremony," Meyer and Rowan (1977) addressed the problem of contradictory environmental demands in which the formal structures of organizations are understood to reflect the institutionalized expectations in their environment. If formal structures that have been developed to address contradictory environmental expectations are not compatible with each other, organizations react with de-coupling (i.e., subunits are functionally differentiated and separated from each other). If de-coupling is not a possible option, conflicts continuously arise. Such conflicts, then, have to be resolved within informal structures— i.e., by individuals: "The organization cannot formally coordinate activities because its formal rules, if applied, would generate inconsistencies. Therefore, individuals are left to work out technical interdependencies informally" (ibid., 357).

The relevance of this theoretical model for the analysis of MNCs, and especially for the transnational type of MNC, is obvious. An increasing functional differentiation and specification of the globally dispersed subsidiaries and their simultaneous ever closer transnational integration, rules out the de-coupling that has been typical for the multinational type of coordination. Along with the quite vague proposition that individuals will have to deal with these contradictions informally, the institutionalist theory of MNCs, however, remains relatively silent about the question of how to resolve the problem of conflicting institutional pulls.[11] What we argue here is that it is primarily expatriate managers who informally balance these tensions resulting from contradicting institutional pulls.

Balancing Contradicting Interests

Whereas the contingency and the institutionalist approaches to the modern MNC have their merits in pointing to fundamental tensions that characterize MNCs, they suffer from a structuralist bias. MNCs neither simply adopt structures institutionalized in their societal environments nor do MNC managers simply execute 'fitting' strategies following a universal economic rationale (Geppert, Matten, and Walgenbach 2006). Against the backdrop of this critique, during the past decade or so, some scholars with more sociological and organization theoretical backgrounds have started to develop an analytical perspective on MNCs that seeks to bring 'the actor back in' in the sense that the focus of research is shifted to the innerorganizational processes of decision making and the way in which organizational actors bring their *interests* in bargaining processes and conflicts to the fore (see Dörrenbächer and Geppert 2006).

Looking at micropolitics and conflicts in MNCs, therefore, has developed into an important new stream in the research on MNCs (see Dörrenbächer and Geppert 2006; Becker-Ritterspach and Dörrenbächer 2011; Dörrenbächer and Geppert 2011; Becker-Ritterspach et al. 2016; Geppert, Becker-Ritterspach, and Mudambi 2016). From this perspective, it becomes clear that expatriate managers are not only executers of an economic or institutional rationality but also micropolitical actors with their own interests and agency rationales.

The merits of this micropolitical approach to MNCs lie in its claim that actors do not simply enact formal structures or strategies derived from market or societal contexts, but that they bring with them their own specific interests and power resources (see Dörrenbächer and Geppert 2006; see also Mense-Petermann 2013). Proponents of the micropolitical approach posit that MNCs' structures and strategies cannot be explained without returning to these interests and power resources. Hence, the micropolitical approach to MNCs sheds light on yet another sort of tension characteristic of MNCs—namely, the various interests of different groups of actors and the conflicts resulting therefrom. Therefore, in our view, this approach adds a third kind of highly important built-in tension of MNCs.

Glenn Morgan (2001b, 9–10) summarized this micropolitical image of the MNC as follows:

> In sociological accounts of the firm, it is perceived as a structured set of relations between a range of actors with their own powers and interests. Decision processes are characterized by political bargaining and negotiation. The outcomes of decision processes do not reflect an underlying economic rationality but the ability of different sorts of actors (endowed with differential powers by the social contextual shaping of organizational structures) to make their interests count in the various arenas of negotiation that exist within and across firms.

Research adopting such a micropolitical perspective on MNCs aims at "examining the conflicts that emerge when powerful actors with different goals, interests and identities interact with each other locally and across national and functional borders (. . .) taking into account their subjective interests in organizing and strategizing" (Dörrenbächer and Geppert 2006, 255). These scholars, thus, conceive of actors as bringing their *pre-existing* interests and power resources with them. This view neglects, however, that interests are not a once and for all stable property of actors, but are constituted, challenged, and changed in interactions. We will come back to this issue in the next subchapter.

Moreover, research on micropolitics in MNCs has predominantly focused on headquarters-subsidiary relationships. As a result, primarily the conflicting interests between headquarters and subsidiary management have been studied (Forsgren, Holm, and Johanson 2005; Clark and Geppert 2006; Dörrenbächer and Gammelgaard 2006; Dörrenbächer and Geppert 2009, 2010;

Blazejewski and Becker-Ritterspach 2011), because "executives from both the HQ and subsidiaries seem to be the main 'political brokers' (March 1962, 672) in MNCs," whereas other groups of actors are by and large neglected.

More critical yet is that this strand of debate tends to derive the interests of actors from their functional and hierarchical positions. Subsidiary managers, thus, are seen as advocating local autonomy and bargaining for mandates for their subsidiaries, whereas headquarters management is equated with an interest in global integration and the overall efficiency of the MNC (for a critical discussion see Dörrenbächer 2007, 322). Hence, this approach suffers from an oversocialized conception of actors (Wrong 1961; for a critique see Granovetter 1985). It furthermore neglects the fact that subsidiaries are often times not managed by local host country management; instead, management consists of expatriate managers from the headquarters whose interests and orientations are not initially very clear because they may display different allegiance patterns (e.g., connected with career interests) (Black and Gregersen 1992; Loveridge 2006).[12] Even though the micropolitical approach to MNCs concentrates on different sorts of managers and their agency, it leaves dealing with expatriate managers and their specific role in micropolitical bargaining to the International Human Resource Management (IHRM) literature.

The micropolitical approach to MNCs represents a major advance with regard to grasping and understanding the complexities of MNCs' structures and internal processes and in making up for lack of consideration of the role of actors in negotiating these structures and propelling these processes. It also stresses the focus on built-in tensions in MNCs by pointing to conflicting *interests* as an additional source of tension in addition to conflicting strategic goals and institutional pulls. Yet in order to develop a more fine-grained picture of MNCs and the micropolitical bargaining within them, it is necessary to shift the level of analysis away from headquarters-subsidiary relations to the level of everyday face-to-face interactions between different sorts of managers and employees in which interpretive schemes and interests are constituted and changed and order is negotiated.

Co-constructing the MNC as a 'Transnational Social Space'

So far, we have discussed three different strands of theorizing the modern MNC, and we have shown that each of these strands puts forward one specific sort of tension which it considers decisive for an adequate understanding of the structures and strategies of MNCs. Concentrating solely on one sort of tension, however, is an oversimplification that hinders a theorization of the complexity of the modern MNC as a whole. We contend that it is exactly this complexity of multidimensional tensions that characterizes MNCs, and—most importantly here—builds the context of expatriate managers' agency and the challenges they are confronted with. What is needed, therefore, is a theoretical approach that is capable of conceiving of these complexities.

In this book, we adapt a theoretical approach suggested by Glenn Morgan (2001c, 2001b) that is able to account in a more nuanced way for the complexities of managing MNCs. He conceives of MNCs as "transnational social spaces" socially constructed by "transnational communities." Morgan borrows the concepts of transnational space (Faist 2000) and transnational communities (Vertovec 1999) from migration studies and 'imports' them into the study of MNCs.

Transnational social space can be defined as an "arena in which (. . .) foreign and local power holders 'meet.' In this social space, their interpretations of economic action come together, local and global knowledge mingle, processes of learning take place, sense is made, power is exercised and the dynamics of consensus, conflict and resistance are played out" (Geppert and Clark 2003, 436). Within this arena, "continued and structured interaction between actors that belong to different organisational units" (Dörrenbächer 2007, 322) takes place. The transnational social space approach to MNCs, hence, constitutes an actor-centered approach that focuses on the everyday interactions of concrete actors and the social relations built up and reproduced by them as well as the order emerging from them.

This approach to MNCs differs from the three approaches discussed earlier in several respects. First of all, it considers a more open-ended set of actors, not only management. It posits that it is not only global business, functional, and country or subsidiary managers that make up for the building of transnational social spaces, but a plurality of different sorts of actors who belong to different units within the MNC. Morgan (2001c) terms these transnational coordination strategies enacted by MNC management "transnationalism from above," which is, however, complemented, countered, changed, or resisted in the everyday interactions in transnational social spaces, hence, by "transnationalism from below."[13]

One important sort of actor in this respect is the expatriate manager, even though not systematically addressed and discussed by Morgan. However, Geppert and Clark (2003), as well as Dörrenbächer (2007), who have adopted the transnational social space approach in empirical studies of MNCs, make clear that expatriate managers are a core sort of actors when it comes to acting in the transnational arena and to building up transnational communities.

A second, and for our understanding of MNCs most important, feature of the transnational social space approach lies in the fact that it stresses the dynamics and changes in identities and interests resulting from *interactions* in transnational social spaces. The interpretive schemes and interests of actors, as Geppert and Clark (2003, 435–6) put it,

> refer to the logics of action or contextual rationalities (. . .) These interpretive schemes are related to the global, local and organizational contexts in which they arise and which they serve to reproduce in some

degree. They are not merely economic rationalities, but reflect the communities in which actors are socially embedded.

This also implies that "social actors can participate in multiple transnational and national communities" (Morgan 2001c, 118). Hence, actors bring identities and interests with them that have been developed in their own units of the MNC, but within transnational social spaces, new identities and interests emerge, "arising from prolonged structured interaction across national boundaries based, for example, on work and economic activity" (ibid.). Thus, as an actor-centered approach, the transnational social space approach to MNCs considers differing orientations, interpretive schemes, and micropolitical interest, whereas yet not deriving them from the functional and hierarchical positions or national origins of actors, but instead catering for the emergent and dynamic properties of these identities and interests.

Having said that actors' identities and interests are not conceived of as fixed, unitary, and stable properties of actors and that actors may participate in different communities, it also becomes clear that the transnational social space approach conceives of MNCs as multilayered entities that embrace different levels of interaction. In this perspective, the transnational social space, as the arena in which actors from different units meet and negotiate, represents a level *sui generis* that "cannot be reduced to the interplay of *pre-existing* national groups or interests" (ibid., 114–15; emphasis added). Hence, this approach is better suited than those discussed earlier in grasping the complexities of social relations within MNCs, and, thus, the complexity of the multilayered order built up at different levels.

In fact, one of the advantages of the transnational social space approach is that it is especially sensitive to the precariousness of building order in and managing MNCs. From this perspective, Morgan (2001b, 10) stresses that in "complex organizations such as multinationals with multiple sites of production, different sorts of managers and workers, and economic processes that need coordinating from across the world, it is probably more appropriate to admit a sense of wonder that organization is accomplished rather than to start with this expectation. Thus, from this point of view, we can open up the multinational as a set of social processes of coordination and control, disorganization and resistance."

Hence, contrary to the normative and optimistic approach of Bartlett and Ghoshal (1989), the transnational social space approach starts with a presupposition stressing the precarity of achieving transnational coordination and integration, and thereby allows for opening up the analysis of MNCs to consider the everyday processes of negotiating order (Strauss 1978) that are ripe with tensions and conflicts that might disturb 'transnationalism from above.' With regard to the role of expatriates in MNCs, this theoretical perspective maintains that expatriate managers are confronted with precisely these kinds of tensions resulting from everyday processes of negotiating order within MNCs that embrace various sorts of actors with differing allegiance patterns, frames of reference, and interests. As Dörrenbächer's (2007, 320) empirical study teaches us,

> the emergence of transnational communities in MNCs is a demanding process. Moreover, the case study shows that transnational communities are precarious entities, because the underlying cross-national organizational identity is constantly threatened by other social relationships in and around the MNC, as well as by changes in the business environment.

This sociologically informed approach contributes to a much more differentiated and fine-grained understanding of MNCs. In this perspective, the expatriate manager is to be seen as a specific sort of actor who contributes to the social construction of the MNC as a transnational social space. This approach mainly stresses that orientations, rationalities, and interests of expatriate managers are not ultimately shaped by their functions and hierarchical positions, but are instead developed in their interactions with other sorts of actors within and outside the MNC. Note that the transnational social space is by no means a peaceful arena in which interactions take place smoothly and without any frictions. It is exactly *within these interactions* that actors are to coordinate and balance their differing orientations, rationalities, and interests, and from which transnational communities *may* be developed. Hence, in this theoretical perspective on MNCs, the expatriate manager emerges as a highly important coproducer of the MNC as a transnational social space, who is, however, placed in an arena full of tensions and conflictual interpretive schemes, orientations, and interests. The empirical Chapters 7 and 8 in this volume will take a look at and reconstruct the ways in which expatriate managers deal with this situation.

Conclusion: The Role of Expatriate Managers in Transnationally Integrated MNCs

In this chapter, we have reconstructed four different strands within the theorization of the modern MNC. We have shown that these strands converge in the way they see the modern MNC as characterized by built-in tensions and contradictions and their recognition that it is exactly these tensions that are most important for understanding the structures and internal processes of MNCs. Yet we have also shown that each of these strands posits its own particular sort of tension which it considers to be of decisive importance in the theorization of MNCs. Whereas we regard this focus solely on one such dimension to represent a simplistic understanding of the MNC, we have identified the transnational social space approach as one that is able to grasp the full complexity of the multidimensional tensions characterizing MNCs. The modern MNC, thus, can be conceived of as a transnational social space embracing different sorts of actors and their (potentially conflictual) interactions in which order is negotiated on an everyday basis.

Thus, the MNC literature in the past decades has convincingly elaborated on the built-in tensions and contradictions characteristic of MNCs. It has, however, not been equally convincing when it comes to answering the question of how MNCs can deal with the challenges connected to these tensions. Whereas Bartlett and Ghoshal explicitly address questions of the management of transnationally integrated MNCs by assigning different roles and functions to different types of managers, they do not address the question of how these managers are to acquire the required skills nor do they address the role global assignments may play for the transnational integration of MNCs. The institutionalist theory of the MNC is even more silent on questions of management. It mainly discusses how the contradicting institutional pulls are dealt with at the level of organizational structure, and it only very briefly touches upon the role of individuals in cases where structural de-coupling is not an option. Finally, the micropolitical approach to MNCs, whereas explicitly claiming to 'bring the actor back in' by focusing on the interests and power resources of specific sorts of actors (mainly headquarters and subsidiary management), tends to equate these interests and power resources with the hierarchical and functional position of the respective actors, thus neglecting the social construction of the latter in processes of interaction, within biographical and specifically career courses, and with respect to the dynamics of change in interactions within transnational social spaces.

Building on the analysis of the MNC as fundamentally characterized by built-in tensions and contradictions as discussed in the literature we have reviewed, we posit that when it comes to dealing with these tensions, expatriate managers are a key sort of actor. Summarizing the debates on the modern MNC and the role of expatriate managers in their (formal and informal) structures and strategies, the expatriate emerges as a sort of actor indispensable for MNCs, but who is confronted with challenges that are extremely hard to meet in the face of multidimensional contradictions, tensions, and conflicts. Expatriates have, however, been dealt with in one strand of literature—namely, in a substream of IHRM that is largely disconnected from the MNC literature (Bonache, Brewster, and Suutari 2001). Therefore, against the backdrop of understanding MNCs as transnational social spaces, as we have developed in this chapter, we will now proceed in the next chapter with an analysis of the role of expatriate managers in MNCs as discussed in the IHRM and expatriate literature.

Notes

1 See Sassen (2001, 23–32) for a more detailed reconstruction of the major "changes in the global flow of factors of production, commodities, and information" (ibid., 23) and the shifts in the geographic dispersal of economic activities

from the 1970s onwards that lead to a "vastly decentralized global production system" (Sassen 2001, 24).

2 For a more detailed discussion, see ibid.

3 For the following, see also Wagner and Mense-Petermann 2006 and Mense-Petermann 2012

4 See Collinson and Morgan (2009, 11) who state, "What was central here was their identification of the problem even if their solution did not go much beyond wishful thinking. Nevertheless the way in which they spelt out the problem has been fundamental to later developments."

5 Therefore, institutionalist scholars have reacted to Bartlett and Ghoshal's contingency-approach based contribution with numerous comparative studies investigating the impact of country-specific institutional settings on the globalization strategies and paths of MNCs (see Hirst and Thompson 1999; Whitley 2001; for a detailed review of this literature, see Geppert, Matten, and Walgenbach 2006). These contributions revealed an enduring embeddedness of MNCs in country-specific institutional settings, as the latter to a large extent impact the quantity, direction, and strategic orientation of FDI; the degree of autonomy granted the subsidiaries; the degree of embeddedness of subsidiaries in their local environments; and, thus, the chances of tapping into host country—specific knowledge and resources (Whitley 2001, 61). Whereas scholars from the comparative institutionalist camp were engaged in stressing the continuous importance and impact of country-specific institutional settings, they failed, however, to account for empirically observable changes in MNCs structures and strategies that proceeded in the 1990s (see Wagner and Mense-Petermann 2006). More recent studies, however, painted a more sophisticated picture of the *inter-play* of embeddedness in country-specific institutional settings and increasing transnational integration of MNCs operations, see (Elger and Smith 1999; Sharpe 2001; Lane 2001; Flecker and Simsa 2001; Morgan 2001c, 2001b).

6 For a detailed discussion of different strands of institutionalist theories of the MNC, see Geppert, Matten, and Walgenbach (2006).

7 From a "New Institutionalism in Organizational Analysis" point of view, formal organizational structures are not understood as resulting from rational decisions of management in reaction to specific problems, but as stemming from adaptation to institutionalized expectations in the environment of organizations. Such expectations and taken-for-granted beliefs are developed in "organizational fields" and disseminated by professionals and their organizations, as well as by management consultancies (see Powell and DiMaggio 1991). DiMaggio and Powell coined the term "organizational field" in order to point to "those organizations that, in the aggregate, constitute a recognized area of institutional life: key suppliers, resource and product consumers, regulatory agencies, and other organizations that produce similar services or products" (DiMaggio and Powell 1991, 64–5).

8 In their seminal article "The Iron Cage Revisited: Institutional Isomorphism and Collective Rationality in Organizational Fields," (1991) DiMaggio and Powell argue that organizations become more similar due to isomorphic pressures. Isomorphism, they explain, "is a constraining process that forces one unit in a population to resemble other units that face the same set of environmental conditions" (1991, 66). The authors "identify three mechanisms through which institutional isomorphic change occurs, each with its own antecedents: (1) *coercive* isomorphism that stems from political influence and the problem of legitimacy; (2) *mimetic* isomorphism resulting from standard responses to uncertainty; and (3) *normative* isomorphism, associated with professionalization" (DiMaggio and Powell 1991, 67).

9 One case example is Arthur Andersen. "'Arthur Andersen with revenues of $3,115 million in 1996 and an international staff of about 44,000 consultants,

has its own "university," the former girls' school at St Charles, Illinois which is known as Andersen Consulting College. There it trains consultants by the thousands and increasingly promotes conferences and video conferences' (Thrift 1998, 172). In turn, consultancies bring packaged solutions to business problems across the world. These solutions may be more or less customized and innovative depending on cases and problems but they remain built on the notion of general management skills as propounded in the Anglo-American framework. Management consultancies propagate the message to managers insecure and uncertain about the environment in which they are seeking to survive" (Morgan 2001c, 126).

10 See Morgan (2001c, 125): "MBAs are increasingly available by distance learning variants supplemented by Internet, e-mail and video conferencing. They are no longer confined to the populations of the core industrial nations either in terms of attendance or location. MBAs of their nature have a standardized curriculum usually aimed to produce the 'general manager'. Most top MBA schools are very conscious of the identity-forming functions of the process. In the USA, in particular (although this is mirrored elsewhere, not least because alumni are a major source of funds for business schools), well-developed alumni associations attempt to maintain and reinforce these identities by offering the benefits to graduates of continued social networking and refresher courses."

11 In fact, Kostova (1999, 317–18) in her study of transnational transfers of organizational practices discusses the role of "transfer coalitions," i.e., the important decision makers at the recipient unit, for a successful transfer. "The transfer coalition serves as a 'bridge' between the recipient unit and the parent company and, as such, is key in understanding and interpreting the practice and its value to the unit. It is responsible for 'selling' the practice to the employees at the recipient unit, and it also determines what is communicated, how it is communicated, and how it is received." Kostova then goes on to discuss the factors that influence the motivation of the transfer coalition to engage in the process of transfer. She does not, however, address the question of *how* the members of the transfer coalition fulfil their bridging role, and *what challenges* they may be confronted with.

12 Dörrenbächer and Geppert (2006, 257) only touch upon this issue very briefly when pointing to specific micropolitical games that capitalize foreignness, without, however, going into further detail.

13 The distinction between transnationalism 'from above' and 'from below' had been introduced by Smith and Guarnizo (1998), who argued for the importance of other actors in globalization process besides MNCs, such as transnational social movements and migrants.

Bibliography

Aharoni, Yair. 1966. *The Foreign Investment Decision Process*. Boston: Division of Research, Graduate School of Business Administration, Harvard University.

Bartlett, Christopher A., and Sumantra Ghoshal. 1987. "Managing Across Borders: New Organizational Responses." *Sloan Management Review* 29 (1): 43–53.

Bartlett, Christopher A., and Sumantra Ghoshal. 1989. *Managing Across Borders: The Transnational Solution*. Boston: Harvard Business School Press.

Bartlett, Christopher A., and Sumantra Ghoshal. 2003. "What Is a Global Manager?" *Harvard Business Review* 81 (8): 101–8.

Becker-Ritterspach, Florian A. A., Susanne Blazejewski, Christoph Dörrenbächer, and Mike Geppert, eds. 2016. *Micropolitics in the Multinational Corporation:*

Foundations, Applications and New Directions. Cambridge: Cambridge University Press.

Becker-Ritterspach, Florian A. A., and Christoph Dörrenbächer. 2011. "An Organizational Politics Perspective on Intra-Firm Competition in Multinational Corporations." *Management International Review* 51 (4): 533–59. doi:10.1007/s11575-011-0083-2.

Black, Stewart, and Hal B. Gregersen. 1992. "Serving Two Masters: Managing the Dual Allegiance of Expatriate Employees." *Sloan Management Review* 33 (4): 61–71.

Blazejewski, Susanne, and Florian Becker-Ritterspach. 2011. "Conflict in the Headquarters-Subsidiary Relations: A Critical Literature Review and New Directions." In *Politics and Power in the Multinational Corporation: The Role of Institutions, Interests and Identities*, edited by Christoph Dörrenbächer and Mike Geppert, 139–90. Cambridge: Cambridge University Press.

Bonache, Jaime, Chris Brewster, and Vesa Suutari. 2001. "Expatriation: A Developing Research Agenda." *Thunderbird International Business Review* 43 (1): 3–20. doi:10.1002/1520-6874(200101/02)43:1<3:AID-TIE2>3.0.CO;2-4.

Clark, Ed, and Mike Geppert. 2006. "Socio-Political Processes in International Management in Post-Socialist Contexts: Knowledge, Learning and Transnational Institution Building." *Journal of International Management* 12 (3): 340–57. doi:10.1016/j.intman.2006.06.004.

Collinson, Simon, and Glenn Morgan. 2009. "Images of the Multinational Firm." In *Images of the Multinational Firm*, edited by Simon Collinson and Glenn Morgan, 1–22. Chichester: Wiley.

DiMaggio, Paul J., and Walter W. Powell. 1991. "The Iron Cage Revisited: Institutional Isomorphism and Collective Rationality in Organizational Fields." In *The New Institutionalism in Organizational Analysis*, edited by Walter W. Powell and Paul J. DiMaggio, 63–82. Chicago: University of Chicago Press.

Dörrenbächer, Christoph. 2007. "Inside the Transnational Social Space: Cross-Border Management and Owner Relationship in a German Subsidiary in Hungary." *Journal for East European Management Studies* 12 (4): 318–39. doi:10.1688/1862-0019_jeems_2007_04_doerrenbaecher

Dörrenbächer, Christoph, and Jens Gammelgaard. 2006. "Subsidiary Role Development: The Effect of Micro-Political Headquarters—Subsidiary Negotiations on the Product, Market and Value-Added Scope of Foreign-Owned Subsidiaries." *Journal of International Management* 12 (3): 266–83. doi:10.1016/j.intman.2006.06.001.

Dörrenbächer, Christoph, and Jens Gammelgaard. 2010. "Multinational Corporations, Inter-Organizational Networks and Subsidiary Charter Removals." *Journal of World Business* 45 (3): 206–16. doi:10.1016/j.jwb.2009.12.001.

Dörrenbächer, Christoph, and Jens Gammelgaard. 2011. "Subsidiary Power in Multinational Corporations: The Subtle Role of Micro-Political Bargaining Power." *Critical Perspectives on International Business* 7 (1): 30–47. doi:10.1108/17422041111103822.

Dörrenbächer, Christoph, and Jens Gammelgaard. 2016. "Subsidiary Initiative Taking in Multinational Corporations: The Relationship between Power and Issue Selling." *Organization Studies* 37 (9): 1249–70. doi:10.1177/0170840616634130.

Dörrenbächer, Christoph, and Mike Geppert. 2006. "Micro-Politics and Conflicts in Multinational Corporations: Current Debates, Re-Framing, and Contributions of this Special Issue." *Journal of International Management* 12 (3): 251–65. doi:10.1016/j.intman.2006.07.001.

Dörrenbächer, Christoph, and Mike Geppert. 2009. "Micro-Political Games in the Multinational Corporation: The Case of Mandate Change." Special Issue: Power in Organizations—Power of Organizations. *Management Revue* 20 (4): 373–91. doi: 10.1688/1861-9908_mrev_2009_04_Doerrenbaecher

Dörrenbächer, Christoph, and Mike Geppert. 2011. "Politics and Power in the Multinational Corporation: An Introduction." In *Politics and Power in the Multinational Corporation. The Role of Institutions, Interests and Identities*, edited by Christoph Dörrenbächer and Mike Geppert, 3–38. Cambridge: Cambridge University Press.

Dunning, John H. 1988. "The Eclectic Paradigm of International Production: A Restatement and Some Possible Extensions." *Journal of International Business Studies* 19 (1): 1–31. doi:10.1057/palgrave.jibs.8490372.

Elger, Tony, and Chris Smith. 1999. "Japanese Inward Investors and the Remaking of Employment and Production Regimes: the British Case." In *Global Players in lokalen Bindungen: Unternehmensglobalisierung in soziologischer Perspektive*, edited by Andrea Eckardt, Holm-Detlev Köhler, and Ludger Pries, 99–134. Berlin: Edition Sigma.

Faist, Thomas. 2000. *The Volume and Dynamics of International Migration and Transnational Social Spaces*. Oxford: Oxford University Press.

Flecker, J., and R. Simsa. 2001. "Co-Ordination and Control in Transnational Business and Non-Profit Organizations." In *New Transnational Social Spaces: International Migration and Transnational Companies in the Early Twenty-First Century*, edited by Ludger Pries, 164–84. London: Routledge.

Forsgren, Mats, Ulf Holm, and Jan Johanson. 2005. *Managing the Embedded Multinational: A Business Network View*. Northampton: Edward Elgar.

Geppert, Mike, F. Becker-Ritterspach, and R. Mudambi. 2016. "Politics and Power in Multinational Companies: Integrating the International Business and Organization Studies Perspectives." *Organization Studies* 37 (9): 1209–25. doi:10.1177/0170840616656152.

Geppert, Mike, and Ed Clark. 2003. "Knowledge and Learning in Transnational Ventures: An Actor-Centred Approach." *Management Decision* 41 (5): 433–42. doi:10.1108/00251740310479287.

Geppert, Mike, and Christoph Dörrenbächer. 2014. "Politics and Power Within Multinational Corporations: Mainstream Studies, Emerging Critical Approaches and Suggestions for Future Research." *International Journal of Management Reviews* 16 (2): 226–44. doi:10.1111/ijmr.12018.

Geppert, Mike, D. Matten, and P. Walgenbach. 2006. "Transnational Institution Building and the Multinational Corporation: An Emerging Field of Research." *Human Relations* 59 (11): 1451–65. doi:10.1177/0018726706072888.

Granovetter, Mark. 1985. "Economic Action and Social Structure: The Problem of Embeddedness." *The American Journal of Sociology* 91: 481–510. doi:10.1086/228311.

Hedlund, Gunnar. 1986. "The Hypermodern MNC—a Heterarchy?" *Human Resource Management* 25 (1): 9–35. doi:10.1002/hrm.3930250103.

Hirst, Paul, and Grahame Thompson. 1999. *Globalization in Question: The International Economy and the Possibilities of Governance*. Cambridge: Polity Press.

Johanson, Jan, and Jan-Erik Vahlne. 1977. "The Internationalization Process of the Firm—a Model of Knowledge Development and Increasing Foreign Market Commitments." *Journal of International Business Studies* 8 (1): 23–32. doi:10.1057/palgrave.jibs.8490676.

Kostova, Tatiana. 1999. "Transnational Transfer of Strategic Organizational Practices: A Contextual Perspective." *The Academy of Management Review* 24 (2): 308–24. doi:10.5465/AMR.1999.1893938.

Kostova, Tatiana, and Kendall Roth. 2002. "Adoption of an Organizational Practice by Subsidiaries of Multinational Corporations: Institutional and Relational Effects." *The Academy of Management Journal* 45 (1): 215–33. doi:10.2307/3069293.

Kostova, Tatiana, and Srilata Zaheer. 1999. "Organizational Legitimacy Under Conditions of Complexity: The Case of the Multinational Enterprise." *The Academy of Management Review* 24 (1): 64–81. doi:10.5465/AMR.1999.1580441.

Lane, Christel. 2001. "The Emergence of German Transnational Companies: A Theoretical Analysis and Emprical Study of the Globalization Process." In Morgan, Kristensen, and Whitley 2001, 69–96.

Loveridge, Ray. 2006. "Embedding the Multinational Enterprise: The Micro-Processes of Institutionalization in Developing Economies." In *Global, National and Local Practices in Multinational Companies*, edited by Mike Geppert and Michael Mayer, 189–219. Basingstoke: Palgrave Macmillan.

March, James G. 1962. "The Business Firm as a Political Coalition". In *Journal of Politics*. 24: 662–678. *doi: 10.1017/s0022381600016169*.

Mense-Petermann, Ursula. 2005. "Unternehmen im Transnationalisierungsprozess—Zum Problem der Herstellung de-facto-akzeptierter Entscheidungen in transnationalen Integrationsprozessen." *Soziale Welt* 4: 381–97. doi:10.5771/0038-6073-2005-4-381.

Mense-Petermann, Ursula. 2006. "Transnationalisierung als glokale Restrukturation von Organisationsgrenzen." In Mense-Petermann and Wagner 2006, 63–84.

Mense-Petermann, Ursula. 2012. "Multinationals, Transnationals, Global Players—Zur Besonderheit grenzüberschreitend operierender Organisationen." In *Handbuch Organisationstypen*, edited by Maja Apelt and Veronika Tacke, 43–61. Wiesbaden: VS Verlag für Sozialwissenschaften.

Mense-Petermann, Ursula. 2013. "Expatriates as Micro-Political Actors: Power Resources and Strategizing on Global Assignments." *Gazdasági élet és társa dalom (Economy and Society)* 1–2: 44–73.

Mense-Petermann, Ursula, and Gabriele Wagner, eds. 2006. *Transnationale Konzerne: Ein neuer Organisationstyp?* Wiesbaden: VS Verlag für Sozialwissenschaften.

Meyer, John W., and Brian Rowan. 1977. "Institutionalized Organizations: Formal Structure as Myth and Ceremony." *American Journal of Sociology* 83 (2): 340–63. doi:10.1086/226550.

Morgan, Glenn. 2001a. "The Development of Transnational Standards and Regulations and Their Impact on Firms." In Morgan, Kristensen, and Whitley 2001, 225–52.

Morgan, Glenn. 2001b. "The Multinational Firm: Organizing Across Institutional and National Divides." In Morgan, Kristensen, and Whitley 2001, 1–24.

Morgan, Glenn. 2001c. "Transnational Communities and Business Systems." *Global Networks* 1 (2): 113–30. doi:10.1111/1471-0374.00008.

Morgan, Glenn, Peer H. Kristensen, and Richard Whitley, eds. 2001. *The Multinational Firm: Organizing Across Institutional and National Divides.* Oxford: Oxford University Press.

Nohria, Nitin, and Sumantra Ghoshal. 1997. *The Differentiated Network: Organizing Multinational Corporations for Value Creation.* San Francisco: Jossey-Bass.

Perlmutter, Howard V., and David A. Heenan. 1974. "How Multinational Should Our Managers Be?" *Harvard Business Review* 52 (6): 121–32.

Powell, Walter W., and Paul J. DiMaggio, eds. 1991. *The New Institutionalism in Organizational Analysis.* Chicago: University of Chicago Press.

Sassen, Saskia. 2001. *The Global City.* Princeton: Princeton University Press.

Sharpe, Diana R. 2001. "Globalization and Change: Organizational Continuity and Change Within a Japanese Multinational in the UK." In Morgan, Kristensen, and Whitley 2001, 196–224.

Smith, Michael P., and Luis Guarnizo, eds. 1998. *Transnationalism from Below.* New Brunswick and London: Transaction Publishers.

Strauss, Anselm, ed. 1978. *Negotiations: Varieties, Contexts, Processes and Social Order.* San Francisco: Jossey-Bass.

Thrift, Nigel. 1998. "Virtual Capitalism: The Globalization of Reflexive Business Knowledge." In *Virtualism: A New Political Economy*, edited by James G. Carrier and Daniel Miller, 161–86. Oxford: Berg.

UNCTAD. 2007. "The World Investment Report." New York and Geneva: United Nations Conference on Trade and Development. http://unctad.org/en/pages/DIAE/World%20Investment%20Report/WIR-Series.aspx. Accessed June 02, 2017.

UNCTAD. 2013. "The World Investment Report." New York and Geneva: United Nations Conference on Trade and Development. http://unctad.org/en/pages/DIAE/World%20Investment%20Report/WIR-Series.aspx. Accessed June 02, 2017.

UNCTAD. 2015. "The World Investment Report." New York and Geneva: United Nations Conference on Trade and Development. http://unctad.org/en/pages/DIAE/World%20Investment%20Report/WIR-Series.aspx. Accessed June 02, 2017.

Vertovec, Steven. 1999. "Conceiving and Researching Transnationalism." *Ethnic and Racial Studies* 22 (2): 447–62. doi:10.1080/014198799329558.

Wagner, Gabriele, and Ursula Mense-Petermann. 2006. "Zur Einleitung: Transnationale Konzerne als neuer Organisationstyp? Glokalität als Organisationsproblem." In Mense-Petermann and Wagner 2006, 9–32.

Westney, D. E. 1993. "Institutionalization Theory and the Multinational Corporation." In *Organization Theory and the Multinational Corporation*, edited by Sumantra Ghoshal and D. E. Westney. 53–76. Basingstoke: St. Martin's Press.

Whitley, Richard. 2001. "How and Why Are International Firms Different? The Consequences of Cross-Border Managerial Coordination for Firm Characteristics and Behavior." In Morgan, Kristensen, and Whitley 2001, 27–68.

Wrong, Dennis H. 1961. "The Oversocialized Conception of Man in Modern Sociology." *American Sociological Review* 26 (2): 183. doi:10.2307/2089854.

3 Expatriate Managers as Boundary Spanners in MNCs

Bastian Bredenkötter

In the previous chapter, we investigated the modern MNC, revealing that it is fundamentally characterized by built-in contradictions, inconsistencies, and conflicts. The fact that the literature on MNCs as organizations has not paid systematic attention to expatriates as a specific sort of manager notwithstanding, we furthermore posited that they are key actors when it comes to dealing with these tensions. Contrary to the MNC literature, expatriates have been increasingly dealt with in another strand of literature—namely, the literature on global mobility in the field of IHRM. The focus of this research is on how MNCs and especially their HRM can successfully use and manage global assignments. In this chapter, we utilize this literature as well as other strands of expatriate research in order to improve our conceptualization of the expatriate manager and to establish our research perspective focusing on the day-to-day work practices of global assignees and the interactive negotiation processes they engage in on-site. Furthermore, we adopt sociological role theory for theorizing expatriate managers' *boundary spanning*. Far from providing a comprehensive review of the countless contributions in the field,[1] we instead discuss our perception of the expatriate literature against the backdrop of our social theoretical basic assumption of structured and structuring agency (Chapter 1) and our understanding of the MNC as transnational social space (Chapter 2).

In the first part of this chapter, we explore the role and function of the expatriate in the MNC and pick up the idea that expatriate managers can theoretically be described as boundary spanners (first Thomas 1994). Regardless of the specific functional and/or hierarchical position of a concrete manager, expatriates occupy boundary roles in which they are expected to bridge intra- and/or interorganizational, as well as cultural boundaries. We then take up several strands of debate to problematize the role of the expatriate in the MNC and show that successful role-*taking*—and in this respect, the stabilization of the MNC—is rather unlikely. We argue that in order to understand expatriates' boundary spanning, it is necessary to conceptualize expatriate managers as resourceful and creative actors with their own specific agency and to empirically inquire into their role-*making* practices. This leads us to a research agenda that is obvious, but surprisingly still under-investigated; instead of taking an HRM perspective and asking questions about how to manage assignments successfully, we propose taking the perspective of the expatriate and exploring questions about how expatriates 'make' their boundary role in practice.

The Boundary Role(s) of Expatriate Managers in MNCs

Increasing globalization of the economy has resulted in rising numbers of global assignments, and surveys by professional service firms indicate that this trend is continuing (Brookfield 2012; Ernst and Young 2012).[2] During the last 50 years, this development has been reflected in a large number of studies in the IHRM literature. Key issues are why and when global assignments occur and the HRM practices and challenges that arise along the expatriation cycle from identification, selection and training via compensation, adjustment, and performance appraisal, through to repatriation and career management (see for an overview Bonache, Brewster, and Suutari 2001; Harvey and Moeller 2009; Bonache et al. 2010; Caligiuri and Bonache 2016). Whereas earlier studies, with a few exceptions (Edström and Galbraith 1977; Boyacigiller 1990), had been criticized for being "anecdotal" (Thomas 1994, 146), "fundamentally descriptive in character and generally lack[ing] a theoretical foundation" (Bonache, Brewster, and Suutari 2001, 3), more recent studies have contributed a better understanding of the roles and functions of expatriate managers within MNCs (see Bonache et al. 2010, 264–5). In this subchapter, we will show that in this literature, the expatriate manager—explicitly or implicitly—emerges as a *boundary spanner*.

Boundary spanning is, independent of the discussion about MNCs and expatriates, a classical concept and research area in organization studies. The concept has its theoretical roots in open-systems theory and role theory (see the literature reviews in Thomas 1994; Mayrhofer 1997; Tacke 1997; Johnson and Duxbury 2010).[3] The classical literature mentions two kinds of linkages that organizations (must) establish at their boundaries: To survive as open systems, they need to adjust to and interact with their outside environments and, therefore, differentiate interorganizational linkages that "detect and respond to any fluctuations in the external environment that might pose a threat to the system" (Johnson and Duxbury 2010, 30). In unfamiliar and uncertain environments, organizations adapt by increasing these linkages at their external boundaries "to support the inward flow of information and to exert outward control over clients, suppliers, partners, and others in their task environments" (ibid., 29). Other studies emphasize that the functioning of organizations also requires linkages at their internal boundaries to coordinate and control the activities between the different subunits. Large organizations with high levels of internal differentiation especially rely on such intraorganizational linkages, given that the emergence of specialized, internally coherent subunits generally leads to differences and conflicts between the individual subunits (see Mayrhofer 1997,

120). In the literature, these inter- and intraorganizational linkages take the form of more or less formalized organizational roles (boundary roles)[4] and depend on the activities (boundary spanning activities) of the individuals who act them out (boundary spanners).[5] It is through the agency of such boundary spanners that organizations are able to gather intelligence and exert influence across internal and/or external boundaries in pursuit of organizational objectives (see Johnson and Duxbury 2010, 29).[6]

MNCs are complex and geographically dispersed organizations embedded in multiple and multilayered economic, institutional and political settings. As such, relevant parts of the internal and external environment are located in different countries, which, in contrast to organizations that only operate in one country, brings influencing factors like geographical distances and cultural differences into play (see Mayrhofer 1997, 118). Accordingly, MNCs are characterized by a high level of boundary complexity and rely on exchanges across these boundaries. This applies especially to the case of the transnational type, as its functional differentiation increases both the need for exchanges between the subsidiaries of the MNC as well as the relevance of external environments of the local operations to the overall organization (see Chapter 2; Mense-Petermann 2006b).[7] It is against this backdrop that several authors have explicitly conceptualized expatriate managers as internal and/or external and, in addition, also as cultural boundary spanners in MNCs (e.g., Thomas 1994; Mayrhofer 1997; Au and Fukuda 2002; Reiche, Harzing, and Kraimer 2009; Mense-Petermann 2014, 2017; Harzing, Pudelko, and Reiche 2016; Mense-Petermann and Spiegel 2016).[8] Furthermore, it seems to be no coincidence that other parts of the expatriate literature also implicitly conceptualize expatriates as boundary spanners by addressing roles and functions that appear to be related to or aspects of the boundary spanning concept (see Johnson and Duxbury 2010, 29). For example, according to the literature investigating the strategic purposes of expatriate assignments, the key reasons for global assignments are, besides management development, knowledge transfer and control (for an overview, see Harzing 2001b, 140–4; Caligiuri and Bonache 2016, 129–30).

Synthesizing the literature, analytically, we can distinguish two classes of interrelated boundary spanning functions and related (sub)roles: *processing information* and *exerting influence*.[9] Both scholars who conceptualize expatriates as boundary spanners and those researchers who describe them as agents of knowledge transfer, "emphasize the importance of the role for *processing information*" (Yagi and Kleinberg 2011, 630, emphasis added) across internal, external and/or also cultural boundaries. For example, building on the classical typology of Ancona and Caldwell (1992) and Au and Fukuda's (2002) work on external boundary spanning behaviors of expatriates, Park and Mense-Petermann (2014, 271), concentrating on internal boundary spanning in MNCs, distinguish subroles that accentuate the directionality of information processing: "The *ambassador* tends to convey knowledge from headquarters to subsidiaries, the *scout* from subsidiaries to headquarters, and the *task coordinator* in both directions" (emphasis added). It could also be added that expatriate managers might also take a "guard" (Ancona and Caldwell 1992) role and buffer an organizational unit from external demands for information.

Other researchers stress how expatriates are important in controlling subsidiaries, making sure that they are pursuing the objectives of the headquarters, or in influencing external environments in the interest of the overall MNC. We label these more power-related functions as *exerting influence*. For example, building on the seminal work of Edström and Galbraith (1977) and a number of German studies, Harzing (2001a) introduces three vivid metaphors to examine the internal control function of expatriate assignments in greater detail. In the *bear* role, expatriates are used as "the long arm of headquarters managers" (ibid., 375), replacing or complementing "HQ centralization of decision-making and direct surveillance of subsidiaries by headquarters managers" (ibid., 369). The metaphor describes "personal centralized control" and "reflects a level of dominance (. . .) associated with this type of expatriate control" (ibid.). As *bumblebees*, expatriates are used to transfer organization culture—they "fly 'from plant to plant' and create cross-pollination between the various offshoots" (ibid.). Thereby, the organization aims to realize indirect control based on "socialization of both expatriate and local managers into the corporate culture" (ibid., 367). In the role of the *spider*, expatriates are expected to realize indirect control by "[w]eaving an informal communication network" (ibid., 369) "that provides links between subsidiaries and headquarters" (ibid., 367).[10] Regarding the directionality of influence exertion, it has to be added that it can also be a latent or manifest function of expatriates to influence the headquarters in terms of pushing it to adapt to external changes and requirements.

From the literature, we can deduce that the expatriate emerges as a boundary spanner. Expatriate managers, regardless of their specific functional and/ or hierarchical position, simultaneously occupy positions at both organizational and cultural boundaries, and they are expected to bridge these boundaries in the performance of their roles. Their specific function, thus, is to ensure flows of information and to exert influence across internal and external boundaries in pursuit of organizational objectives.[11] However, the execution of organizational expectations and successful role performance cannot be taken for granted.

From Role-Taking to Role-Making: Expatriate Managers as Creative Actors

Structural-functional role theory, as part of the normative paradigm in social theory, conceives of role performance as a relatively unproblematic "role-taking" (Turner 1990). Actors internalize the role senders' expectations and play their roles without major complications. Such a smooth role-taking, of course, depends on several preconditions. For example, the role incumbent must have the necessary resources under their disposal to be able to perform the role, and the role must be compatible with the interests and orientations of the role occupant (see detailed Schimank 2010, 66–76). Yet the interpretive paradigm in social theory radically rejects the understanding of role performance as a widely unproblematic execution of expectations by pointing out that these preconditions can by no means be taken for granted. It stresses the fundamental importance of the *creative* contributions of the individual occupying a role in dealing with the complications that arise when the social prerequisites of the structural-functional model are not given (ibid.). The role occupant "is creating and modifying roles as well as merely bringing them to light; the process is not only role-taking but *role-making*" (Turner 1990, 86, emphasis in original). As a consequence, the interpretive paradigm conceptualizes the role incumbent as a resourceful and creative social actor, not as someone slavishly following a script. It is the involved actors as persons who, through role-making, sustain social order under critical circumstances (see Schimank 2010, 78).

In accordance with our idea of structured and structuring agency (e.g., Giddens 1984; Chapter 1) we adopt this theoretical perspective and argue that it is precisely the role-making practices of expatriates—as creative actors embedded in concrete social contexts and involved in constant negotiations with other actors—that must be put at the focus of empirical research. By accepting global assignments, expatriate managers accept taking on organizational and, at the same time, cultural boundary roles. Yet the social preconditions of successful boundary spanning cannot be taken for granted. Instead, the literature reveals that neither the necessary *resources* for successful role performance nor the compatibility of the role with the *interests and orientations* of the expatriate manager are self-evident. An uncomplicated role-taking is unlikely under these circumstances and has to be conceived of as an interactive and open-ended process that can fail and is susceptible to faults (see Wagner 2006, 225, 228; Wagner and Vormbusch 2010).

First, regarding the necessary *resources* of boundary spanning work, several bodies of literature show that processing information and exerting influence across organizational and cultural boundaries are complex enterprises that confront the expatriate with hard to meet challenges, whose fulfillment require highly subjective capabilities as well as sufficient power resources.

Processing information is not an unproblematic and neutral transfer of factual information. The classical (not expatriate or MNC-related) literature on boundary spanning already highlights the importance of role incumbents' subjective capabilities when they engage in uncertainty absorption by gathering relevant information in the external environment and communicating it to the organization. Aldrich and Herker (1977, 218–19) argue that the success of the organization in adapting to environmental fluctuations depends in part on the expertise of boundary role occupants in "selecting," "summarizing," and "interpreting" information originating from the environment and in "determining who gets what information". The burgeoning research on intraorganizational knowledge transfer in MNCs has shown that knowledge transfer is "a more arduous task than was predicted by the models of transnational firms where information flowed freely" (Caligiuri and Bonache 2016, 131). Much of the relevant knowledge is "tacit as it cannot be coded or set out in manuals, but instead is steeped in the experience and skills of the organization's members (Polanyi 1962)" (ibid., 130). In this context, Choi and Johanson (2012, 1148) suggest "a paradigmatic shift from knowledge transfer without loss, to knowledge translation as a matter of modification of knowledge when transferred from one context to another" see also Czarniawska and Joerges 1996). They describe knowledge transfer as a socio-cultural process in which expatriates play an import role as moderators and translators. Thereby, they show that personal characteristics, like expatriation experience and relationship development capabilities, have positive effects on the transfer of knowledge from the headquarters to foreign subsidiaries.

Exerting influence across organizational boundaries, too, is a challenging task. It must be seen as a precarious micropolitical process that depends on role incumbents' power resources as well as on their subjective and social capabilities. This also applies to the intraorganizational case, where the expatriate manager has direct control rights. MNCs are arenas in which expatriates find themselves placed within a multidimensional field of conflicting interests and rationalities (Mense-Petermann 2013, 45; see also Chapter 2). Expatriates' capacities to exert influence in the local subsidiary depend on their disposal over various power resources (see ibid., 49–50). Whereas they may dispose over formal authority, they, at least in the beginning—like every 'new boss' (Luhmann 1962)—do not control the informal communication channels on-site (see Wagner 2006). Their capacity to generate the necessary willingness to cooperate of the local employees thus depends in part on their ability to balance interests, achieve compromises, and gain trust.

We can summarize that processing information and exerting influence are socio-cultural processes that depend on the creative contributions (e.g., selecting, interpreting, translating, moderating, negotiating, balancing) of the expatriates. These contributions require highly subjective capabilities as well as power resources, neither of which can be taken for granted.

Second, not only the necessary resources for boundary spanning but also expatriate managers' own *interests and orientations* have to be taken into consideration. Expatriates' subjectivity is more than just a required resource for successful boundary spanning. As the transnational social space perspective of the MNC has already indicated (see Chapter 2), it is insufficient to conceptualize expatriates only from their function and the 'functional part' of their subjectivity. Expatriates are not only fulfillers of organizational expectations or agents of the headquarters; they are, rather, actors with their own interests, and their agency is contingent on these interests. For example, career orientations and allegiance patterns should be considered as important contingencies with regard to the 'agency' and willingness to bring in capabilities that cannot be subject to a contract.

Expatriates are "serving two masters"—the parent firm and the local operation—and, as Black and Gregersen (1992) show, different "patterns of allegiance" are conceivable: Expatriates can leave their "hearts at home" (commitment to the headquarters), they can "go native" (commitment to the subsidiary), see themselves as "dual citizens" (commitment to both), or even as "free agents" (low commitment to both). Especially expatriates who see themselves as "free agents" seem to be particularly committed to their own career orientations. In this context it is worth mentioning that in the career literature the dominant concepts of the "boundaryless" (Arthur and Rousseau 1996) and the "protean career" (Hall 1976, 2004) describe a continuing rise in the importance of career orientations that are not bound to a specific organization. Loveridge (2005) differentiates three types of expatriate careers (diplomats, fast-trackers/tourists, locals), each implying different degrees of immersion into the host countries' business and social environment and culture. We assume that the career orientations and organizational allegiances of expatriates affect their micropolitical strategizing (see Mense-Petermann 2013) and boundary spanning capacities (see Park and Mense-Petermann 2014) as they "are connected, for example, with levels of willingness to learn the local language, to engage in local communication and conflict, to form relationships with local businesses, government officials (Heikkliä 2012) and other individuals, and generally to absorb the local worldview" (ibid., 273).

The possibilities for expatriates to advance their individual interests not always in line with those of the headquarters depend—as do their possibilities to control internal and external environments—on their power resources, in this case, their power resources in relation to that of the headquarters. Aldrich and Herker (1977, 227) propose, "The power of boundary role incumbents will vary inversely with boundary role routinization, and directly with their own expertise in accomplishing role requirements and with the costliness and unpredictability of organizational transactions". Following this proposition and taking into account the complexity of MNCs and their environments and the required subjective capabilities of boundary spanning, we can assume that expatriates have considerable power resources to advance their own interests. To conclude, expatriates can be expected to reinterpret or even undermine the organizations' expectations, depending on their own interests, orientations, and power resources.

So far, the boundary spanning of expatriates has been problematized from an organizational perspective that defines the boundaries in question as intra- and/or inter*organizational* boundaries. There is, however, a separate strand of literature that defines boundaries that have to be spanned by expatriates as *cultural* boundaries. Here, expatriates are conceived of as

"culture carriers" (Björkman and Lu 2001). The IB and management literature focusing on the cultural dimension of boundary spanning posits that a
cosmopolitan orientation—also labeled as a "global mindset" or "geocentric orientation" (see the literature review in Levy et al. 2007)—is a necessary management resource for putting the modern MNC—especially the
transnational form—into practice. For example, Kanter (1995, 23) portrays
"world class" managers as interculturally competent "cosmopolitans" who
are "[c]omfortable in many places and able to understand and bridge the
differences among them". However, the occurrence of the allegedly necessary orientation and an unproblematic spanning of cultural boundaries cannot be taken for granted. Authors from a more sociological perspective have
stressed the complexity and problems of intercultural communication and
transnational cooperation (e.g., Klemm and Popp 2005; Mense-Petermann
2005a, 2005b, 2006a, 2017; Yagi and Kleinberg 2011; Mense-Petermann
and Spiegel 2016). In addition, authors from critical management studies
have attacked the picture of expatriate managers as cosmopolitan boundary
spanners by portraying them rather as anti-cosmopolitan boundary makers
(e.g., Ybema and Byun 2009; Leonard 2010; see the literature review in
Chapter 4).

Our discussion of the necessary resources for successful role-making and
the individual interests and orientations of expatriate managers has shown
that neither organizational nor cultural boundary spanning can be understood as unproblematic role-*taking*. Instead, the role-*making* of the expatriate has to be shifted into focus and empirically investigated.

Conclusion

The expatriate manager can be conceived of as an actor who can contribute
to the construction of the MNC as a transnational social space by successfully acting as a *boundary spanner*.

In the first part of this chapter, we discussed the literature addressing
boundary roles and functions of expatriates. In this literature, the expatriate
manager emerges as a boundary spanner; expatriates occupy roles on organizational and, at the same time, cultural boundaries, and it is their central
function to exert influence and process information across these boundaries.
It is through the agency of expatriates that MNCs can adjust to their external environments and coordinate the activities of their subunits.

In the second part of this chapter, we problematized this role by collecting various theoretical and empirical indications deriving from IB, IHRM,
and more sociologically oriented expatriate literature as well as sociological theory. We argued that processing information and exerting influence
across organizational boundaries are socio-cultural processes that require
highly demanding subjective and social capabilities like expertise in selecting, interpreting, and translating information and in balancing different
interests, rationalities, and cultures. We then argued that the successful

boundary spanning of expatriates cannot be taken for granted, as they are actors with own interests, orientations, and loyalties, which might influence their boundary spanning capabilities. In this sense, we are always simultaneously dealing with both: the expatriate manager's organizational role and also the actor inhabiting this role (see Wagner and Vormbusch 2010, 221).

We can summarize that expatriates take crucial roles in the organizational structure, but in terms of stabilizing the MNC, their contribution in successfully performing these roles is contingent on a series of prerequisites that cannot be taken for granted. Against this backdrop, the role-*making* practices of expatriates—as *creative actors* embedded in concrete social contexts and involved in constant negotiations with other actors—must be shifted into greater focus. Although many of the issues we have raised in this chapter are not new to IB and IHRM researchers and practitioners, our actor-centered perspective leads to a research agenda—which is employed in Chapters 7 and 8—that is clearly important but surprisingly still underresearched: *How* do expatriate managers attempt to balance the tensions and manage the challenges they are confronted with *in practice*? *How* do they interpret and enact their boundary roles in their *everyday work* at the subsidiary? *How* do they deal with cultural difference in their *daily interactions* with local colleagues and subordinates? By taking this focus, we turn away from examining the 'inputs' and 'outcomes' of global assignments and move to a more detailed investigation of the *complex processes* in which MNCs as transnational social spaces are (co)constructed and stabilized by expatriate managers as boundary spanners.

Notes

1 Several textbooks (e.g., Dowling, Festing, and Engle 2013; Harzing and Pinnington 2014), introductions to special issues (e.g., Bonache, Brewster, and Suutari 2001; Bonache et al. 2010), and literature reviews (e.g., Harvey and Moeller 2009; Caligiuri and Bonache 2016) provide an overview of the debates and developments in this research area. The launch of the Journal of Global Mobility in 2013 underlines the agile and ongoing research activities in this field.
2 The 2012 Global Relocation Trends Survey report states, that "growth in international assignee populations continues to be strong and, in fact, has strengthened well beyond what has been reported in the last three Global Relocation Trends Survey reports" (Brookfield 2012, 9). Sixty-four percent of the 123 participating companies indicated that their assignee population increased. In the 2012 Global Mobility Effectiveness Survey, on average, the more than 520 survey respondents "forecast that both short-and long-term assignments will continue growing over the next two years by 20% and 11% respectively" (Ernst and Young 2012, 16).
3 See also Luhmann's (1976) work on boundary positions.
4 In the literature, the terms 'boundary role' and 'boundary-spanning role' are often used synonymously.
5 "Boundary spanning personnel are, therefore, those personnel that cross internal and/or external organizational boundaries in the performance of their roles" (Thomas 1994, 147).

6 In their article, Johnson and Duxbury (2010) only deal with boundary spanning across external boundaries.

7 In the multinational enterprise, the individual subsidiary could be described as a functionally complete and almost autonomous operating organization. The boundaries between the widely independent subunits and the headquarters as well as between the locally dispersed operations almost take the form of external boundaries. The boundaries of the individual subsidiary to its external environments are almost only relevant to the local unit itself. Against this backdrop, transnationalization and the switch to a functional division of labor can be understood as a '*glocal* restructuring of organizational boundaries' (Mense-Petermann 2006b).

8 Other authors in the IB and management literature use the boundary spanning concept, but not in the specific context of expatriate managers in MNCs: Johnson and Duxbury (2010) apply it to expatriates who work as foreign service professionals, not as managers in MNCs. Other authors apply different aspects of the boundary-spanning concept to MNCs without referring exclusively to expatriate managers. For example, Yagi and Kleinberg (2011) empirically investigate the boundary-spanning work of expatriates with long host country experience and theoretically refer to them as biculturals; Kostova and Roth (2003) develop a theoretical model to explain how the private social capital of an individual boundary spanner is created and how it is transformed into unit-level social capital; Beechler et al. (2005) speak of boundary spanning as a necessary skill of global managers; Schotter and Beamish (2011) and Barner-Rasmussen et al. (2014) empirically identify individuals who successfully act as boundary spanners—independent of their expatriate/non-expatriate status.

9 We borrow the terms "processing information" and "exerting influence" from different authors: Aldrich and Herker (1977, 218–21) distinguish two classes of functions performed by boundary roles: "external representation" and "processing information." Johnson and Duxbury (2010, 29) write, "It is through the agency of such boundary-spanning employees that the organization is able to gather local intelligence and exert influence over external constituents in pursuit of organizational objectives (Adams, 1976; Thompson, 1967)." It seems to be appropriate to use the notions 'exerting influence' and 'processing information' because they seem to be the most general terms. They are neither restricted to internal or external boundary spanning, nor do they prescribe a direction of information and/or influence flows.

10 Because of their role in the establishment of networks, expatriates have also been labeled as "network architects" (Wagner 2006; Wagner and Vormbusch 2010).

11 As well as flows of other resources not explicitly mentioned here (e.g., goodwill, image, financial, or human resources; Johnson and Duxbury 2010, 34).

Bibliography

Aldrich, Howard, and Diane Herker. 1977. "Boundary Spanning Roles and Organization Structure." *The Academy of Management Review* 2 (2): 217–30. doi:10.5465/AMR.1977.4409044.

Ancona, Deborah G., and David F. Caldwell. 1992. "Bridging the Boundary: External Activity and Performance in Organizational Teams." *Administrative Science Quarterly* 37 (4): 634–65. doi:10.2307/2393475.

Arthur, Michael B., and Denise M. Rousseau, eds. 1996. *The Boundaryless Career: A New Employment Principle for a New Organizational Era.* New York: Oxford University Press.

Au, Kevin Y., and John Fukuda. 2002. "Boundary Spanning Behaviors of Expatriates." *Journal of World Business* 37 (4): 285–96. doi:10.1016/S1090-9516(02)00095-0.

Barner-Rasmussen, Wilhelm, Mats Ehrnrooth, Alexei Koveshnikov, and Kristiina Mäkelä. 2014. "Cultural and Language Skills as Resources for Boundary Spanning Within the MNC." *Journal of International Business Studies* 45 (7): 886–905. doi:10.1057/jibs.2014.7.

Beechler, Schon, Orly Levy, Sully Taylor, and Nakiye A. Boyacigiller. 2005. "Does It Really Matter If Japanese MNCs Think Globally?" In *Japanese Firms in Transition: Responding to the Globalization Challenge (Advances in International Management, Volume 17)*, edited by Thomas W. Roehl and Allan Bird, 261–88. Bingley: Emerald.

Björkman, Ingmar, and Yuan Lu. 2001. "Institutionalization and Bargaining Power Explanations of HRM Practices in International Joint Ventures: The Case of Chinese-Western Joint Ventures." *Organization Studies* 22 (3): 491–512. doi:10.1177/0170840601223005.

Black, Stewart, and Hal B. Gregersen. 1992. "Serving Two Masters: Managing the Dual Allegiance of Expatriate Employees." *Sloan Management Review* 33 (4): 61–71.

Bonache, Jaime, Chris Brewster, and Vesa Suutari. 2001. "Expatriation: A Developing Research Agenda." *Thunderbird International Business Review* 43 (1): 3–20. doi:10.1002/1520-6874(200101/02)43:1<3:AID-TIE2>3.0.CO;2–4.

Bonache, Jaime, Chris Brewster, Vesa Suutari, and Petra de Saá. 2010. "Expatriation: Traditional Criticisms and International Careers: Introducing the Special Issue." *Thunderbird International Business Review* 52 (4): 263–74. doi:10.1002/tie.20349.

Boyacigiller, Nakiye. 1990. "The Role of Expatriates in the Management of Interdependence, Complexity and Risk in Multinational Corporations." *Journal of International Business Studies* 21 (3): 357–81. doi:10.1057/palgrave.jibs.8490825.

Brookfield. 2012. "Global Relocation Trends: 2012 Survey Report." https://esprit-globallearning.com/wp-content/uploads/2011/03/2012-Brookfield-Global-Relocations-Trends-Survey.pdf. Accessed September 04, 2016.

Caligiuri, Paula, and Jaime Bonache. 2016. "Evolving and Enduring Challenges in Global Mobility." *Journal of World Business* 51: 127–41. doi:10.1016/j.jwb.2015.10.001.

Choi, Soon-Gwon, and Jan Johanson. 2012. "Knowledge Translation Through Expatriates in International Knowledge Transfer." *International Business Review* 21 (6): 1148–57. doi:10.1016/j.ibusrev.2012.01.002.

Czarniawska, Barbara, and Bernward Joerges. 1996. "Travel of Ideas." In *Translating Organizational Change*, edited by Barbara Czarniawska-Joerges and Guje Sevón, 13–48. Berlin and New York: De Gruyter.

Dowling, Peter J., Marion Festing, and Allen D. Engle. 2013. *International Human Resource Management*. Andover: Cengage Learning.

Edström, Anders, and Jay R. Galbraith. 1977. "Transfer of Managers as a Coordination and Control Strategy in Multinational Organizations." *Administrative Science Quarterly* 22 (2): 248–63. doi:10.1177/017084069101200215.

Ernst & Young. 2012. "Driving Business Success: Global Mobility Effectiveness Survey 2012." http://www.worldwideconnect.com/documents/resources/Tax_Global_Mobility_Effectiveness_S_24EC21CA2E7E5.pdf. Accessed September 04, 2016.

Giddens, Anthony. 1984. *The Constitution of Society: Introduction of the Theory of Structuration.* Berkeley: University of California Press.

Hall, Douglas T. 1976. *Careers in Organizations.* Santa Monica: Goodyear.

Hall, Douglas T. 2004. "The protean career: A quarter-century journey." *Journal of Vocational Behavior* 65 (1): 1-13. doi:10.1016/j.jvb.2003.10.006.

Harvey, Michael, and Miriam Moeller. 2009. "Expatriate Managers: A Historical Review." *International Journal of Management Reviews* 11 (3): 275–96. doi:10.1111/j.1468-2370.2009.00261.x.

Harzing, Anne-Wil. 2001a. "Of Bears, Bumble-Bees, and Spiders: The Role of Expatriates in Controlling Foreign Subsidiaries." *Journal of World Business* 36 (4): 366–79. doi:10.1016/S1090-9516(01)00061-X.

Harzing, Anne-Wil. 2001b. "Who's in Charge? An Empirical Study of Executive Staffing Practices in Foreign Subsidiaries." *Human Resource Management* 40 (2): 139–58. doi: 10.1002/hrm.1004.

Harzing, Anne-Wil, and Ashly H. Pinnington. 2014. *International Human Resource Management.* London: Sage.

Harzing, Anne-Wil, Markus Pudelko, and B. S. Reiche. 2016. "The Bridging Role of Expatriates and Inpatriates in Knowledge Transfer in Multinational Corporations." *Human Resource Management* 55 (4): 679–95. doi:10.1002/hrm.21681.

Johnson, Karen L., and Linda Duxbury. 2010. "The View from the Field: A Case Study of the Expatriate Boundary-Spanning Role." *Journal of World Business* 45 (1): 29–40. doi:10.1016/j.jwb.2009.04.002.

Kanter, Rosabeth M. 1995. *World Class: Thriving Locally in the Global Economy.* New York: Simon & Schuster.

Klemm, Mathias, and Michael Popp. 2005. "Škoda als 'learning community.' Empirische Befunde zu kulturell-kommunikativen Bedingungen von Wissensaustausch im 'Tochter'-Konzernverhältnis." In *Deutsche Autoproduktion im globalen Wandel: Altindustrie im Rückwärtsgang oder Hightech-Branche mit Zukunft?* edited by Ludger Pries and Markus Hertwig, 125–46. Berlin: Edition Sigma.

Kostova, Tatiana, and Kendall Roth. 2003. "Social Capital in Multinational Corporations and a Micro-Macro Model of Its Formation." *The Academy of Management Review* 28 (2): 297–317. doi:10.5465/AMR.2003.9416356.

Leonard, Pauline. 2010. *Expatriate Identities in Postcolonial Organizations: Working Whiteness.* Studies in Migration and Diaspora. Farnham and Burlington: Ashgate.

Levy, Orly, Schon Beechler, Sully Taylor, and Nakiye A. Boyacigiller. 2007. "What We Talk About When We Talk About 'Global Mindset': Managerial Cognition in Multinational Corporations." *Journal of International Business Studies* 38 (2): 231–58. doi:10.1057/palgrave.jibs.8400265.

Loveridge, Ray. 2005. "Embedding the Multinational: Bridging Internal and External Networks in Transitional Institutional Contexts." *Asian Business and Management* 4 (4): 389–409. doi:10.1057/palgrave.abm.9200143.

Luhmann, Niklas. 1962. "Der neue Chef." *Verwaltungsarchiv* 53: 11–24.

Luhmann, Niklas. 1976. *Funktionen und Folgen formaler Organisation.* Berlin: Duncker & Humblot.

Mayrhofer, Wolfgang. 1997. "Auslandseinsatz als Instrument des informationellen Grenzmanagements international tätiger Unternehmen—eine systemtheoretisch orientierte Analyse." In Schreyögg and Sydow 1997, 111–57.

Mense-Petermann, Ursula. 2005a. "Transnationale Kulturalität—Ein konzeptioneller Vorschlag zum Problem der Sozialintegration transnationaler Konzerne am

Beispiel der Automobilindustrie." In *Und es fährt und fährt: Automobilindustrie und Automobilkultur am Beginn des 21. Jahrhunderts*, edited by Gert Schmidt, 173–200. Berlin: Edition Sigma.

Mense-Petermann, Ursula. 2005b. "Unternehmen im Transnationalisierungsprozess—Zum Problem der Herstellung de-facto-akzeptierter Entscheidungen in transnationalen Integrationsprozessen." *Soziale Welt* 4: 381–97. doi:10.5771/0038-6073-2005-4-381.

Mense-Petermann, Ursula. 2006a. "Micro-Political or Inter-Cultural Conflicts? An Integrating Approach." *Journal of International Management* 12 (3): 302–17. doi:10.1016/j.intman.2006.07.002.

Mense-Petermann, Ursula. 2006b. "Transnationalisierung als glokale Restrukturation von Organisationsgrenzen." In Mense-Petermann and Wagner 2006, 63–84.

Mense-Petermann, Ursula. 2013. "Expatriates as Micro-Political Actors: Power Resources and Strategizing on Global Assignments." *Gazdasági élet és társa dalom (Economy and Society)* 1–2: 44–73.

Mense-Petermann, Ursula. 2014. "'Bridging the Differences'—Die Arbeit des 'Boundary Spanning' und ihre Regulierung in Transnationalen Unternehmen." In *Vielfalt und Zusammenhalt. Verhandlungen des 36. Kongresses der Deutschen Gesellschaft für Soziologie in Bochum und Dortmund 2012, Teil 1*, edited by Martina Löw, 297–311. Frankfurt/Main and New York: Campus.

Mense-Petermann, Ursula. 2017. "Die Arbeit des 'boundary-spanning – Der Expatriate als Protagonist transnationalen Arbeitens? In Globalisierung als Auto-Kapitalismus. Studien zur Globaliät moderner Gesellschaften, edited by Philipp Hessinger, and Markus Pohlmann, 179–95. Wiesbaden: Springer VS.

Mense-Petermann, Ursula, and Anna Spiegel. 2016. "Global Mobility Policies, Social Positioning and Boundary Spanning Work of Expatriate Managers." *Bielefelder Beiträge zur Wirtschafts- und Arbeitssoziologie (bi.WAS Working Paper)* 1. Bielefeld: Faculty of Sociology, Bielefeld University.

Mense-Petermann, Ursula, and Gabriele Wagner, eds. 2006. *Transnationale Konzerne: Ein neuer Organisationstyp?* Wiesbaden: VS Verlag für Sozialwissenschaften.

Park, Kathleen, and Ursula Mense-Petermann. 2014. "Managing Across Borders: Global Integration and Knowledge Exchange in MNCs." *Competition & Change* 18 (3): 265–79. doi:10.1179/1024529414Z.00000000060.

Reiche, B. S., Anne-Wil Harzing, and Maria L. Kraimer. 2009. "The Role of International Assignees' Social Capital in Creating Inter-Unit Intellectual Capital: A Cross-Level Model." *Journal of International Business Studies* 40 (3): 509–26. doi:10.1057/jibs.2008.86.

Schimank, Uwe. 2010. *Handeln und Strukturen: Einführung in die akteurtheoretische Soziologie*. Weinheim and München: Juventa.

Schotter, Andreas, and Paul W. Beamish. 2011. "Performance Effects of MNC Headquarters—Subsidiary Conflict and the Role of Boundary Spanners: The Case of Headquarter Initiative Rejection." *Journal of International Management* 17 (3): 243–59. doi:10.1016/j.intman.2011.05.006.

Schreyögg, Georg, and Jörg Sydow, eds. 1997. Managementforschung 7: *Gestaltung von Organisationsgrenzen*. Berlin and New York: De Gruyter.

Tacke, Veronika. 1997. "Systemrationalisierung and ihren Grenzen—Organisationsgrenzen und Funktionen von Grenzstellen in Wirtschaftsorganisationen." In Schreyögg and Sydow 1997, 1–44.

Thomas, David C. 1994. "The Boundary-Spanning Role of Expatriates in the Multinational Corporation." In *Advances in International Comparative Management* 9: 145–70.

Turner, Ralph H. 1990. "Role Taking: Process Versus Conformity." In *Life as Theater: A Dramaturgical Sourcebook*, edited by Dennis Brissett and Charles Edgley, 85–100. New York: Aldine de Gruyter.

Wagner, Gabriele. 2006. "Expatriates als Netzwerkarchitekten." In Mense-Petermann and Wagner 2006, 225–48.

Wagner, Gabriele, and Uwe Vormbusch. 2010. "Informal Networks as "Global Microstructures": The Case of German Expatriates in Russia." *Critical Perspectives on International Business* 6 (4): 216–36. doi:10.1108/17422041011086823.

Yagi, Noriko, and Jill Kleinberg. 2011. "Boundary Work: An Interpretive Ethnographic Perspective on Negotiating and Leveraging Cross-Cultural Identity." *Journal of International Business Studies* 42 (5): 629–53. doi:10.1057/jibs.2011.10.

Ybema, S., and H. Byun. 2009. "Cultivating Cultural Differences in Asymmetric Power Relations." *International Journal of Cross Cultural Management* 9 (3): 339–58. doi:10.1177/1470595809346600.

4 Cosmopolitans or Parochial Anti-Cosmopolitans?

Expatriate Managers' Resources, Social Positions, and Orientations

Anna Spiegel and Ursula Mense-Petermann

Introduction

As we have argued in the preceding chapters, expatriate managers are core protagonists of economic globalization and boundary spanners in transnationally integrated MNCs. Drawing on IB and management, IHRM as well as organization studies, we have discussed their role and agency in the transnationalization of MNCs. In this chapter, we want to broaden the perspective on expatriate managers by asking how their agency in global economic activities is entangled with their everyday lives and their orientations and practices toward cultural Others. Can expatriate managers be conceived of as interculturally open and competent cosmopolitans as argued by dominant parts of the relevant literature (Kanter 1995; Sklair 2001)?

In order to answer this question, we have to focus on the relation between spheres of work and non-work. The professional performance and working practices of expatriates are strongly impacted by their embeddedness in the non-work environment. In the case of corporate expatriates, then again, their position in the local context is itself institutionally shaped by the employing MNCs and their global mobility policies. We will show in this chapter that MNCs equip their expatriate managers with extraordinary material and symbolic resources and thus allocate them to privileged social positions in the host localities. This privileged social position, in turn, also shapes expatriate managers' orientations toward the Other as well as their working and management practices. The aim of this chapter, thus, is to work out this complex entanglement of work and non-work spheres by discussing the link between the social positions of expatriate managers as defined by the material and symbolic resources and privileges they have at their disposal, and the emergence of cosmopolitan, or parochial anti-cosmopolitan orientations, respectively.

In a first step, we will refer back to the literature on *global mobility policies* of MNCs. These have been addressed by the IHRM literature, which is mainly concerned with describing different types of policies and with discussing the effects of different policies on the motivation to accept an assignment and perform well on it. We argue, however, that this perspective is too narrow, and we suggest that these global mobility policies instead be considered the most important institution contributing to how expatriate managers are equipped with the material and symbolic resources that make up an elite social position and to a vast extent shape expatriate managers' lifestyles and everyday practices on their stints. A review of this literature offers a vivid picture of the privileges expatriate managers enjoy on their stints and of the lifestyles they are able to afford. In a second step, we will then discuss two opposing strands of literature positing a link between these resources and privileges on the one hand, and cosmopolitanism—i.e. orientations and social and spatial practices of expatriate managers—on the other (see Chapter 1): the *transnational elite* thesis (Kanter 1995; Sklair 2001) and the *expatriate 'bubble'* thesis (Fechter 2007). Finally, building on the critical discussion of this literature, we end by suggesting a new approach for empirically studying, first, the link between resources and possible elite positions of expatriate managers and, second, their orientations, lifestyles, and working and management practices, stressing the role of agency—i.e., of the ways in which expatriate managers deal with resources granted by global mobility policies in structuring their everyday private and work life on their stints abroad.

The Global Mobility Policies of MNCs and Their Impact on the Social Positions of Expatriate Managers

In the IB and IHRM literature, global mobility policies of MNCs have been mainly discussed with regard to their role in motivating expatriates to accept a global assignment, to their impact on expatriates' job performance on their stints, and to evaluating different approaches of global mobility policies in these regards (Bonache, Brewster, and Suutari 2001; Phillips and Fox 2003; Bonache 2006; Harvey and Moeller 2009). In the following, we will introduce MNCs' global mobility policies as a mobility regime governing the transnational mobility of corporate expatriate managers based on this literature. Yet we go beyond this perspective and discuss global mobility policies also as the main institution shaping the social position and lifestyles of expatriate managers on their stints. Thereby, following our proposition of an entanglement of the professional and the non-work spheres (see Chapter 1), we extend our perspective on expatriates to beyond the professional sphere and focus also on their lifeworlds in the non-work sphere.

Corporate expatriate mobility is *organized* mobility. It is part of MNCs' transnational organizational strategies and, thus, it is initiated, framed, structured, organized, and operated by MNCs.[1] In MNCs, global assignments are regulated by specific global mobility divisions and their highly formalized global assignment programs, based on a core of global mobility policies. These global mobility policies are analyzed as a mobility regime—i.e.,

> a specific set of principles, norms and rules that govern the mobility practice of its members within and on behalf of a company. They

discipline mobile subjects by means of a framework for action that dictates who is allowed to move, how and under which terms.

(Kesselring 2014, 6)[2]

Initially, the concept of mobility regimes had been coined for the regulation of international migration by ILO conventions, OECD-Guidelines, and EU-frameworks (see Pries 2010, 41–4). In contrast to these mobility regimes, the scope of global mobility policies in MNCs is limited; global mobility policies are developed by an MNC in order to regulate the transnational mobility of its own employees only on an intraorganizational level. However, the specific principles, norms, and regulations of the respective global mobility policies transcend the level of the single company, as human resources and global mobility divisions of MNCs mutually observe one another and adjust their policies accordingly in institutionalized arenas. Bonache (2006) reports that most MNCs deploy "state of the art" expatriate packages because they match their policies with those of other MNCs. This either takes place by organizing inter-enterprise expert circles or by consulting the IHRM literature or other publications[3] (Phillips and Fox 2003; Bonache 2006; Harvey and Moeller 2009; Mense-Petermann 2014). This is also supported by the fact that, strikingly, our interviewees from the global mobility departments of German MNCs often and uniformly used English expressions that frequently appear in the IHRM literature, like "home-country approach," "cost of living allowance (COLA)," "housing allowance," etc. Moreover, MNCs' global assignment strategies and global mobility policies are embedded in a "global mobility industry" (Cranston 2014) consisting of service providers in the global mobility realm. It "provides services in immigration, tax compliance, relocation management, accommodation services, household goods removal, and cross-cultural training" (Cranston 2014, 1126).[4] Hence, this industry, too, contributes to isomorphism regarding the global mobility policies of MNCs. Thus, global mobility policies constitute a mobility regime of their own, being applied at the company level but evolving in wider organizational fields (Powell and DiMaggio 1991).

Global mobility policies contain basic rules and regulations for global assignments in MNCs (Harvey and Moeller 2009). They regulate (1) how much an expatriate earns while being abroad (this includes regulations for taxation, insurances, as well as for bonuses); (2) which other financial benefits the expatriate gets, such as moving, housing and mobility allowances; (3) which other services the company offers the expatriate and his/her family, such as so-called look and see trips prior to the assignment, the organization of the relocation, and the processing of the tax declaration by an external provider; and finally (4) which services and benefits the company offers to accompanying spouses and children, such as meeting the costs for language classes, tuition fees, offering day nursery facilities and specific programs for spouses, etc. (Bonache, Brewster, and Suutari 2001; Phillips and

Fox 2003; Harvey and Moeller 2009). In combination with global mobility divisions in charge of concrete handling of global assignments and applied formalized assignment procedures, global mobility policies form a mobility regime enabling the company to administer and process numerous assignments within a limited time-frame (Harvey and Moeller 2009).[5]

The global mobility policies not only allow for administering global assignments in large numbers and help MNCs to standardize and rationalize the assignment process, though. They also shape the social positions expatriate managers and their families occupy in their host localities as defined by the material and symbolic resources they have at their disposal to a considerable extent. These resources, however, depend on the specific policies implemented by the employing MNCs. The IHRM literature differentiates between three different approaches: the host country approach, the home country approach, and the global approach (Phillips and Fox 2003; Bonache 2006).

The *host country approach* aims to position the expatriate into the host locality social environment in terms of income and resources. In this case, a host country or locality basket of goods is the basis for calculating expatriates' income and benefits. Given the fact that most assignments go from advanced economies to emerging economies with lower standards of living, deploying a host country approach is only possible if there are enough eligible prospective expatriates available who do not have to be persuaded to accept an assignment through financial benefits but who are instead perhaps interested because of career perspectives or a general interest in experiencing foreign countries.[6] Therefore, in most cases, this approach is adopted for very young employees or for so-called local hires who are already living in the host country anyway.

The *global approach* is used mostly for cases of multiple assignments—e.g., in project work in the global oil or power plant industry. In this case, a global basket of goods is taken as basis for the calculation of income and benefits, and the expatriate package would be irrespective of the respective host country.

Finally, the *home country approach* aims to equip the expatriate with a purchasing power equivalent to the home country and with appropriate resources to allow for a home country lifestyle.[7] To mention an example from our own study, for the German expatriates in our sample, a German basket of goods builds the basis for the calculation of the compensation. So, if German import products like a German 'Erdinger Weißbier' (Bavarian beer) cost much more in Shanghai or in Boston than would be the case in Germany, this difference is compensated for in the basic income granted for the time of assignment (see also Hindman 2008). Bonache (2006, 162), citing the "Worldwide Survey of International Assignment Policies and Practices" (WIAPP) of 2002, reports that the home country approach is the most common one. According to this report, it is adopted by 70 percent of the European, 65 percent of the Asian, and 79 percent of the North

American firms. And both KPMG (2010) and WIAPP 2012 stress that the "home balance sheet approach remains by far the prevalent compensation approach for typical long-term assignees worldwide except Latin America" (Velaszquez Duchanoy 2015). These figures point to the fact that the global mobility policies of MNCs, in addition to their regulative function, also serve to motivate eligible employees to accept global assignments by offering financial benefits, especially to less attractive host localities. As Harvey and Moeller (2009, 278) put it,

> The refusal rate for managers to expatriate has been growing at a steady pace in many countries (. . .). Reducing the level of apprehension relative to relocating to an expatriate assignment frequently necessitates increasing the benefits/compensation to the expatriate.
>
> (ibid., see also Phillips and Fox 2003; Bonache 2006)

The result of this is that the large majority of expatriates are equipped with material and symbolic resources that lift them up regarding their social position compared to their situation at home and put them in an elite position on their stints. Bonache, for example, states, "In China, it was estimated that expatriates earned between 20 to 50 times more than local employees," and that the "average compensation package of expatriates (. . .) is two to five times as much as that received by their counterparts at home, and a great deal more than that received by the local nationals in the developing countries" (2006, 163).

Thus, the global mobility policies of MNCs allow their expatriates to conduct a typical 'expat-lifestyle,' which, at least in the case of Western expatriates assigned to host countries in the Global South, has been characterized in the literature as 'neocolonial.'[8] This neocolonial lifestyle is, first of all, characterized by elite consumption patterns made possible by the different allowances and benefits granted by the global mobility policies, especially in the case of a home country approach. The latter also allow for the renting of luxurious residences—e.g., in gated communities or compounds equipped with gatekeepers and security services, gardening services, and recreation facilities like swimming pools, gyms, tennis courts, as well as shopping centers.[9] The neocolonial lifestyle of expatriates is also characterized by access to housemaids, gardeners, and drivers, and by the fact that the children are attending expensive private or international schools.

To sum up, MNCs' global mobility policies put expatriates in a position allowing them to afford a lifestyle that can justifiably be termed neocolonial with respect to their luxurious consumption, disposal over services and domestic servants, and housing conditions. This lifestyle markedly sets them apart from the local population (and thus also from their local colleagues and subordinates). And this lifestyle is also very much different from the lifestyle they practiced back home[10] (and thus also different from the lifestyles of their immobile colleagues back at the headquarters).[11]

Yet the global mobility policies not only define the material and symbolic resources at their disposal—they also intervene into the everyday lives of expatriates and their families in a far-reaching way. For example, the standardized 'expatriate packages' define not only the housing budget but also pre-select specific residential offers. In addition to specifying the relocation services, the package also determines the specific relocation agency that is to be employed. Whereas the MNCs pay for childcare, they also specify one or a small number of 'contracted schools' for the expatriates' kids, and sometimes run their own kindergartens. Many also engage in the placement of housemaids and drivers, etc. Hence, as previous research done by the author has revealed (see Mense-Petermann 2014), in many cases, the expatriates themselves no longer decide where and how they would like to reside; they do not have a choice regarding schooling and childcare for their kids; a housemaid is hired for them (regardless of whether they want to employ one or not). All of this represents an invasion into the nonprofessional life of the expatriates and their families, going far beyond the standard HR management measures (ibid.).

As such, the global mobility policies of MNCs constitute a specific relationship between the expatriate and their employing organization that could thus—for the sake of sharpening the argument—be termed "neo-feudalistic" (ibid., 301). This pointed expression is meant to shed light on the fact that MNCs tend to incorporate the whole person of the expatriate without allowing for role differentiation as a standard feature of modern societies. Hence, MNCs' global mobility policies play an important part in the entanglement of professional and non-work spheres of expatriate lives.[12]

Our review of the IHRM literature regarding the global mobility policies of MNCs has shown that the latter typically equip expatriate managers with extraordinary material and symbolic resources compared to what they receive on their posts at home. These resources put them in a very wealthy position on their stints and allow for elite lifestyles. The global mobility policies of MNCs represent a mobility regime that on the one hand allows for global placement of expatriates in large numbers by *standardizing* and *routinizing* global assignments and by *homogenizing* expatriates' working and living conditions at the globally dispersed sites of MNCs. On the other hand, however, they also create new differences and inequalities between the mobile expatriates and between different groups of immobile people: the local staff of the globally dispersed subsidiaries, and the local populations in the host localities in general, as well as the immobile colleagues in the headquarters and other immobile professionals with the same set of skills in the home country (Bonache 2006; Harvey and Moeller 2009). These inequalities are being observed by the expatriates themselves and also by the other groups. Additionally, the orientations of the latter toward the expatriates do not go unaffected by these observations. As Bonache (2006, 159) puts it,

> Finally, the generous incentives designed to help attract overseas employment have the side-effect of creating large pay gaps between expatriates

and local employees. The less fortunate position of the local employees relative to that of the expatriate may damage their perceptions of the company's procedural and distributive justice.

(ibid.)

And it can be expected that also the orientations of the expatriates toward the local Others do not go unaffected by the resources and the privileged position they have at their disposal on their stints. Here, the global mobility policies literature implicitly points to the entanglement of the professional and the non-work spheres, and it foreshadows possible implications for the boundary spanning capacities of expatriates without however going into further detail, not to mention an empirical investigation of such implications. We will come back to this in the empirical parts of this book.

In the next two subchapters, we will go on with our literature review and discuss two approaches that explicitly deal with the question of how this elite position may be linked to expatriate managers' orientations.

Expatriate Managers as Members of a Cosmopolitan 'World Class'? The Transnational Elite Thesis

In this subchapter, we discuss a growing strand of literature that posits the emergence of a new transnational economic elite (Kanter 1995; Sklair 2001; Rothkopf 2009; Freeland 2011; Robinson 2012; McKenna, Ravishankar, and Weir 2015; Useem 2015), which is explicitly considered to be a *cosmopolitan* elite. Hence, the 'transnational elite' thesis explicitly deals with the question of cosmopolitanism and links it to questions of status, privilege, and lifestyle. It is put forward by authors from different disciplines and—accordingly—takes different shapes.

From an IB and management background, Kanter (1995) argues the emergence of a new "world class" of top executives. She introduces this thesis by explaining,

> "World class" is a play on words suggesting both the need to meet the highest standards anywhere in order to compete and the growth of a social class defined by its ability to command resources and operate beyond borders and across wide territories.

(Kanter 1995, 22)

From a functionalist perspective, the managers constituting this 'world class' are portrayed as a new type of economic actor, which is the sine qua non for successfully managing border-crossing networks of MNCs and in assuring competitiveness in global markets (Bartlett and Ghoshal 1989; Black, Gregersen, and Mendenhall 1992; Kanter 1995; Bossard and Peterson 2005).[13]

Also, from a Marxist politico-economic perspective, the view is held that a "transnational capitalist class" (TCC) is emerging (Sklair 2001; Carroll

2010). For Sklair, the "transnational capitalist class is the main driver of a series of globalizing practices in the global economy. It is, therefore, the leading force in the creation of a global capitalist system" (Sklair 2001, 3). Corporate executives, for Sklair, form the most important and dominant fraction of this TCC because they control transnational corporations, which are the basis of the global capitalist system, whereas other fractions like globalizing bureaucrats and politicians ("the state fraction"), globalizing professionals ("the technical fraction"), and merchants and media ("the consumerist fraction") are considered supporting members of the TCC (ibid., 17).

Finally, social anthropology and sociology also have investigated "the privileged, bourgeois, politically uncommitted elites" (Vertovec and Cohen 2002b, 6). This transnational economic elite is considered as a—physically and virtually—*mobile* elite (Urry 2007). For Elliot and Urry, today "membership of the global elite is reconfigured in terms of both the 'new flexibility' of the weightless, information economy and (perhaps above all) the speed of mobilities" (2010, 65). In their seminal book on "The New Spirit of Capitalism," Boltanski and Chiapello also maintain that the "mobility/immobility differential" is the central explanatory variable of inequality in today's capitalism:

> In fact, in a connexionist world, mobility—the ability to move around autonomously not only in geographical spaces, but also between people, or in mental space, between ideas—is an essential quality of great men, such that the little people are characterized primarily by their fixity (their inflexibility).
>
> (2007, 361)

Despite theoretical and methodological differences, the studies cited above all promote the view that we are witnessing the emergence of a new transnational economic elite. They go beyond just pointing to the resources and privileges that the individual transnationally mobile manager disposes of—as elaborated in the preceding subchapter—but posit that these managers (together with other globalizing fractions, see Sklair 2001) build a coherent social class of its own. Next to the extraordinary material and symbolic resources, this transnational elite is seen to be characterized by (1) a *homogeneous lifestyle* that is irrespective of their national origin or country of residence, (2) *transnational networks*, and (3) last but not least, *cosmopolitan orientations* (Kanter 1995; Sklair 2001; Urry 2007; for an overview see Goxe and Belhoste 2015).

The *homogeneous lifestyles* that the members of the transnational elite are said to share have been portrayed as 'neocolonial,' as elaborated in the previous subchapter. Integral parts of it are

> exclusive clubs and restaurants, ultra-expensive resorts in all continents, private as opposed to mass forms of travel and entertainment and,

ominously, increasing residential segregation of the very rich secured by armed guards and electronic surveillance. These gated communities are being studied all over the world.

(Sklair 2001, 20f)

Not only can expatriate managers afford a neocolonial lifestyle, in this perspective, they also share the same segregated dwelling and consumption spaces. And these authors implicitly suggest that these spaces are shared by managers from different home countries—i.e., they are segregated socially, but not nationally or ethnically.

Beside homogeneous lifestyles, *transnational networks* are seen as a primary feature of the newly emerging transnational elite (Kanter 1995; Sklair 2001; Urry 2007; Carroll 2010). For Kanter (1995), connections form part of the most important intangible assets members of the 'world class' are rich in and increase their influence over locals (ibid., 23). Beaverstock argues that expatriates are part of dense global-local corporate networks, due to their interaction with expatriates as well as with Western educated/experienced local coworkers and clients (Beaverstock 2002, 536). Sklair (2001) also points to the occasions and structural interfaces where members of the transnational elite meet and socialize: "A crucial component of the integration of the TCC is that most of the senior members of its inner circle will occupy a variety of interlocking positions" (ibid., 21) on the boards of corporations, think-tanks, charities, and the like.[14] Here again, the members of the transnational elite are portrayed as not only individually disposing over social capital, but as being connected with and knowing one another, socializing in shared spaces, developing class consciousness and political unity,[15] as well as common vocabularies and shared worldviews (Kanter 1995). Hence, to use Marxist categories, they are conceived of as a class in-itself and for-itself.

And last but not least, the members of the transnational elite are also said to have *cosmopolitan orientations* (Hannerz 1990b; Calhoun 2002; Skrbis 2004) or—as management scholars have put it—dispose of a "global mindset" (Kanter 1995; Estienne 1997; Kedia and Mukherji 1999; Levy et al. 2007), a "transnational mentality" (Bartlett and Ghoshal 1989), or a "geocentric orientation" (Perlmutter and Heenan 1974; Beechler et al. 2005). As Levy et al. (2007) have worked out, it was the concept of cosmopolitanism—being associated with flexibility, openness, and the capacity to conceive of one's own knowledge as contextually bounded—that served as a theoretical foundation—be it explicit or implicit—for these new kinds of managerial mindsets. However, the different variations of the 'transnational elite' thesis display very different understandings of cosmopolitanism.

For Kanter, cosmopolitanism "is a mindset that finds commonalities across places," and cosmopolitans "spread universal ideas" (Kanter 1995, 61). She explicates: "They are familiar with many places and aware of distinctively local characteristics but see beyond the interests of any one place because they are linked to a wider world and can move between and among places. (. . .) Cosmopolitans face decentralizing pulls in their own organizations, such as reasons why an idea from one place won't work in another, resentment of world concepts because they restrict local identity and options, and legitimate concerns about how well concepts from other places fit local needs. The job of cosmopolitans is to bridge such differences and resolve them so that companies can operate efficiently on a global basis" (ibid.). Therefore, Kanter also terms these cosmopolitans "global integrators" (ibid., 80).

As becomes clear from these quotes, Kanter locates cosmopolitanism on a supralocal level (ibid., 24). Cosmopolitans move in spaces that are disembedded from specific places. The members of the 'world class' are confronted with differences, but differences are seen as *barriers* for global integration and therefore have to be 'resolved.' They are not supposed to embrace differences, but to make "places more similar" (ibid., 61) by bringing "alternatives from one place to another" (ibid., 60).

Yet sociology and social anthropology offer an opposing understanding of cosmopolitanism. Here, it is equated with an *appreciation* of cultural difference (Hannerz 1990a; Calhoun 2002; Skrbis 2004). Members of the transnational elite are said to develop a fundamental intellectual and aesthetic openness toward divergent cultural experiences and the willingness to personally appropriate these practices into their everyday life practices and their habitus. What is implicitly suggested here is that the homogeneous lifestyle of the transnational elite is one that is detached from home as well as host country reminiscences and instead is a hybrid one constructed by selectively incorporating and combining products, services, and practices of different origin. This, then, is considered to be linked to cosmopolitan orientations. Note that this understanding of cosmopolitanism refers to the adoption of *objects* and *practices* stemming from host environment and to the integration of such objects and practices into actors' lifestyles. Yet it remains silent on the *sociabilities*—i.e., on the social relations with other individuals—of such cosmopolitans, and with regard to the question of to what extent locals are integrated into these sociabilities.

These differences notwithstanding, however, both understandings of cosmopolitanism implicitly attribute it to transnational, locally disembedded and segregated spaces. These spaces either are identified in the professional sphere—the transnational network of MNCs or the wider organizational field (Kanter 1995)—or in the non-work sphere—luxurious resorts, expensive hotels, restaurants and bars, first-class airport business lounges, etc. In both cases, these spaces are inhabited by the members of the 'world class' who segregate themselves from local spaces and the 'locals' who inhabit the latter.

Hence, regarding the question of where the cosmopolitan orientations of the members of the transnational elite come from, the proponents of the 'transnational elite' thesis stress the three mechanisms of mobility, transnational connections and networks, and shared consumption patterns and spaces: First, the members of the transnational elite are portrayed as being *hypermobile* and this *hypermobility* is conceived of as a precondition for cosmopolitan openness (Szerszynski and Urry 2002, 2006; Elliott and Urry 2010; Bühlmann, David, and Mach 2013). Kanter characterizes cosmopolitans as "multilingual, well-traveled, at ease in many places" (Kanter 1995, 81). However, she does not elaborate how traveling advances cosmopolitanism or how exactly one gets at ease in many places.[16] The new mobility paradigm (Urry 2007; Elliott and Urry 2010) theorizes more explicitly on the ways how mobility, be it corporal, imaginative or virtual, contributes to the emergence of cosmopolitan orientations. Szerszynski and Urry, for example, have rightly pointed out that mobility has dramatically reconfigured the social, cultural, and spatial fabric of contemporary life, producing connectivity and proximity where there was formerly separation and distance (Szerszynski and Urry 2002, 2006). Being mobile thus allows for coming in contact with cultural Others and to experience difference. Elliott and Urry argue that movement "enables people to be connected with each other, to meet and to re-meet over time and across space. Movement makes *connections*" (2010, 45; emphasis in original). Consequently, mobility is seen as a basic "condition for a cosmopolitan mode of being-in-the-world" (Szerszynski and Urry 2006, 115–16).

Making *connections* and socializing with cultural Others, thus, is considered a second mechanism of developing cosmopolitan orientations. However, the cultural Others considered here also are members of the 'world class.' As Kanter points out, "[m]embers of the world class are not only cosmopolitan in outlook; they are also highly interconnected with each other. They may start with loose social ties within industry sectors and regions, but then, as their companies link their fates more tightly through alliances, joint ventures, cross shareholding, or exchange of people, cosmopolitans become more tightly connected to their *counterparts* around the world. The interactions that occur through these networks create a need for common vocabularies, tools, and systems, and they encourage transfer or sharing of capabilities" (Kanter 1995, 84, emphasis added). This is also why interlocking directorates are considered a prime space for network building, socializing, and developing cosmopolitan orientations (Sklair 2001; Carroll 2010; Useem 2015).

And last but not least, sharing *the same (disembedded) luxurious consumption spaces* is considered to be a third mechanism for developing cosmopolitan orientations. Hannerz, thus, clearly understands cosmopolitanism as a unique privilege linked to other privileges such as education, mobility, leisure time, and material recourses (Hannerz 2011, 198). And in his article with the telling title "The Class Consciousness of Frequent Travelers," Calhoun also—although critically—links cosmopolitanism back to mainly economic privileges of a global elite by saying that the cosmopolitan curiosity "is based on the privileges of wealth and perhaps, citizenship in certain states" (Calhoun 2002, 108). Consumption practices based on the diversity of choices made possible by a privileged social position are seen as an important social condition for developing a cosmopolitan openness to difference (Vertovec and Cohen 2002b, 7). As Skrbiš puts it, "the patterns of consumption of these emerging omnivores suggest affinities between them and what we term 'cosmopolitan consumers'" (2004, 130).

As becomes clear from this review of the 'world class' or 'transnational elite' thesis, the proponents of this thesis, even though anchored in different disciplines and paradigms, all advance the view that transnationally mobile corporate expatriates dispose of extraordinary privileges, display homogeneous elite lifestyles, and maintain border spanning networks and sociabilities, and that these characteristics are linked to cosmopolitan orientations. Cosmopolitan orientations emerge because the members of the transnational elite have extraordinary material and symbolic resources at their disposal that allow for being hypermobile and thus for encounters with numerous places, for making connections across borders, and for practicing cosmopolitan consumption patterns in dwelling and leisure spaces shared with other members of the transnational elite. Hence, in this view, cosmopolitanism inevitably is linked to the privileges of the elite and automatically goes along with them.

This thesis of a cosmopolitan transnational class, however, has been criticized for having various shortcomings. First of all, many of these contributions are prescriptive in character and not very well grounded in empirical data (Goxe and Belhoste 2015).[17] Most of the literature on global mindsets has concentrated on defining what a global mindset is, focusing on how the managers *should* be and what they *should* know (Kedia and Mukherji 1999; Baruch 2002), on its positive results on managerial performance (Au and Fukuda 2002; Bruning, Sonpar, and Wang 2012), and on suggesting practical ways for how to develop such a mindset through training and other educational activities (Estienne 1997). Especially in the case of Kanter it remains unclear whether the picture she paints of the "global manager" as the protagonist of a cosmopolitan elite represents an empirically grounded type of manager or a prescriptive role model. Also, Sklair (2001) postulates more than he empirically investigates the sociabilities of the TCC.[18] And from the position of uncritically assuming an automatic positive relation between mobility and openness to difference, as in the mobility paradigm, the question of how people deal with the perceived and experienced blurring of established boundaries and whether it produces openness or closure, is not answered and cannot even be asked adequately. Studies that have in fact empirically investigated transnationally interlocking directorates— discussed in the literature as a key mechanism for the transnational socialization of corporate leaders[19]—have shown that "most corporate networkers remained national, and most transnationalists participated primarily in one national network" (Carroll 2010, 227–8). Hence, Carroll summarizing the findings of his network analysis, states that "the TCC exists neither as a free-standing entity (it is deeply embedded in national business communities) nor as a homogeneous collectivity" (ibid., 228). And even for the Eurozone, Vion, Dudouet, and Grémont (2015) state,

> The structural basis for the formation of a corporate elite in the Euo-rozone has not been achieved given the evidence from the interlock-ing directorships. Even though the national anchorage of business elites has declined, transnational linkages have not grown much and thus the capacity for acting cohesively at moments of crisis does not exist.
>
> (ibid., 185)

Therefore, at best, as "a class-for-itself, the transnational capitalist class is in the making, but not (yet) made" (ibid., 233), and what has emerged on a Eurozone level only are "specific pockets of interconnectedness" (ibid., 168).

Moreover—and most importantly—the 'transnational elite' thesis is based on a rather narrow understanding of cosmopolitanism, locating it in disembedded transnational spaces secluded from localities and locals. As Kendall, Woodward, and Skrbiš (2009) critically note, Kanter mainly focuses on forms of intellectual, social, and cultural capital that "are highly valued in the global economy" (ibid., 16) and that Kanter's global manag-ers are rich in (see also Goxe and Belhoste 2015). This understanding leads, however, to a bias toward managers stemming from the Global North "whose identification is largely with Western ideals" (Kendall, Woodward, and Skrbiš 2009, 16). Hence, cosmopolitanism is implicitly equated with Western mindsets. Therefore, the literature discussed in this subchap-ter leaves open the questions of how cosmopolitan orientations that can help expatriates to successfully act as boundary spanners in subsidiaries localized in concrete geographic, political, and cultural environments can emerge in secluded *elite 'bubbles.'* Although it explicitly addresses entan-glements of the elite lifestyles in the non-work sphere and the cosmopolitan orientations that can help expatriate managers in the professional sphere, it does not, however, empirically ground and elaborate these entanglements sufficiently.

Expatriate Managers as Members of a Parochial Anti-Cosmopolitan Elite? The Expatriate 'Bubble' Thesis

Taking up the notion of living in a secluded *elite 'bubble,'* a second strand of literature that is equally interested in both the link between elite positions and lifestyles, on the one hand, and the orientations and practices of trans-nationally mobile managers, on the other, challenges the 'transnational elite' thesis with its implied elite cosmopolitanism. Primarily scholars in the field of anthropology and human geography (Willis, Yeoh, and Fakhri 2002; Ley 2004; Fechter 2007; Bayat 2008; Meier 2015a, 2016) have argued that the lives of mobile elites have little to do with the celebrations found in the 'transnational elite' literature, putting forward the contrasting thesis of a pronounced elite anti-cosmopolitanism. This expatriate 'bubble' thesis argues that material and symbolic privileges are invested into creating and maintaining boundaries and to establishing exclusionary sociabilities and anti-cosmopolitan closure.[20]

These two approaches—the 'transnational elite' thesis and the expatriate 'bubble' thesis—are characterized by important methodological and conceptual differences regarding their understandings of boundaries and cosmopolitanism. The first difference is a methodological one. Whereas the 'transnational elite' thesis is built on the analysis of professional networks of expatriates, most scholars arguing for an *expatriate 'bubble'* apply an ethnographic and everyday life oriented approach, which traces expatriates' modes of dealing with difference in different dimensions of everyday life, such as dwelling, consumption, and home making, beyond mere self-descriptions. They are thus able to shed light on the intricacies of the everyday life of mobile elites. A second difference is conceptual. Whereas the 'transnational elite' thesis has emphasized professional networks with other elite members from a variety of countries and the disconnection from the Local as the constitutive feature for cosmopolitanism, the expatriate 'bubble' thesis puts the emphasis precisely on the expatriate's relation with the Local for defining cosmopolitan openness and anti-cosmopolitan closure, respectively. How mobile elites relate to the Local becomes the test case for their cosmopolitanism. Most of the expatriate 'bubble' studies rather neglect the professional contacts among members of the global elite from different countries in their analysis of elite cosmopolitanism, as they see the cultural and national 'Otherness' within the global elite itself as already transcended by the 'sameness' and homogeneity regarding their lifestyles and everyday practices. Instead, it is the locals who appear as the actual Others and the orientations and practices toward these actual Others which qualifies the cosmopolitan. Analyzing cosmopolitanism from this perspective, however, expatriate 'bubble' studies offer a contradicting picture of the global elite: Instead of conceiving of them as cosmopolitan, they stress their parochial anti-cosmopolitan orientations.

First, empirical studies highlight that the private everyday life of expatriates is characterized by practices and strategies of *self-exclusion from local spaces* (Fechter 2007; Bayat 2008; Walsh 2015). To describe this lifestyle based on establishing rather than transgressing spatial and social boundaries to the Local, Fechter takes up the metaphor of the "expat bubble" (2007, 28). This 'bubble' life, it is argued, is directly related to expatriates' privileged economic situation. The economic and symbolic resources provided to them by their membership in powerful transnational corporations convert their mobility into "privileged" (Kunz 2016; Polson 2016) or "elite mobilities" (Birtchnell and Caletrío 2014). In particular, expatriate privileges such as residing in specific Western or foreign oriented gated housing estates are said to provide the spatial and material basis for expatriate self-exclusion from local spaces (Glaze and Alkhayyal 2002; Fechter 2007; Bayat 2008; Walsh 2015) and thus for a globally standardized and "transportable" yet locally disconnected anti-cosmopolitan lifestyle (Glaze and Alkhayyal 2002, 326). In her pioneering ethnographic study on Western expatriates in Jakarta, Fechter (2007) shows that the spatially segregated everyday life of privileged Western expatriate professionals—living in exclusive expatriate high-rise buildings in the city center or in secluded luxury gated communities in the outskirts—is the outcome of expatriates' everyday practices aimed at the production and maintenance of boundaries in relation to the host country. She argues, "a main concern in expatriates' use of space is to distance themselves from 'Indonesia',," and that "most of expatriates' dwelling tend to disconnect the inhabitants from ordinary Jakartan surroundings" (ibid., 63). Additionally, consumption and home-making practices of expatriates have been identified as contributing to the attempts of expatriate professionals to distance themselves from the locality (Gordon 2008; Hindman 2008; Johnston 2014). Hindman, for example, shows how much effort, especially by accompanying wives, is put into keeping the Local from invading into their domestic spaces. She argues that they "exclude culture by relegating it to accessories and doing the hard work required to ensure that the domestic remains traditional—looking like a typical home from their nation of origin" (Hindman 2008, 51). The presence of those local accessories in the domestic space, however, are interpreted as a form of distancing and controlling the Other by objectifying it and as an excuse to not actually engage in durable sociabilities with locals (Coles and Fechter 2008; Meier 2016; Meier and Frank 2016). Besides the spatial segregation of the expatriate domestic sphere from the locality, several studies highlight that this segregation also continues for the leisure sphere because expatriates tend to nearly exclusively use 'meeting places' which are directly related to the expatriates' economic privileges (Beaverstock 2002; Willis and Yeoh 2002; Beaverstock 2005). Among such typical disembedded expatriate leisure spaces are exclusive sporting clubs, restaurants, or bars, all characterized by their non-accessibility to locals.

Second, for the sphere of work, where a spatial and social self-exclusion from the Local is seldom a solution, the relatively new and ever-growing research stream of postcolonial critical management research and organizational studies (Banerjee and Prasad 2008; Mir, Banerjee, and Mir 2008; Alcadipani et al. 2012; Boussebaa and Morgan 2014) deconstructs the image of the cosmopolitan expatriate manager by highlighting *practices of dominance* regarding the Other. Research about expatriate workspaces such as corporate offices of MNCs suggests that they tend to contribute to "the making of difference and augment the raced/national aspect of identity"

(Leonard 2010, 133).[21] Postcolonial scholars argue that despite normative discourses on the global and cosmopolitan mindset in management studies, modern MNCs are embedded in neocolonial power relations. Such neocolonial arrangements are characterized by a systematic persistence of discourses and practices stabilizing the economic and symbolic superiority of the West and the inferiority of the former colonized countries in modern MNCs. The mechanisms through which Western dominance is stabilized today, however, are no longer "traditional mechanism of expanding frontiers and territorial control", but instead are more complex, operating through "political, economic and *cultural* control" (Mir, Banerjee, and Mir 2008, 223, emphasis added). Boussebaa and Morgan (2014) have addressed the MNC as a "neo-imperial space." Not only the locational patterns of MNCs—headquarters in the West and subsidiaries in former colonies—mirror old colonial power geographies (ibid., 99); the hierarchical and asymmetrical knowledge flows also suggest a reproduction of colonial hierarchies within the modern MNC (Boussebaa, Morgan, and Sturdy 2012; Boussebaa and Morgan 2014, 100; Boussebaa, Sturdy, and Morgan 2014). "Some parts of the MNC are 'peripheral'", acting mostly as recipients rather than producers of skills and knowledge, while others are 'central' to the firm, operating more as exporters than importers of such capabilities" (Boussebaa and Morgan 2014, 100). Mir, Banerjee, and Mir (2008) highlight the hegemonic character of such knowledge flows, arguing they are only made possible by destroying and devaluating already existing local knowledge at the subsidiary. These processes of devaluation reflect colonial hierarchies of knowledge and power. Postcolonial scholars, in highlighting that knowledge transfer is in many cases based on coercion and not on dialogue (Mir, Banerjee, and Mir 2008, 222; Mir and Mir 2009, 106) and that headquarters' attempts to establish a knowledge hegemony (Mir, Banerjee, and Mir 2008, 222) deconstruct the image of the modern MNC as a nonhierarchical and polycentric networked organization. In addition, postcolonial perspectives have attacked the notion of the cosmopolitan manager. Studies analyzing the professional lives of expatriates, largely ethnographic, show that managers continue to use predominantly ethnocentric approaches (Black and Porter 1991; Selmer 2001; Leonard 2010, 2012). For expatriates in British MNCs in Hong Kong, Leonard argues, "British 'ways of doing things' are still expressed as the norm, which the Chinese are seen to have 'problems with'" (Leonard 2010, 77). Leonard also describes expatriate workspaces characterized by an absence of interaction between expatriates and local employees, because expatriates work in areas where their most relevant colleagues are also expatriates (ibid., 121). Black and Porter (1991, 109) showed that the management styles of U.S.-American managers in Hong Kong was not significantly different from the management styles of U.S.-American managers in the U.S., even when they had already been in Hong Kong for longer periods. Cheung (2008, 278) argues for an "asymmetrical understanding," as she found that most expatriate managers in China did not possess solid knowledge about China prior to their assignment and were also not actively engaging in the project of understanding Chinese work and management practices. Chinese employees, instead, were indeed trained in Western management approaches and were eager to develop a deeper understanding of the expatriate managers' management practices and approaches (ibid., 301). Analyzing corporate offices of MNCs as "spaces of transnational encounter," Leggett concludes that "the colonial imaginary permits— and legitimizes even—the persistence of race-based hierarchical structures within today's transnational organizations" (Leggett 2012, 88). He found that expatriates continued using colonial imaginations about the backwardness of non-Western societies to make sense of their migration experiences by framing their work in typical colonial terms of adventure, exoticism, and danger. He also showed how colonial racial politics still shaped organizational life, such as staffing practices (Leggett 2012, 2013).

Third, the image of expatriate managers as a transnational cosmopolitan elite is deconstructed by highlighting the *"hypernationalized"* (Hindman 2008, 41, emphasis added) character of expatriate space and communities. Expatriates are not only seen as trying to limit their exposure to the Local by practices and strategies of self-exclusion and dominance, as elaborated earlier. Additionally, the spaces expatriates inhabit are said to be anything but cosmopolitan and international, but instead clearly organized along national lines (Willis and Yeoh 2002, 560). Empirical studies have identified national expatriate communities resulting from spatial clustering of specific expatriate nationalities in specific gated communities, neighborhoods, or areas of the city. For example, in their ethnographic study on Danish expatriate everyday compound life in Saudi Arabia, Lauring and Selmer (2009) demonstrate that living in the spatially segregated compound among conationals produces nationally homogeneous forms of sociability. In his study on German finance expatriates in London and Singapore, Meier analyzes the spatiality of the expatriate managers and their residential patterns and showed how these choices reinforce the emergence of a German national community (Meier 2015b, 2015a, 2016; Meier and Frank 2016) and the reproduction of exclusive male, white and elite identities within these spaces. He speaks of a nearly "automatic integration into the German community" (Meier 2015b, 70). Leisure spaces are also in many cases associated with one specific national expatriate community (Beaverstock 2002, 535; Willis and Yeoh 2002), such as British or U.S.-American clubs. Spaces such as schools, too, contribute to the formation of national communities, as the most prominent schools among expatriates are national enclave schools such as the German, French, U.S.-American, or British foreign schools (Moore 2008; Mulholland and Ryan 2015). And finally, most of the work spaces are characterized by a dominance of expatriates of the same nationality, based on the national character and identity of most MNCs.

To conclude, in these studies the global elite are conceived of as anti-cosmopolitans because they either *exclude* or *dominate the Local* and moreover gather in *hypernationalized 'communities of transnationals.'* Expatriates are said to be "bounded within the physical safety and cultural purity of their own reclusive collectives" (Bayat 2008, 5) and thus typically neither develop an intellectual nor an aesthetic openness toward divergent cultural experiences nor the willingness to personally appropriate these practices into their everyday life practices and their habitus. The expatriate 'bubble' thesis thus rejects describing expatriates as cosmopolitans, highlighting, however, that they have to

> be considered as a diasporic group in the age of global capitalism, as they congregate in national communities, are driven by a sense of nostalgia for their native country, [and] engage in the re-creation of national or regional cultures in their host country.
>
> (Fechter 2007, 162)

The everyday life of expatriates in this perspective is characterized by an "exaggerated geographical boundedness" (Ley 2004, 157). On a theoretical level, this significantly relativizes the idea that mobility automatically leads to the development of cosmopolitan openness in terms of sociabilities or identities (Kendall, Woodward, and Skrbiš 2009; Kennedy 2010; Vertovec 2010; Glick Schiller, Darieva, and Gruner-Domic 2011; Radice 2014). Depending on the context, mobility can both produce openness and closure.[22] However, as it is the case for the 'transnational elite' thesis also the expatriate 'bubble' thesis tends to produce rather homogenized images of the group of the mobile professional.

Conclusion

The aim of this chapter was to work out the complex entanglement of work and non-work spheres of expatriate managers and to elaborate on how the literature discusses the link between the social positions of expatriate managers as defined by the material and symbolic resources and privileges they dispose over and the emergence of cosmopolitan, or parochial anti-cosmopolitan orientations, respectively. By investigating the influence of global mobility policies and the resources provided by them on expatriate managers' lifeworlds and their social positions in their host localities, we have shown that global mobility policies constitute a key mechanism in the (re)production of elite positions of expatriate managers.

Next, we discussed two strands of literature positing a link between these resources and privileges, for one, and the orientations and social and spatial practices of expatriate managers. The 'transnational elite' thesis, to sum it up briefly, argues that material and symbolic privileges translate smoothly into cosmopolitan openness and transnational sociabilities. The expatriate 'bubble' thesis, however, criticizes exactly this equation of an elite social position and cosmopolitan orientations (Fechter 2007; Fechter and Walsh

2012). On the contrary, these authors argue that material and symbolic privileges are invested in creating and maintaining boundaries and establishing nationally homogeneous sociabilities and anti-cosmopolitan closure. Despite significant differences in their understandings of cosmopolitanism, however, both approaches share the proposition that specific social positions automatically evoke specific orientations and practices.

To sum up, the literature has thus far delivered a rather split and incomplete image of the lifeworlds of those expatriates who occupy leading positions in the globalizing economy. Thus, the polarizing question of whether corporate expatriates are to be described as interculturally open and competent cosmopolitans or, on the contrary, as pronounced anti-cosmopolitans and 'parochial jet-setters' remains unanswered.

All of the strands of literature discussed in this chapter stress how expatriate managers are equipped with extraordinary material and symbolic resources and privileges that put them in an elite position on their stints. However, resources and privileges are only one side of the process of elite (re)production (Salverda and Abbink 2013, 4). Following Giddens's idea of structuration (Giddens 1984), in our approach to expatriate managers' social positions and lifestyles, we stress the role of the agency of expatriates (see Chapter 1). Global mobility policies do indeed influence everyday practices and lifestyles, but they neither determine them, nor do they pre-describe specific habitus re-formations. Instead, social actors, such as expatriates and their families, have to deal with these institutionally shaped resources in order to position themselves within the new social context. Also the question whether mobility leads directly to the emergence of cosmopolitan orientations and practices remains open. It is thus necessary to conceptually separate privileges and mobility from openness and cosmopolitanism and to theoretically deconstruct "teleological connections among mobility, transnational networks and cosmopolitanism" (Glick Schiller, Darieva, and Gruner-Domic 2011, 414). We argue that it is an empirical question as to whether people react to the new connectivities and proximities brought to their lives by their own and others' complex mobilities by drawing new symbolic and social boundaries or by positively appropriating these new configurations. Our focus, thus, is on the *practices* of social positioning and resource enactment by expatriates.

Therefore, in the empirical part of this book that now follows, we will address the questions of how expatriate managers make use of these resources, what kind of agency they develop, and how they negotiate their institutionally framed elite position on an everyday level. We show how in the sphere of their everyday life, their elite status is simultaneously both maintained and contested by the managers themselves (see Skovgaard Smith 2013). With this focus on the everyday lifeworlds of expatriate managers, we go beyond the analysis of how the elite status of expatriate managers is institutionally constituted and highlight the ambivalent interplay of institutional formation of elite positions and the everyday negotiations of such social positions. We show that expatriate managers, indeed, form part of the transnational economic elite with regard to the resources they have access to. However, they represent a *transitory elite*,[23] and their lifeworlds are characterized by a number of ambivalences due to this transitory character of their social status.

Secondly, we challenge the idea that elite positions determine specific orientations and practices as implicitly put forward in both the 'transnational elite' and the expatriate 'bubble' theses. Instead, we critically reconsider this idea by offering empirically grounded accounts of expatriate managers' everyday life. These empirically grounded accounts, however, turned out to go way beyond the dichotomies of cosmopolitanism, for one, and the hermetically sealed 'bubble' life, for another, as the literature has suggested. The aim of the following empirical chapters is, thus, to work out and make sense of the ambivalences and contradictions we have found in our ethnographic data.

Notes

1 The fact that expatriate mobility is organized and operated by MNCs differentiates this type of transnational mobility from other forms—e.g., from self-initiated transnational mobility. And it also differentiates expatriates and their lifeworlds and lifestyles abroad from those of other kinds of 'migrants'.
2 Kesselring (2014) explains that to "determine the socially structuring dynamic of spatial mobilities, the concept of mobilities regimes was developed with reference to the political science concept of regimes" (Kesselring 2014, 6). He thereby stresses the aspect of dominance and control that MNCs exercise over the mobilities of their employees.
3 Consultancies like KPMG, for example, conduct surveys about the global mobility policies of MNCs worldwide and publish results so that their clients can orient their own policies towards those of their competitors.
4 Cranston (2014, 1124) reports on trade shows in this industry that "act as an arena in which the latest trends, products, services, and opportunities within an industry are presented. The Expat Show that I attended was an opportunity for the GMI to publicize and sell their services to their potential transnational organization clients. It was advertised as 'everything HR need to plan and manage their expatriate programs.'"
5 See Harvey and Moeller (2009, 281): "While this system is still in its early stages of approval from the larger organizational society, it has the potential substantially to replace significant human interaction and thus keep the resulting labour costs to a minimum. The primary objective of this system is to provide an organization with a system capable of handling an employee's compensation on a global spectrum."
6 This applies in cases where the 'ordinary' living standard in the host country is equal to or lower than that of the home country. This approach may also be adopted in cases where the living standard in the host country is higher than in the home country—e.g., when emerging economy MNCs dispatch expatriates to European countries or the U.S. This is, however, quite a new phenomenon and does not yet happen very frequently.
7 For the complicated and gendered procedure of how such market baskets for the home country approach are calculated see Hindman (2008).

8 Fechter (2007, 27), citing Cohen (1977), stresses the similarities between the lifestyle of former colonial officers and today's expatriates: "In many respects there is considerable sociological similarity and sometimes even historical continuity between European colonial society and the expatriate communities in contemporary neo-colonial countries."

9 See the descriptions of compounds for Western expatriates in Glasze and Alkhayyal (2002, 324–7; Saudi-Arabia) and Fechter (2007, 63–7; Indonesia). Glasze and Alkhayyal (2002, 326) term such compounds "enclaves of Western lifestyles."

10 See also Harvey and Moeller (2009, 283): "The 'perks' have become 'a way of life', or a lifestyle has been developed to which the family has become accustomed over an extended period. When these fringe benefits are recalibrated for the domestic environment, a 'reality shock' for the manager, and most particularly for the family, results."

11 The IHRM literature, too, discusses problems of inequalities caused by global mobility policies: Harvey and Moeller (2009, 280) state that a central feature of international compensation systems is "to be fair with respect to local employees and other expatriates from either the same or a different nationality or with respect to those located in another location." See also Phillips and Fox (2003).

12 See also the thesis of the "incorporated wife" (Callan and Ardener 1984), referring to the traditional constellation of a male expatriate manager and an accompanying wife, showing that not only the expatriate is managed by the global assignment department in a way that encroaches far more into his private life than is the case for 'normal' jobs, but that the members of his family—and especially the trailing spouses, too, are addressed by the global mobility policies and thereby managed by the MNC—without however being a member of the organization.

13 See also the detailed literature review in Goxe and Belhoste (2015).

14 Network analysis investigating interlocking directorates has been a most important approach to study economic elites on a national basis in the past, and the interlock network has been considered to represent "a reliable map of elite power" (Chu and Davis 2016).

15 This is how Chu and Davis (2016) put the role of interlock networks in the U.S. context.

16 For Kanter (1995, 89), cosmopolitans "reproduce themselves. Cosmopolitans create conditions that require additional cosmopolitan leaders with boundary-crossing skills." She leaves open, however, where the initial cosmopolitans who should be assigned by MNCs to fill "global integrator" roles would come from.

17 Some are not at all based on research, but instead on observations, personal chats, or on journalist interviews (Rothkopf 2009; Freeland 2011).

18 See Carroll (2010, 2): Sklair's and others' contributions "rely primarily on aggregated statistical evidence, supplemented by citation of instances of transnational corporate mergers and quotation of corporate CEOs, rather than on sociological analysis of class organization."

19 For a discussion of the transnational interlocking studies, see Vion, Dudouet, and Grémont (2015, 169–70).

20 Note, however, that some scholars from IB have also developed critical perspectives on the 'global elite'. Goxe and Belhoste (2015, 192), for example, have investigated the processes through which the global elite constitutes itself by strategies of segregating and excluding 'outsiders'.

21 Some authors even highlight that expatriate workplaces are completely disconnected from local social networks (Willis and Yeoh 2002, 558). Hindman even found examples of expatriates working in office spaces, where locals where nearly totally absent (2008, 41).

22 It has also been argued that nonelite forms of mobility and even non-mobility can lay the foundations for cosmopolitan practices and aspirations (Amit 2015; Amit and Barber 2015).
23 Fechter argues that expatriates elite status is "situational and temporary, insofar as they often did not possess it before being posted, and they are likely to lose it as soon as they are being repatriated" (2007, 163).

Bibliography

Abbink, Jon, and Tijo Salverda, eds. 2013. *The Anthropology of Elites: Power, Culture, and the Complexities of Distinction.* New York: Palgrave Macmillan.
Alcadipani, Rafael, Farzad Rafi Khan, Ernesto Gantman, and Stella Nkomo. 2012. "Southern Voices in Management and Organization Knowledge." *Organization* 19 (2): 131–43. doi:10.1177/1350508411431910.
Amit, Vered. 2015. "Circumscribed Cosmopolitanism: Travel Aspirations and Experiences." *Identities* 22 (5): 551–68. doi:10.1080/1070289X.2014.975709.
Amit, Vered, and Pauline G. Barber. 2015. "Mobility and Cosmopolitanism: Complicating the Interaction Between Aspiration and Practice." *Identities* 22 (5): 543–50. doi:10.1080/1070289X.2014.975714.
Au, Kevin Y., and John Fukuda. 2002. "Boundary Spanning Behaviors of Expatriates." *Journal of World Business* 37 (4): 285–96. doi:10.1016/S1090-9516(02)00095-0.
Banerjee, Subhabrata B., and Anshuman Prasad. 2008. "Introduction to the Special Issue on 'Critical Reflections on Management and Organizations: A Postcolonial Perspective.'" *Critical Perspectives on International Business* 4 (2/3): 90–98. doi:10.1108/17422040810869963.
Bartlett, Christopher A., and Sumantra Ghoshal. 1989. *Managing Across Borders: The Transnational Solution.* Boston: Harvard Business School Press.
Baruch, Yehuda. 2002. "No Such Thing as a Global Manager." *Business Horizons* 45 (1): 36–42. doi:10.1016/S0007-6813(02)80008-8.
Bayat, Asef. 2008. "Everyday Cosmopolitanism." *ISIM Review* 22 (1): 5.
Beaverstock, Jonathan. 2002. "Transnational Elites in Global Cities: British Expatriates in Singapore's Financial District." *Geoforum* 33 (4): 525–38. doi:10.1016/S0016-7185(02)00036-2.
Beaverstock, Jonathan. 2005. "Transnational Elites in the City: British Highly-Skilled Inter-Company Transferees in New York City's Financial District." *Journal of Ethnic and Migration Studies* 31 (2): 245–68. doi:10.1080/1369183042000339918.
Beechler, Schon, Orly Levy, Sully Taylor, and Nakiye A. Boyacigiller. 2005. "Does It Really Matter If Japanese MNCs Think Globally?" In *Japanese Firms in Transition: Responding to the Globalization Challenge (Advances in International Management, Volume 17)*, edited by Thomas W. Roehl and Allan Bird, 261–88. Bingley: Emerald.
Birtchnell, Thomas, and Javier Caletrío. 2014. *Elite Mobilities.* Changing Mobilities. London and New York: Routledge.
Black, J. Stewart, Hal B. Gregersen, and Mark E. Mendenhall. 1992. *Global Assignments: Successfully Expatriating and Repatriating International Managers.* San Francisco: Jossey-Bass.
Black, Stewart, and Lyman W. Porter. 1991. "Managerial Behaviors and Job Performance: A Successful Manager in Los Angeles May Not Succeed in Hong Kong."

Journal of International Business Studies 22 (1): 99–113. doi:10.1057/palgrave. jibs.8490294

Boltanski, Luc, and Eve Chiapello. 2007. *The New Spirit of Capitalism.* London: Verso.

Bonache, Jaime. 2006. "The Compensation of Expatriates: A Review and a Future Research Agenda." In *Handbook of Research in International Human Resource Management*, edited by Gunther K. Stahl and Ingmar Björkman, 158–75. Northampton: Edward Elgar.

Bonache, Jaime, Chris Brewster, and Vesa Suutari. 2001. "Expatriation: A Developing Research Agenda." *Thunderbird International Business Review* 43 (1): 3–20. doi:10.1002/1520-6874(200101/02)43:1<3:AID-TIE2>3.0.CO;2–4.

Bossard, Annette B., and Richard B. Peterson. 2005. "The Repatriate Experience as Seen by American Expatriates." *Journal of World Business* 40 (1): 9–28. doi:10.1016/j.jwb.2004.10.002.

Boussebaa, Mehdi, and Glenn Morgan. 2014. "Pushing the Frontiers of Critical International Business Studies: The Multinational as a Neo-Imperial Space." *Critical Perspectives on International Business* 10 (1/2): 96–106. doi:10.1108/ cpoib-11-2013-0046.

Boussebaa, Mehdi, Glenn Morgan, and Andrew Sturdy. 2012. "Constructing Global Firms? National, Transnational and Neocolonial Effects in International Management Consultancies." *Organization Studies* 33 (4): 465–86. doi:10.1177/0170840612443454.

Boussebaa, Mehdi, Andrew Sturdy, and Glenn Morgan. 2014. "Learning from the World? Horizontal Knowledge Flows and Geopolitics in International Consulting Firms." *The International Journal of Human Resource Management* 25 (9): 1227–42. doi:10.1080/09585192.2013.826711.

Bruning, Nealia S., Karan Sonpar, and Xiaoyun Wang. 2012. "Host-Country National Networks and Expatriate Effectiveness: A Mixed-Methods Study." *Journal of International Business Studies* 43 (4): 444–50. doi:10.1057/jibs.2012.5

Bühlmann, Felix, Thomas David, and André Mach. 2013. "Cosmopolitan Capital and the Internationalization of the Field of Business Elites: Evidence from the Swiss Case." *Cultural Sociology* 7 (2): 211–29. doi:10.1177/1749975512473587.

Calhoun, Craig. 2002. "The Class Consciousness of Frequent Travelers: Toward a Critique of Actually Existing Cosmopolitanism." In Vertovec and Cohen 2002, 86–109.

Callan, Hilary, and Shirley Ardener. 1984. *The Incorporated Wife.* London: Croom Helm.

Carroll, William K. 2010. *The Making of a Transnational Capitalist Class: Corporate Power in the Twenty-First Century.* London and New York: Zed Books.

Cheung, Lenis L. 2008. "Let the "Other" Speak for Itself: Understanding Chinese Employees from Their Own Perspectives." *Critical Perspectives on International Business* 4 (2/3): 277–306. doi:10.1108/17422040810870024.

Chu, Johan S. G., and Gerald F. Davis. 2016. "Who Killed the Inner Circle? The Decline of the American Corporate Interlock Network." *American Journal of Sociology* 122 (3): 714–54. doi:10.1086/688650.

Cohen, Eric. 1977. "Expatriate Communities." *Current Sociology* 24 (3): 5–90. doi:10.1177/001139217702400301.

Coles, Anne, and Anne-Meike Fechter, eds. 2008a. *Gender and Family Among Transnational Professionals.* London and New York: Routledge.

Coles, Anne, and Anne-Meike Fechter. 2008b. "Introduction." In Coles and Fechter 2008, 1–20.

Cranston, Sophie. 2014. "Reflections on Doing the Expat Show: Performing the Global Mobility Industry." *Environment and Planning A* 46 (5): 1124–38. doi:10.1068/a46249.

Elliott, Anthony, and John Urry. 2010. *Mobile Lives.* London and New York: Routledge.

Estienne, Marion. 1997. "The Art of Cross-Cultural Management: An Alternative Approach to Training and Development." *Journal of European Industrial Training* 21 (1): 14–18. doi:10.1108/03090599710156393

Fechter, Anne-Meike. 2007. *Transnational Lives: Expatriates in Indonesia.* Aldershot and Burlington: Ashgate.

Fechter, Anne-Meike, and Katie Walsh, eds. 2012. *The New Expatriates: Postcolonial Approaches to Mobile Professionals.* London and New York: Routledge.

Freeland, Chrystia. 2011. "The Rise of the New Global Elite." *The Atlantic*, January/February.

Giddens, Anthony. 1984. *The Constitution of Society: Introduction of the Theory of Structuration.* Berkeley: University of California Press.

Glasze, Georg, and Abdallah Alkhayyal. 2002. "Gated Housing Estates in the Arab World: Case Studies in Lebanon and Riyadh, Saudi Arabia." *Environment and Planning B: Planning and Design* 29: 321–36. doi:10.1068/b12825t

Glick Schiller, Nina, Tsypylma Darieva, and Sandra Gruner-Domic. 2011. "Defining Cosmopolitan Sociability in a Transnational Age: An introduction." *Ethnic and Racial Studies* 34 (3): 399–418. doi:10.1080/01419870.2011.533781.

Gordon, Leonie. 2008. "The Shell Ladies' Project: Making and Remaking Home." In Coles and Fechter 2008, 21–39.

Goxe, Francois, and Nathalie Belhoste. 2015. "Showing Them the Door (Nicely): Rejection Discourses and Practices of a Global Elite." *Critical Perspectives on International Business* 11 (2): 189–206. doi:10.1108/cpoib-10-2012-0048.

Hannerz, Ulf. 1990a. "Cosmopolitans and Locals in World Culture." In *Global Culture: Nationalism, Globalization and Modernity: A Theory, Culture & Society Special Issue*, edited by Mike Featherstone, 237–51. London, Newbury Park, and New Delhi: Sage.

Hannerz, Ulf. 1990b. "Cosmopolitans and Locals in World Culture." *Theory, Culture & Society* 7 (2): 237–51. doi:10.1177/026327690007002014.

Hannerz, Ulf. 2011. "Kosmopolitismus." In *Lexikon der Globalisierung*, edited by Fernand Kreff, Eva-Maria Knoll, and Andre Gingrich, 197–201. Bielefeld: Transcript.

Harvey, Michael, and Miriam Moeller. 2009. "Expatriate Managers: A Historical Review." *International Journal of Management Reviews* 11 (3): 275–96. doi:10.1111/j.1468-2370.2009.00261.x

Hindman, Heather. 2008. "Shopping for a Hypernational Home: How Expatriate Women in Kathmandu Labour to Assuage Fear." In Coles and Fechter 2008, 41–61.

Johnston, Barbara. 2014. "Making and Unmaking Difference: A Study of Expatriate Women's Relationship with Domestic Workers in Singapore." Doctoral thesis (PhD). University of Sussex.

Kanter, Rosabeth M. 1995. *World Class: Thriving Locally in the Global Economy.* New York: Simon & Schuster.

Kedia, Ben L., and Ananda Mukherji. 1999. "Global Managers: Developing a Mindset for Global Competitiveness." *Journal of World Business* 34 (2): 230–51.

Kendall, Gavin, Ian Woodward, and Zlatko Skrbiš. 2009. *The Sociology of Cosmopolitanism: Globalization, Identity, Culture and Government.* London: Palgrave Macmillan UK.

Kennedy, Paul T. 2010. *Local Lives and Global Transformations: Towards World Society.* Basingstoke and New York: Palgrave Macmillan.

Kesselring, Sven. 2014. "Corporate Mobilities Regimes: Mobility, Power and the Socio-Geographical Structurations of Mobile Work." *Mobilities* 10 (4), 1–21. doi: 10.1080/17450101.2014.887249.

KPMG. 2010. "International Executive Services: Global Assignment Policies and Practices Survey." www.kpmg.com/ZA/en/IssuesAndInsights/ArticlesPublications/Tax-and-Legal-Publications/Documents/GAPP-Survey-2010.pdf. Accessed August 17, 2015.

Kunz, Sarah. 2016. "Privileged Mobilities: Locating the Expatriate in Migration Scholarship." *Geography Compass* 10 (3): 89–101. doi:10.1111/gec3.12253.

Lauring, Jakob, and Jan Selmer. 2009. "Expatriate Compound Living: An Ethnographic Field Study." *The International Journal of Human Resource Management* 20 (7): 1451–67. doi:10.1080/09585190902983215.

Leggett, William. 2012. "Institutionalising the Colonial Imagination: Chinese Middlemen and the Transnational Corporate Office in Jakarta, Indonesia." In Fechter and Walsh 2012, 77–90.

Leggett, William. 2013. *The Flexible Imagination: At Work in the Transnational Corporate Offices of Jakarta, Indonesia.* Lanham: Lexington.

Leonard, Pauline. 2010. *Expatriate Identities in Postcolonial Organizations: Working Whiteness.* Studies in Migration and Diaspora. Farnham and Burlington: Ashgate.

Leonard, Pauline. 2012. "Work, Identity and Change? Post/Colonial Encounters in Hong Kong." In Fechter and Walsh 2012, 59–75.

Levy, Orly, Schon Beechler, Sully Taylor, and Nakiye A. Boyacigiller. 2007. "What We Talk About When We Talk About 'Global Mindset': Managerial Cognition in Multinational Corporations." *Journal of International Business Studies* 38 (2): 231–58. doi:10.1057/palgrave.jibs.8400265.

Ley, David. 2004. "Transnational Spaces and Everyday Lives." *Transactions of the Institute of British Geographers* 29 (2): 151–64. doi:10.1111/j.0020-2754.2004.00122.x.

McKenna, Steve, Mayasandra-Nagaraja Ravishankar, and David Weir. 2015. "Critical Perspectives on the Globally Mobile Professional and Managerial Class." *Critical Perspectives on International Business* 11 (2): 118–21. doi:10.1108/cpoib-10-2014-0043.

Meier, Lars. 2015a. "Introduction: Local Lives, Work and Social Identities of Migrant Professionals in the City." In Meier 2015, 1–17.

Meier, Lars. 2015b. "Learning the City by Experiences and Images: German Finance Managers' Encounters in London and Singapore." In Meier 2015, 59–74.

Meier, Lars, ed. 2015c. *Migrant Professionals in the City: Local Encounters, Identities and Inequalities.* New York: Routledge.

Meier, Lars. 2016. "Dwelling in Different Localities: Identity Performances of a White Transnational Professional Elite in the City of London and the Central Business District of Singapore." *Cultural Studies* 30 (3): 483–505. doi:10.1080/09502386.2015.1113636.

Meier, Lars, and Sybille Frank. 2016. "Dwelling in Mobile Times: Places, Practices and Contestations." *Cultural Studies* 30 (3): 362–75. doi:10.1080/09502386.2015.1113630.

Mense-Petermann, Ursula. 2014. "'Bridging the Differences'—Die Arbeit des 'Boundary Spanning' und ihre Regulierung in Transnationalen Unternehmen." In *Vielfalt und Zusammenhalt. Verhandlungen des 36. Kongresses der Deutschen Gesellschaft für Soziologie in Bochum und Dortmund 2012, Teil 1*, edited by Martina Löw, 297–311. Frankfurt/Main and New York: Campus.

Mir, Raza, Subhabrata B. Banerjee, and Ali Mir. 2008. "Hegemony and Its Discontents: A Critical Analysis of Organizational Knowledge Transfer." *Critical Perspectives on International Business* 4 (2/3): 203–27. doi:10.1108/17422040810869990.

Mir, Raza, and Ali Mir. 2009. "From the Colony to the Corporation: Studying Knowledge Transfer Across International Boundaries." *Group & Organization Management* 34 (1): 90–113. doi:10.1177/1059601108329714.

Moore, Fiona. 2008. "The German School in London, UK: Fostering the Next Generation of National Cosmopolitans?" In Coles and Fechter 2008, 85–102.

Morgan, Glenn, Paul Hirsch, and Sigrid Quack, eds. 2015. *Elites on Trial*. Bingley: Emerald.

Mulholland, Jon, and Louise Ryan. 2015. "'Londres Accueil': Mediations of Identity and Place Amongst the French Highly Skilled in London." In Meier 2015, 157–74.

Perlmutter, Howard V., and David A. Heenan. 1974. "How Multinational Should Our Managers Be?" *Harvard Business Review* 52 (6): 121–32.

Phillips, Larry, and Mark A. Fox. 2003. "Compensation Strategy in Transnational Corporations." *Management Decision* 41 (5): 465–76. doi:10.1108/00251740310479313.

Polson, Erika. 2016. *Privileged Mobilities: Professional Migration, Geo-Social Media, and a New Global Middle Class*. Intersections in Communications and Culture: Global Approaches and Transdisciplinary Perspectives Vol. 34. New York: Peter Lang.

Powell, Walter W., and Paul J. DiMaggio, eds. 1991. *The New Institutionalism in Organizational Analysis*. Chicago: University of Chicago Press.

Pries, Ludger. 2010. *Erwerbsregulierung in einer globalisierten Welt*. Wiesbaden: VS Verlag für Sozialwissenschaften.

Radice, Martha. 2014. "Micro-Cosmopolitanisms at the Urban Scale." *Identities* 22 (5): 588–602. doi:10.1080/1070289X.2014.975711.

Robinson, William. I. 2012. "Global Capitalism Theory and the Emergence of Transnational Elites." *Critical Sociology* 38 (3): 349–63. doi:10.1177/0896920511411592.

Rothkopf, David J. 2009. *Superclass: The Global Power Elite and the World They Are Making*. New York: Farrar Straus and Giroux.

Salverda, Tijo, and Jon Abbink. 2013. "Introduction: An Anthropological Perspective on Elite Powers and the Cultural Politics of Elites." In Abbink and Salverda 2013, 1–28.

Selmer, Jan. 2001. "Coping and Adjustment of Western Expatriate Managers in Hong Kong." *Scandinavian Journal of Management* 17 (2): 167–85. doi:10.1016/S0956-5221(99)00040-8.

Sklair, Leslie. 2001. *The Transnational Capitalist Class*. Oxford: Blackwell.

Skovgaard Smith, Irene. 2013. "Management Consultants at Work with Clients: Maintenance and Contestation of Elite Status." In Abbink and Salverda 2013, 207–26.

Skrbiš, Zlatko. 2004. "Locating Cosmopolitanism: Between Humanist Ideal and Grounded Social Category." *Theory, Culture & Society* 21 (6): 115–36. doi:10.1177/0263276404047418.

Szerszynski, Bronislaw, and John Urry. 2002. "Cultures of Cosmopolitanism." *Sociological Review* 50 (4): 461–82. doi:10.1111/1467-954X.00394

Szerszynski, Bronislaw, and John Urry. 2006. "Visuality, Mobility and the Cosmopolitan: Inhabiting the World from Afar." *The British Journal of Sociology* 57 (1): 113–31. doi:10.1111/j.1468-4446.2006.00096.x.

Urry, John. 2007. *Mobilities*. Cambridge: Polity Press.

Useem, Michael. 2015. "From Classwide Coherence to Company-Focused Management and Director Engagement." In Morgan, Hirsch, and Quack 2015, 399–421.

Velazquez Duchanoy, Ana. 2015. "Worldwide Survey of International Assignment Policies and Practices (WIAPP): Highlights and Trends—Latin America." www.imercer.com/uploads/LatinAmerica/pdfs/LACBF/WIAPPLACBF.pdf. Accessed February 03, 2017.

Vertovec, Steven. 2010. "Cosmopolitanism." In *Diasporas: Concepts, Intersections, Identities*, edited by Kim Knott and Seán McLoughlin, 63–69. London and New York: Zed Books.

Vertovec, Steven, and Robin Cohen, eds. 2002a. *Conceiving Cosmopolitanism: Theory, Context, and Practice*. Oxford: Oxford University Press.

Vertovec, Steven, and Robin Cohen. 2002b. "Introduction: Conceiving Cosmopolitanism." In Vertovec and Cohen 2002, 1–23.

Vion, Antoine, Francois-Xavier Dudouet, and Eric Grémont. 2015. "The Euro Zone Corporate Elite at the Cliff Edge (2005–2008): A New Approach of Transnational Interlocking." In Morgan, Hirsch, and Quack 2015, 165–87.

Walsh, Katie. 2015. "British Transnational (Be)longing: Emplacement in the Life of Skilled Migrants in Dubai." In Meier 2015. 232–350

Willis, Katie, and Brenda Yeoh. 2002. "Gendering Transnational Communities: A Comparison of Singaporean and British Migrants in China." *Geoforum* 33 (4): 533–65. doi: 10.1016/S0016-7185(02)00039-8

Willis, Katie, Brenda Yeoh, and S. M. A. K. Fakhri. 2002. "Transnational Elites." *Geoforum* 33 (4): 505–7. doi:10.1016/S0016-7185(02)00038-6.

Part II

Negotiating Difference in the Private Sphere

Part II is dedicated to the empirical analysis of expatriate managers' living abroad *in the non-work sphere*. As we have argued in Part I, expatriates' positions and self-positioning in the private sphere is strongly impacted by their equipment with resources and privileges granted by MNCs' global mobility policies. The case study based reconstructions of Part II take up this suggestion and explore empirically how the expatriate managers of our sample make sense and make use of these resources. The chapters of this Part focus on the question of how expatriate managers negotiate difference in their private everyday spaces, the urban space, and their homes on the basis of our ethnographic case studies.

Chapter 5 explores how expatriates deal with cultural difference in different spheres of their everyday life. We show that (1) the urban social space of expatriate managers is constituted by an ambivalent mix of local and translocal as well as national and international connections and by belonging simultaneously to both nationally exclusive and cosmopolitan communities, (2) expatriate managers live in spatially segregated areas based on paradoxical practices of immersion in and distance from the host locality, and (3) the identities displayed in material practices at their homes oscillate between celebrating and avoiding cultural difference.

Chapter 6 enters the debates on the relation of cosmopolitanism and mobility from a gender perspective by exploring the gendered division of labor regarding practices of enabling, shaping, and stabilizing mobility and cosmopolitan lifestyles. For this purpose, we compare two different expatriate arrangements—namely, male expatriate managers and female accompanying partners on the one hand and female expatriate managers and male accompanying partners on the other. Our empirical reconstruction speaks for a simultaneous persistence and transformation of gender relations through mobility.

Part II, thus, offers a differentiated, empirically grounded picture of the emerging paradoxes of the everyday practices and orientations of expatriate managers and their families in the non-work sphere.

5 Difference, Spatiality, and Sociability in the Everyday Life of Expatriate Managers

Anna Spiegel

In the first part of our book, we have set the scene for our research on corporate expatriates' practiced cosmopolitanism by characterizing them as organizational, spatial, and cultural boundary spanners in the transnational social space of MNCs and by working out global mobility policies of MNCs as endowing them with privileged resources. In this chapter, we will now in a first step examine the ways corporate expatriates deal with difference in their nonprofessional everyday life and how they negotiate their institutionally shaped privileged position.

Over the past decade, interest in the analysis of the everyday life of globally mobile business elites has been steadily growing. As already discussed in Chapter 4, many of the existing studies have drawn rather binary and simplistic pictures of these expatriate professionals, who as a group are either portrayed as interculturally open and competent cosmopolitans and global managers (Kanter 1995; Hannerz 2000; Sklair 2001) or, on the contrary, as pronounced anti-cosmopolitans and 'parochial jet-setters' who insist "on fortifying spatial and social divides" (Fechter 2007, 80) and live in segregated 'bubbles.' The aim of this chapter is to reassess these polarized images by shedding light on corporate expatriates' everyday social and spatial practices regarding the ways in which they deal with cultural difference. This endeavor is supported by the works of a relatively new generation of studies in cosmopolitanism oriented around the everyday life of expatriate professionals that highlights ambivalences and contradictions within practiced cosmopolitanisms (Beaverstock 2002; Ley 2004; Datta 2009; Kendall, Woodward, and Skrbiš 2009; Dharwadker 2011; Glick Schiller, Darieva, and Gruner-Domic 2011; van Bochove and Engbersen 2013). However, these inherent contradictions have not yet been sufficiently theorized.

Our approach of practiced cosmopolitanism (see introduction) with a focus on corporate expatriates' spatialities and sociabilities contributes to fill this research gap. It builds on Beck's notion of cosmopolitanism as being related to "new kinds of space-time experience and of human sociability" (Beck 2006, 30). In the following we concentrate on corporate expatriates' *sociability* and *spatiality* in the private sphere (Johanson and Lundberg 2016)—such as choices of residence, dwelling, and establishing friendships—where spatial and social boundaries are negotiated with multiple cultural Others, including locals and other expatriates.

The first analytical dimension considered here is the *everyday spatiality* of expatriate managers and their families, that is, how they position themselves within the local space through the selection of their place of residence (Meier 2015), their housing (Blunt and Dowling 2006), and their urban mobility practices. For relatively mobile actors, the home becomes a critical place, as it has to be reproduced in the new environment under conditions of temporality (Coles and Fechter 2008b; Bilecen 2015; Meier and Frank 2016). This process is related to practices of dealing with the Other in so far as symbols and artifacts selected for the new home can be differently attached to the place of origin, the host locality or other meaningful places in the world.

The second analytical dimension is the *sociability* of expatriate managers and their families. We explore the extent to which the sociabilities that the expatriate managers and their families build up can be described as cosmopolitan, that is, as crossing the categories and boundaries between 'us' and 'them,' and how these social practices are related to the residential and dwelling arrangements of the expatriate families. This focus on sociabilities incorporating the friends, families, and colleagues expatriate managers engage with is based on an understanding of space as socially constituted by social actors and their interactions with others (Berger and Luckmann 1967; Schütz 1972; Bourdieu 1985; Lefebvre 1991; Löw 2008). Focusing on the interconnection of social and spatial practices furthermore puts an "emphasis (. . .) on material culture in theorization of cosmopolitanism" (Kendall, Woodward, and Skrbiš 2009, 32) and subscribes to the idea that "cosmopolitanism can never simply be understood as a mental phenomenon" (ibid.) but must instead be understood as centrally constituted by social practices and material culture.

The remainder of this chapter is structured as follows: The main empirical part of the chapter explores the everyday spatiality and sociability of corporate expatriates using ideal-typical ethnographic cases and works out three types of practiced cosmopolitanisms found in the ethnographic data which are all characterized by inherent contradictions: *selective cosmopolitanism, unaccomplished cosmopolitanism* and *conditional cosmopolitanism*. In the conclusion, we systematize on the *diversity* and the *inherent contradictions* regarding the modes of dealing with cultural difference found in the corporates' expatriates diverse spheres of everyday life.

Expatriate Everyday Life Beyond the 'Bubble' and Cosmopolitanism: Ambivalences and Contradictions

In our research, we have indeed found examples that correspond more or less to the two opposing descriptions—transnational class thesis and expatriate 'bubble' thesis'—of expatriates' spatial and social practices. On the one hand, we have found a few rather cosmopolitan expatriates who had minimal social and spatial distance to the population of their host country and some expatriates who lived a typical 'bubble' life who avoided cultural difference and contact to the local population and uncritically embraced the privileged expatriate lifestyle as described by Fechter (2007), on the other. However, most of our cases did not fit one of these patterns. Instead, an ethnographic exploration of the relationship between spatiality, sociability, and cosmopolitanism showed that ambivalences and inherent contradictions were constitutive features of the everyday lives of most of the managers who participated in this study, and their families. Three typical inherent contradictions will be worked out in the following. These types are analytical differentiations. They have been observed in specific subgroups of our sample. In the following, they are illustrated with an exemplary case, but it would also be possible that several of them occur at the same time in the case of one single manager.

Selective Cosmopolitanism: Breaking the National, Not the Expatriate 'Bubble'

The first inherent contradiction that was present in the everyday lives of many of the managers participating in our study, and one which made it impossible to clearly label them as either cosmopolitans or anti-cosmopolitans, was that they were simultaneously open to some cultural Others and reluctant to others. They were socially and spatially distant to cultural Others who were associated with the host locality while at the same time, they displayed extreme openness and curiosity to cultural difference within the expatriate community present at their host locality. The Winkelmanns, a German-Japanese binational couple, are an ideal-typical case with which to elaborate on this practice of differentiating and hierarchizing between multiple cultural Others.

Mr. Winkelmann, a German manager in his 40s assigned to a global city in China, had begun his current position in the higher management of the Chinese subsidiary of a Swiss MNC four years prior. He pursued his career at a German MNC, which included a three-year assignment to Korea. Mrs. Winkelmann is Japanese, and they got to know each other on Mr. Winkelmann's frequent business trips to Japan during his Korea assignment. Mrs. Winkelmann had worked at a subsidiary of Mr. Winkelmann's company, but she became a housewife when they moved to Germany and got married. They now have two children.

As was the case for many German and U.S.-American expatriate managers assigned to China who participated in this study, the *spatiality* of Mr. Winkelmann's everyday life was characterized by practices of *spatially distancing* himself from the local surrounding. Their residential choice, a gated community with the telling name "World Class Gardens," located approximately 20 km outside of the city center in an area with other gated communities, spatially segregating him and his family from the locality. He experienced this segregation from the surrounding locality—physically through walls and high bushes preventing him glimpses of the inside as well as through gated entries and ritually by security personnel controls, granting access only to inhabitants or those with legitimate association to inhabitants— to such a degree that he perceived the space inside his gated community as not even belonging to Chinese territory anymore, comparing entering the compound to crossing a national border. When we approached the controlled gate of his compound together, Mr. Winkelmann commented with an ironic undertone, "and now we are leaving China." Thus, the Winkelmanns experienced the urban space in different zones with varying degrees of 'Chineseness,' oscillating between hostility and comfort. Hostility zones— perceived as purely Chinese—are the highways and roads to the city, and the Winkelmanns tried to avoid these as much as possible. The 'zones of bear- able discomfort'—perceived as having a lesser degree of 'Chineseness'—were the ways between their own compound, other compounds, and the German school their children attended. Whereas Mrs. Winkelmann is entirely reluc- tant to drive in the hostility zones, she occasionally manages these less hostile routes without a driver. The 'extended comfort zones' of the Winkelmanns— perceived as not or only partly Chinese—are the German school, other com- pounds nearby where mainly German friends live, specific areas in the city catering to the needs of the Western expatriate population (such as restau- rants and shopping areas), and most importantly, the international church they attend. The space that is the center of the Winkelmanns' social life and their main comfort zone is, however, the 'non-Chinese' space of the compound. The "World Class Gardens" is a relatively exclusive compound with large integrated green spaces and water areas, equipped as well with a 24-hour management and security service and additional indoor and out- door sports facilities. The Winkelmann villa has about 350 square meters— sizable, yet still one of the smaller villas in the compound—and a big garden. For Mr. Winkelmann and his family, the compound is a safe haven within a local Chinese surrounding that they describe as dirty, dangerous, and hostile. In her research on Western expatriates in Jakarta, Fechter found a similar structure of urban space dominated by binary juxtapositions (2007, 62–63). Mr. Winkelmann stresses how he and his family enjoy the calm in the compound, where they can "even hear the birds sing," far away from the hectic and loud city environment. And the only way Mrs. Winkelmann tries to reduce the distance to the local Chinese surroundings is to take "City Walks" with her group of expatriate wives. Together, they stroll around Chinese neighborhoods to try to get a glimpse into "real Chinese life." How- ever, these quasi-touristic attachments to local Chinese life only produce dis- tanced, ephemeral, and nonreciprocall relationships and barely change her modes of dealing with the Other from observational to interactive.

The *home* of the Winkelmanns is characterized by a *distinction between different types of cultural Others and hence different orientations to these cultural Others.* When the research team entered the Winkelmanns' house for the first time, Mr. Winkelmann opened the door saying, "Welcome to Asia." What is important to Mr. Winkelmann and his family is that they do not live in a purely German home. With their domestic practices and the material artifacts in the house, they perform a hybrid German-Japanese identity. The whole house is decorated with objects that reference both the German and the Japanese origin of the family. As the family language is German, most of the children's toys, books, and compact disks are German and relate to German children's TV shows. On the shelf next to the compact disk player, several German CDs with German classical music for children are stored, such as "Mozart für Kinder" (Mozart for Children). In the guest bathroom, there are dozens of German women's magazines. Because it is December, they have a typical German wooden Nativity scene on a sideboard in the dining room. During the field research, the family attended the annual Christmas market at the German school, where the main purpose was to 'snatch' one of the highly sought-after typical German Christmas decorations. Besides these objects and practices referring to a nostalgic belonging to Germany, there are also many nostalgic objects with a Japanese identity. They have several typical Japanese wooden cabinets with delicate carvings and art prints showing drawings of medicinal plants. As Mrs. Winkelmann explains, these are reprints from drawings by a Japanese female artist from the fifteenth century who was interested in the healing power of plants and who is very famous in Japan. In the living room, the Winkelmanns have put up a huge educational poster with select Japanese characters for the children to learn Japanese. Mrs. Winkelmann says that any Japanese person would recognize that a Japanese family lives in this home. However, whereas there are strong references to the binational setup of the family and they even attribute their home space an 'Asian' identity, it is nevertheless clear that this hybrid space of the home is—as is the whole compound—somehow located outside of China. When the Winkelmanns moved to China, they liquidated their apartment in Germany entirely and took all of their furniture and other possessions with them. Their home in China is more or less a replication of their home in Germany. They have not integrated any objects into their home which display attachments to local China. *Keeping local references out of the home space* must be interpreted as an attempt to "create a zone of 'normalcy'" (Hindman 2013, 77) by maintaining the home unaltered by the locality.

Mr. Winkelmann's *sociability* is directly affected by the spatial distance to local spaces. Besides the fact that his housing situation is a marked contrast to the typical housing of the average local Chinese population, the feeling of being 'outside China' also refers to the fact that the compound is exclusively inhabited by other expatriates, mostly Taiwanese, French, and some German, and thus represents a social space which is spatially segregated from the local Chinese population. If Mr. Winkelmann comes into regular contact with local Chinese people, they are nearly always in a subordinate position. The Winkelmanns have a gardener who comes once per week, a domestic worker who comes five days per week and a personal driver who is at their permanent disposal. The employment of personal servants, such as gardeners, house maids, nannies, and drivers, is typical of a neocolonial lifestyle, as allowed for by the global mobility policy of his employing MNC (see also Chapter 4). Mr. Winkelmann visibly enjoys his new position as "lord of the manor," which he never would have been able to afford in Germany. He enjoys being driven to his business appointments without having to search for parking, and he enjoys "sitting on the porch on Sunday for breakfast and watching the gardener sweep the leaves." Although he has started weekly Chinese classes, he does not speak Chinese at a level that would be useful in his everyday life. In his personal and home life, his wife assumes the role of translator, speaking Chinese with cab drivers, salespeople, and waiters at restaurants, whereas he does not take up any interaction with them. This specific broker role to the local environment of the so-called trailing spouses will be discussed in detail in the following Chapter 6.

The Winkelmanns' everyday life is characterized by a pronounced *social and spatial distance to difference associated with the territorially defined culture of their host country.* They have organized their everyday life in such a way that they avoid the zones that are perceived to be Chinese and carry out their everyday life in zones of limited contact with the local Other. Given what has been said so far, they appear to be pronounced anti-cosmopolitans. However, at a closer look, the Winkelmanns have a persistent discomfort with this specific social positioning. More specifically, it is very important to the Winkelmanns that they transcend the boundaries of a purely German expatriate community. Here, it becomes relevant that the Winkelmanns are a German-Japanese binational couple.

Most of the U.S.-American and German managers in China lived in what, according to Fechter (2007), could be called a spatial *Western expatriate 'bubble,'* comprised of residential areas exclusively geared toward professionals from the Global North without Chinese neighbors. In contrast, because they wanted their children to have exposure to cultural difference, the Winkelmanns have deliberately opted for a compound which could be referred to as a *global expatriate 'bubble'* within a gated community with a global composition of residents coming from both Western countries and also other Asian and, in some cases, also African countries. According to both Mr. and Mrs. Winkelmann, "it is really good that this compound is not entirely German or Western, so the children get an impression of diversity." When Mr. Winkelmann commented about his gated community not belonging to China, one of the researchers then asked him in what ways he would describe the space then, if not as belonging to China. With a proud undertone, he said, "Well. I don't know; it's not China, but it's not Germany either." His quotation highlights the value he puts on the fact that he does not live in a German-dominated compound, but instead in an international one. Networks to other expatriate families living in the compound, including families from African countries, were easily established, as Mrs. Winkelmann tells; she was immediately approached by other expatriate mothers while she was waiting for the school bus to pick up her children. Mrs. Winkelmann quickly became part of an international group of expatriate wives in the compound who regularly organize parties and other activities with other families. Despite remaining segregated from the locality, the compound provides the space for *cosmopolitan sociability* among expatriates from different countries, among them even non-Western expatriates from several African and Asian countries.

A second space, where Mr. and Mrs. Winkelmann practice a cosmopolitan sociability, is the internationally oriented Pentecostal Church they attend. Although there is both a German Catholic congregation and a Japanese Protestant congregation, the Winkelmanns have finally decided against attending one of their own national diaspora churches in China. The have opted, instead, to attend an internationally oriented Pentecostal Church with an U.S.-American minister and a mixed Asian-Anglo-Saxon congregation because of the international setup of the congregation. The majority of the congregants come from the U.S. and other European countries, but there is also a significant proportion coming from Asian countries, such as the Philippines, Singapore, and Malaysia, as well as Chinese return-migrants with foreign passports. And for the Winkelmanns, it is precisely this international setup of the congregation, which is attractive to them. This attraction includes the U.S.-American style of the church service with a lot of "worshipping and singing," as well as to the religious practices of the Asian members of the group and the everyday life of the other members, as Mr. Winkelmann elaborates in the following quotation:

> You don't see churches like this one in Germany. When you see this kind of internationality, you can't even imagine ever going back to Germany. It's just too German in Germany. Here, you are even able to gather a bit about how other people live. That's the case again now; I am in a group where there are many people from Korea, which is a place that I am somewhat familiar with, and it is very interesting to see how they approach certain things. And it is totally fascinating for me to see how widespread Christianity actually is here in Asia, given that we really only ever see Christianity in Europe or maybe America, but it is lived with such intensity here, which is something we hardly even see anymore, so that is definitely impressive to see.

In the context of the international church, Mr. Winkelmann displays curiosity and openness to cultural difference and to different lifeworlds. Whereas he refuses speaking Chinese, he actively tries to improve his command of English and enjoys the challenge of reading and discussing the Bible in English. Whereas he had mostly tried to avoid local Chinese culture, he talks about other religious styles encountered at his international church with approval and enthusiastically integrates them into his own practices. In the context of the international church, cultural difference is nothing he claims to experience as separating him from others, seeing it instead as a source for exchange, communication, and sociability. Regarding the conversations and discussions in the weekly Sunday men's group he attends, he explains,

> Against a different cultural background, that is very interesting, because we have people from, one is from Northern Ireland, one from Australia, another is from Hong Kong, then we've got Americans originating from China, and other Americans, and one guy from England, three Germans, each with a different cultural background, but here in the same city. Similar positions, a little bit different, (. . .) each essentially holding managerial positions here in the city, (. . .) but it is very exciting to see how . . ., because you do gain a bit of insight into the lives of other people, and then you meet up every Sunday and talk to each other.

The basis for this positive appropriation of difference is that the members of the church, despite being different, are at the same time bound together by specific commonalities. The community that Mr. Winkelmann describes is constituted by joint religious rituals and practices of exchange and through similar everyday life and professional situations. Our argument here is that within such communities based on specific commonalities, difference becomes manageable and, thus, attractive.

To sum up, while trying to avoid differences related to the Chinese locality as much as possible, the Winkelmanns do indeed move in extremely cosmopolitan spaces, without, however, any attachment to the Chinese locality. In contrast to other expatriates with solely national networks, the Winkelmanns maintain international social networks that are not restricted to Western expatriate circles. They have made a point not to live in a *national 'bubble'*; however, they do not problematize their social position of living spatially and socially 'outside China.'

Unaccomplished Cosmopolitanism: The Power of the Locality

The second inherent contradiction present in the everyday lives of a smaller number of the managers was their desire to be immersed in the local culture and the impossibility to realize this desire. These expatriate managers were very critical of the *social and spatial segregation from the host country* typical for the expatriate 'bubble' life. Instead of embracing the privileged lifestyle and avoiding the locality, they consciously *rejected social and spatial segregation from the host country and looked for immersion to the locality*. However, they were not able to achieve their cosmopolitan ideals because of the closed character of the local communities and other specificities of the local context and, thus, remained unaccomplished cosmopolitans. The Kellys, a U.S.-Korean binational expatriate couple, are an ideal-typical case with which to elaborate on this unaccomplished attempt to overcome the social and spatial segregation from the locality.

Mr. Kelly is an U.S.-American expatriate manager in his 60s, assigned to a global city in China. He had been working in the higher ranking management position in a subsidiary of a German MNC in China for approximately ten years. Prior to his current assignment, he had worked in Austria. Mrs. Kelly works as a business consultant for a representation office of a U.S. business services firm. They have three children.

The *spatiality* of the Kellys' everyday life is characterized by practices of minimizing *spatial distance to the host country* and, thus, stands in stark contrast to the spatiality of the majority of U.S.-American and German expatriate managers assigned to China who participated in this study. The Kellys have employed this localizing strategy during both their assignment to Austria and their assignment to China. Whereas most of the managers in Chinese cities only traveled in their company cars with a professional driver, the Kellys have rejected the company car and only use public transportation and bicycles for getting around in the city. In contrast to the majority of expatriate managers who did not think about alternatives to sending their children to national enclave schools such as Mr. Winkelmann or international schools, they had initially sent their children to a regular Chinese school. However, the children had severe problems, and as a result, they had to change to an international school. But especially in their decisions about the location and style of their local place of residence, this longing for local attachment and exposure to local people and culture played a major role. Instead of living in one of the expatriate compounds in the suburbs, as, for instance, the Winkelmanns, they have opted to live in a renovated so-called courtyard house in a predominantly Chinese neighborhood in the city center with predominantly local middle-class residents:

> Well, we have opted against living in a compound, because if you live like this, then you don't live in . . . you could easily think that you're in Dallas, in Texas, walking around in such a compound. And the same is for these Western style high rise buildings in the city center. But we wanted to be in the middle of a Chinese neighborhood, you know, just a totally normal neighborhood. So first we lived in a courtyard, our cleaning lady lived just across the street, and here where we live now, people are taxi drivers or you know, blue collar workers, or even just retired. And when you walk on the street, you can see them. They just sit on the street, because the apartments are too small, so where we have our courthouse they would live with ten families. So we were the only ones to be renovated, the others just remained as they were, with the public toilets. But we decided that we wanted to experience Chinese life, not

only an expat life. So OK, yeah, I also do my grocery shopping at an expat supermarket, because I don't know about the quality at the local produce market, but we otherwise just like being ordinary people here.
(Mrs. Kelly)

In contrast to expatriates living 'outside China,' the Kellys seek exposure to difference and local everyday life through their dwelling practices and actively work on positioning themselves 'in the middle of China.' They refuse the idea of a globally standardized home shaped according to the aesthetics of a stereotypical U.S.-American home and instead strive for immersion into what they conceive to be the local normal Chinese life. The Kellys frame their attempts at being exposed to difference not only from a cultural dimension but also from a socio-structural dimension. By *seeking spatial proximity to normal, 'ordinary' people*, they also construct themselves as ordinary people. This attempt of undoing their elite status (see Chapter 4) by spatial proximity puts them in a position where they can observe normal Chinese life on an everyday basis. Other expatriate managers and their families instead had to organize these everyday 'observations' in the aforementioned 'City Walks' in a touristic way. For the Kellys, the decision to live in the city center was one possible instrument for explicitly practicing an alternative lifestyle to the one usually connected with expatriates in China.

The interior of their *home*, similarly to the location of their home, represents their *attempts to live a 'normal life.'* Despite the high-ranking positions of both Mr. and Mrs. Kelly and their respective economic resources, the style of their home is surprisingly unpretentious and modest. The house is partly furnished, and the Kellys have added some of their own pieces. They have decorated the home with unique handicrafts made by friends from their prior assignment. Mr. Kelly has decorated the apartment with his collection of historic world maps, a typical form of 'banal cosmopolitanism' (Szerszynski and Urry 2002, 467).

However, looking at their forms of *practiced sociability*, the limits to their ambitions to live an ordinary life 'in the middle of China' become evident, as was indicated in the quotation noted earlier. Whereas they have opted for a dwelling location where they are constantly confronted with locals and especially with locals of different socio-structural background and enjoy this exposure as part of an intercultural learning process, this *spatial proximity has not directly led to a social proximity*. Although they live in the same street with their local Chinese neighbors, the actual living conditions could not be more different. Due to their privileged financial resources, as a family of five, they are able to live in the same space typically occupied by several Chinese families. As they told us regretfully, in spite of having lived in their first neighborhood for six years and although all of them spoke at least basic Chinese, contact to their neighbors there had never gone beyond greeting. Only when their son carried out a school research project, which included interviewing their neighbors, did the situation change. The following quotation from an interview with one of the sons makes visible the social and emotional distance toward their neighbors.

> I couldn't really call them neighbors until after the interviews (. . .) it was strange, before that I didn't have any interaction with my neighbors, it was just kind of like a hello in the morning and "Who's that weird foreign youngster?" and then after the interviews we had little chats.

What is illustrated in this quotation is the fact, that in the cosmopolitan encounter, both parties involved have a specific degree of power in determining the outcome of this encounter. The young boy describes the skepticism and the reserve of the local neighbors, which prevented more intensive interactions. In the new neighborhood, they are again socially distant to their neighbors. Even their wider social networks do not reflect the spatial proximity to China. Mrs. Kelly, for instance, very self-critically reflects on the fact that she has no Chinese friends or acquaintances who she would consider important to her:

> And then it is very difficult to make Chinese friends here, who, and maybe it's because of the language, because Chinese is a very difficult language and I don't have the time like I did in Austria to meet up regularly with a tutor or a teacher. For the first three years, I did have one, but we didn't meet regularly, and then, well, now my Chinese is a kind of everyday basic Chinese, good enough for everyday situations.

Although both Mr. and Mrs. Kelly have put strong emphasis on learning local languages during both of their assignments (Austria, China), and although they have achieved fluency in German, they are very frustrated by their only basic Chinese language competences. Whereas in Austria they had both local and international friends, they have not made any local friends in China. All the people Mrs. Kelly would consider to be her friends are either located in Austria, the place of their prior assignment, or in the U.S., which is her husband's home country, or they are other expatriates located in China.

A similar case highlighting the frustrations of not being included in local sociabilities is the Müller family—a German expatriate family living in the U.S. Mr. Müller is in his 40s and is part of the middle management level of his company, a leading German MNC. He started his career at the company approx. 20 years ago and has continuously climbed up the management ladder, coordinating first national and, later, international projects from the German headquarters. He came to the U.S. two years ago when he was offered the position of head of a newly established unit of the U.S. subsidiary. In this position, he is responsible for the coordination of joint projects with U.S.-American cooperation partners. He is married and has two children.

Like in the case of the Kellys, the *spatiality* of the Müllers' everyday life is characterized by a certain proximity to the local population. However, unlike in China, where most of the Western expatriates lived in residential areas with no local residents, most of the German managers in the U.S. lived in *mixed elite 'bubbles,'* that is, residential areas inhabited by local elites. The Müllers live in a rather small subdivision—a bounded residential area with an entry gate and technical surveillance, but without restricted entry— with a clear upper-middle to upper-class character without any other German expatriates. Their two children attend the 'company reference school,' a local, very exclusive private school with regional reputation. The Müllers report enthusiastically about the excellent opportunities that the local school offers to their children.

However, although living in a local neighborhood and attending a local school, the Müllers' *sociability* is characterized by contacts within the German expatriate community. The area, where the company subsidiary is located, is described by the Müllers as a 'boom region' with a lot of international professionals and as a region with 'old money' and wealthy traditional families.[1] Although being fascinated with the affluence of their surroundings and enjoying all the privileges that are related to their status as a German expatriate family, the social position of the Müllers in this local elite space is rather problematic. Local interaction partners put their belonging within this local elite space into question. The Müllers emphasize the closed character of the local elite milieu. They report that it is very difficult, if not impossible, to establish contact with local U.S.-American children and their parents. The Müllers explain that, first, local elite parents do not think that the German expatriate families really belong to this expensive private school. German families were only able to send their children to this school because "their company paid for it" and not because of their own prosperity. Second, the Müllers explain, how they are not considered to be full members of the community because of their temporary limited presence. To emphasize the closed character of the local elite milieu, the Müllers also tell us about subdivisions where it is not enough for potential buyers to be able to afford the highly priced houses, but they must also be personally invited by other families living in the subdivision. In their own subdivision, they have indeed been able to establish closer contact to some of their local U.S.-American neighbors. However, the Müllers' main reference persons and those of their children are other expatriate families from the same company.

The cases of the Kellys and the Müllers show a specific ambivalence. They actively seek local attachment and exposure to local everyday life through their housing and schooling practices. Spatially, they live neither in a national nor in a *Western expatriate 'bubble,'* and in this respect, they display what could clearly be identified as cosmopolitan openness. Nevertheless, this proximity remains spatial, and is not directly translated into social proximity, because in the case of the Kellys, they are confronted with distancing practices of the local population, due to their being conceived as elite members who do not fit into a local nonelite space, and in the case of the Müllers, this is because they are conceived of as nonelites who do not fit into a local elite space. In this sense, they are unaccomplished cosmopolitans.

Conditional Cosmopolitanism: Consuming the Other in Intermediary Spaces

A third type of constitutive contradiction in the everyday lives of expatriate managers lies in the fact that some of them indeed look for an immersion into the locality but try to control this immersion as much as they can. Their everyday life spatiality and sociability are characterized by a controlled proximity to the locality and the local population and mostly takes place in intermediary spaces. Mr. Hoffmann, a young German professional in his late 20s living in China, is an ideal-typical case with which to elaborate on this ambivalence. Mr. Hoffmann had been assigned to a global city for a middle management position for a medium-sized German company. In his self-description, career orientation and flexibility play significant roles. Although he had studied International Management with a regional focus on East Asia and had even taken Mandarin language classes at the university in Germany, he did not want to be identified as the "China guy" and was constantly looking for ways how to counter this regional specialization.

Mr. Hoffmann's *everyday spatiality* is characterized by a *strong ambivalence toward the locality*. He deliberately decided against living in the gated communities far away from the city center because he had the feeling of being in a "holiday resort in Tenerife" there and not in China. Living like a tourist in spatially segregated compounds far away from what he conceived to be the authentic city life, as Mr. Winkelmann did, was not an option for him. This pattern of different rationales for families and single professionals has been discussed by Meier (2015). Whereas he turned down this distant compound housing, he likewise decided against a house in a traditional neighborhood. He had actually looked at such renovated houses in the old town area, but they were, according to his standard, too small and too expensive for him as a single person. Also, he said, they did not have double glazing windows to keep out the urban noise, and they were not safe enough. He comments, "In those houses that I saw, the entrance area and halls were quite run-down, Chinese though, this is why I preferred a modern apartment." Mr. Hoffmann indeed lives in a *local elite 'bubble,'* that is, a high-rise compound with mixed local and foreign elite residents only a few kilometers away from his office on the fringes of the global city's "urban glamour zone" (Sassen 1998). He describes the residents of his high-rise compound as "Chinese nouveaux riches" and reports with amusement about the high number of luxury cars—Ferrari, BMW, Mercedes—which can be found in the car park and the eccentric colors of some of these cars. He has opted for living in the city center as a strategy to minimize spatial distance to what he conceives of as the authentic locality. He, however, also enjoys the amenities of the *elite 'bubble'* for keeping the unpleasant features of the global city life—noise, risk—at a distance. He did not want to live 'outside China'; however, he also did not want to be too immersed.

This same ambivalence can be found in his everyday practices of moving in the urban space. He describes himself as an adventurer in an urban space where he is confronted with irritating and incomprehensible bodily practices of Chinese Others. He is both fascinated and disgusted by these practices, which he describes as strange and even dangerous. He reports very negatively about the subway in the global city, which he refuses to use because of people having to squeeze together and the risk of infections. He is extremely irritated by the practices of openly snorting and spitting, especially when he observes them in young women. Nevertheless, he constantly seeks exposure to this partly incomprehensible urban space in his everyday life. For movement throughout the city, Mr. Hoffmann has opted to buy an electric scooter, as they are popular in urban China these days. Driving the scooter is a practice of participating in Chinese urban everyday life, and he is markedly proud of being so local and courageous. Several other expatriates in our sample consciously decided against a driver, opting instead for scooters, bicycles, tuk tuks, or other local forms of transportation. By adopting the local way of driving his scooter—driving without a helmet, using not only the streets but also the pedestrian lanes, and honking continuously and energetically—he has gained local competence. With regard to honking, he explains that before he himself started to drive an electric scooter, he had found the never-ending cacophonic chorus of horns unbearable. However, driving a silent electric scooter by himself, he quickly learned that honking is the only way to not be overlooked by other drivers and pedestrians. By participating in these local practices, he is situationally able to take up the local perspective and to acquire practical knowledge, which helps him understand practices of the Chinese Others that were previously incomprehensible. In addition, he regularly has lunch at very small Chinese "hole-in-the-wall-restaurants," as he calls them, proudly highlighting that no other expatriates usually go there.

Mr. Hoffmann's *home* could be described as a *flexible home*. He lives in a fully furnished 60 square meter apartment. Although his company offered him the possibility to move all of his belongings to China in a container, he turned this down, instead moving with only two small boxes. Although the style of the apartment does not correspond to his taste, he has not tried to rearrange or modify the apartment in any significant way by, for example, changing the furniture or by adding personal items to the apartment. The only objects that he has added are his iMac, placed on one side of the dining table next to the entrance, and an impressive collection of DVDs with U.S.-American TV shows placed on a sideboard under the oversized flat screen TV. He says,

> I was at home here from the very first day. And will be until my last day. My home is where my computer is, although today with laptops it's

not so clear. That's why wherever I park my underwear, that is where my home is. (. . .) Because when I go visit my family, I always carry my suitcase, and for me, all the places where I have to go with my suitcases are not my home, and the place where the suitcases are empty, this is my home.

He shows a tremendous flexibility in his capacity to build up a sense of belonging to the new place, and objects do not seem to be important for his kind of belonging; he has actually minimized the objects that belong to him, and there are neither nostalgic nor local objects that would evoke a sentimental attachment to a specific locality. The only artifacts that seem to be important to him, the computer and the DVDs, are related to a global media culture and to technologies associated with the disentanglement of physical and social spaces. Mr. Hoffmann's sense of belonging is temporary and flexible and can be deliberately and easily activated and deactivated. This type of belonging is enacted through practices and images of hypermobility, such as packing and unpacking the suitcase. The hypermobile home is where he unpacks his most intimate belongings, his underwear. This belonging is indeed not cosmopolitan in terms of openly embracing difference, but instead in terms of ignoring perceived differences. This indifference toward difference, however, makes it easy for Mr. Hoffmann to quickly feel at home in many places.

Additionally, Mr. Hoffmann's *sociability* is characterized by a *limited, controlled immersion with the local Other in intermediary spaces*. Interestingly, Mr. Hoffmann has not built up friendships within what he calls the "expatriate scene." Disillusioned, he explains,

But here in the city, the expat-scene, well, anyone who says they've been able to make long-term friends, they're kidding themselves. Because if you do meet someone and think, wow, he was really nice or she was really nice, maybe this could turn into something, well then they'll say to you, "Oh, by the way, the day after tomorrow is my last day here in China after three years of being here." Or I'm the one who has to tell people that I won't be here much longer. Private contacts here are rubbish, because even I myself know that I am only going to be here until July, and I only had one and a half years here from the beginning, so why even try.

Establishing friendships within communities consisting of mobile people is highly problematic, as not only one's own residence in the locality is temporarily limited but also the residence of the others. Consequently, Mr. Hoffmann has retracted from a wider expatriate community and has concentrated on establishing contacts with his colleagues from the company. Some of these acquaintances are Germans; others are indeed Chinese. However, all of these Chinese acquaintances have a biographical or educational trajectory that involves long periods of time in Germany. Mr. Hoffmann elaborates:

> Well, Stefan is from Munich, Florian is from Hamburg, even if he is Chinese by birth, ah actually, his parents are Chinese, he himself was born in Hamburg I believe, and that's why we're just somehow automatically close to each other. The female colleagues here too, they speak German, so with them I'm . . ., Mrs. Sun lived in Munich for 14 years, so we are just simply closer to each other. It's not that I dislike the Chinese people here, per se, but I just don't seem to quite, it's not as if I would go out and grab a beer with them in the evening. We just simply have different opinions on that, or then it's the language barrier. I just somehow have more things in common with the others and so that's why I'll meet up with them for a beer in the evening.

Mr. Hoffmann distances himself socially from the expatriate community because of its hypermobility and volatility. However, he also distances himself socially from the average local population that he defines as not having international experiences. What characterizes Mr. Hoffmann's sociability is the search for intermediary spaces, that is, sociabilities with locals who, according to his interpretation, are not entirely local (see Chapter 8 regarding his work life). The company and the internationally experienced local employees constitute one such intermediary space where he can control the amount and degree of the Local that is bearable for him.

The ways Mr. Hoffmann deals with difference and immerses himself in the local space, his social and spatial practices, have ambivalent consequences. On the one hand, they stand for a general openness to participation in local practices and to imitating what locals do in a very embodied way, including taking up corporeal risk. This offers him a greater opportunity to gain deeper understanding of the locality than staying in a strictly observational position. On the other hand, his adventurous attitude does not create permanent and reciprocal engagement in the sense of a cosmopolitan sociability with local people. In both his dwelling arrangements and his sociability, he looks for a limited and controlled immersion with the local Other in intermediary spaces.

Conclusion

Against the background of studies that have either taken cosmopolitanism of mobile elites for granted or, on the contrary, have emphasized their anti-cosmopolitan practices of self-exclusion from spatialities and sociabilities of intercultural encounters, the aim of this chapter was to critically reconsider the idea of elite cosmopolitanism and to empirically ground different types of ambivalences and inherent contradictions in the everyday lives of expatriate managers. We examined dimensions of the expatriate everyday spatiality—such as place of residence (Meier 2015), housing (Blunt and Dowling 2006), and urban mobility practices—and of sociability.

First, ethnographically exploring the relationship between sociability, spatiality, and cosmopolitanism has revealed a *diversity* of modes of dealing with difference in everyday spatiality and sociability with varying degrees of exposure to and immersion with the Other going way beyond the dichotomy of cosmopolitan versus anti-cosmopolitan. Thus, the notion of expatriate managers as a group with a uniform and homogeneous habitus has to be reconsidered. Regarding the *spatiality of everyday life*, we found a diversity of residential patterns regarding their spatial location in the city as well as their social and cultural composition. A first group of managers in our sample lived in *Western expatriate 'bubbles,'* that is, residential areas exclusively geared toward professionals from the Global North with no local neighbors. These *Western expatriate 'bubbles'* were mainly found in China. However, none of the expatriate managers in our sample lived in nationally homogeneous compounds or gated communities, although these do indeed exist. We were frequently told about such compounds that are dominated by expatriates from one nationality. A second group of managers in our sample lived in residential areas that could be referred to as *global expatriate 'bubbles'*—that is, gated communities and high-rise buildings with a global composition of residents but without local residents. A third group of managers and their families lived in *mixed elite 'bubbles'*—that is, residential areas inhabited by both local and foreign elite residents and—thus, socio-structurally very different from the average residential patterns of the locality. This pattern could be mostly found for German expatriate managers and their families in both China and the U.S. And finally, a fourth group of managers lived in *local neighborhoods* with predominantly local middle-class residents, such as Hutongs in China or local middle-class neighborhoods in the U.S. and in Germany. In addition to the diversity of residential patterns, we also found a diversity of reasons for a specific residential choice. Some embedded the choice of their place of residence into an individual cosmopolitan project, thus clearly contradicting the image of practiced self-exclusion. But also those who indeed lived in a residential spatial 'bubble' did not only do so because they wanted to distance themselves from the locality in an anti-cosmopolitan way, as many of the earlier cited authors suggest (Fechter 2007; Hindman 2008, 2013). Many of the managers, especially those with families and children, highlighted that practicability was the main reason for their location choice. Additionally, a considerable number of them were indeed struggling with the segregation from the local population this produced. Finally, our analysis of the dwelling spaces in the empirical data revealed a diversity of modes used for dealing with difference, such as ignoring it and enacting flexible belonging in the flexible home, selectively integrating difference and nostalgic belonging in the replicated home, or forms of banal cosmopolitanism.

The data also suggests *diversity* in the sphere of *sociability*. The negotiation of social boundaries was more complex than the emphasis on either boundary spanning or self-exclusion would suggest. Some of the managers were indeed very critical of what they conceived to be the parochial and closed character of their home country culture and of the continuation of this culture within *national expatriate 'bubbles.'* However, their attempts to transgress and deconstruct these national boundaries did not automatically make them open to the local culture in a cosmopolitan sense. They simultaneously distanced themselves from the *national 'bubble'* and the locality. The empirical cases discussed here represent sociabilities with different degrees of immersion into local sociabilities. *Transnational Pentecostal churches* created ambivalent "cosmopolitan moments" (Krause 2011, 430), as they served as spaces for practicing sociabilities beyond national and even Western communities, but were totally detached from the local population. *MNCs and their partly transnationally educated local workforce* constituted another intermediary space that enabled expatriates to engage in sociabilities with local coworkers and colleagues. However, these sociabilities were highly conditional in the sense that these viable local Others first had to prove distance to the local culture in order to be considered for social inclusion. Only those coworkers with international experiences were integrated into the expatriate managers' networks. Also, *binational relationships and private spaces* enabled the expatriate managers to go beyond forms of exclusive national spatialities and sociabilities.

Second, in addition to the diversity of modes of dealing with difference, the research has shown that *ambivalences* and inherent *contradictions* are constitutive features of the everyday life of most corporate expatriates. Their everyday life was highly ambivalent, with highly contrasting, if not paradoxical, ways of relating to cultural Others. In the analysis of sociability and spatiality patterns, three types of self-contradictory cosmopolitanisms of the corporate expatriates became visible. First, *culturally selective cosmopolitanism* is ambivalent, as it combines openness to cultural difference within international expatriate communities defined by a joint professional and religious culture, on the one hand, and distance to difference associated with a territorially defined culture of the respective host country on the other. Second, *unaccomplished cosmopolitanism* contains ambivalence because of the discrepancy of cosmopolitan ambitions and their realization within the specific local contexts. And, third, *conditional cosmopolitanism* is ambivalent because is it generally open to the local Other, but at the same time sets a precondition of the local actors being themselves somehow distant from the local culture in order to be included into joint sociabilities, thus trying to control and reduce the amount of difference. Both diversity and inherent inconsistencies contradict the image of a homogeneous *expatriate 'bubble life'* as well as the image of a cosmopolitan transnational class. We will come back to these inherent contradictions in the conclusion (Chapter 10), by introducing the concept of 'paradoxical cosmopolitanisms.'

Note

1 Indeed, the medium yearly family income of the area in which the Müllers live ($52,000) is significantly higher than the national average U.S. family income ($37,007).

Bibliography

Beaverstock, Jonathan. 2002. "Transnational Elites in Global Cities: British Expatriates in Singapore's Financial District." *Geoforum* 33 (4): 525–38. doi:10.1016/S0016-7185(02)00036-2.

Beck, Ulrich. 2006. *The Cosmopolitan Vision*. Cambridge: Polity Press.

Berger, Peter L., and Thomas Luckmann. 1967. *The Social Construction of Reality: A Treatise in the Sociology Of knowledge*. Garden City, New York: Doubleday.

Bilecen, Basak. 2015. "Home-Making Practices and Social Protection Across Borders: An Example of Turkish Migrants Living in Germany." *Journal of Housing and the Built Environment* 32 (1): 77–90. doi:10.1007/s10901-015-9490-1.

Blunt, Alison, and Robyn M. Dowling. 2006. *Home*. Key Ideas in Geography. London: Routledge.

Bourdieu, Pierre. 1985. "The social space and the genesis of groups." Theory and Society 14 (6): 723–44. doi:10.1177/053901885024002001

Coles, Anne, and Anne-Meike Fechter, eds. 2008a. *Gender and Family Among Transnational Professionals*. London and New York: Routledge.

Coles, Anne, and Anne-Meike Fechter. 2008b. "Introduction." In Coles and Fechter 2008, 1–20.

Datta, Ayona. 2009. "Places of Everyday Cosmopolitanisms: East European Construction Workers in London." *Environment and Planning A* 41 (2): 353–70. doi:10.1068/a40211.

Dharwadker, Vinay. 2011. "Diaspora and Cosmopolitanism." In *The Ashgate Research Companion to Cosmopolitanism*, edited by Maria Rovisco and Magdalena Nowicka, 125–44. Aldershot: Ashgate.

Fechter, Anne-Meike. 2007. *Transnational Lives: Expatriates in Indonesia*. Aldershot, Burlington: Ashgate.

Glick Schiller, Nina, Tsypylma Darieva, and Sandra Gruner-Domic. 2011. "Defining Cosmopolitan Sociability in a Transnational Age: An Introduction." *Ethnic and Racial Studies* 34 (3): 399–418. doi:10.1080/01419870.2011.533781.

Hannerz, Ulf. 2000. *Transnational Connections: Culture, People, Places*. London and New York: Routledge.

Hindman, Heather. 2008. "Shopping for a Hypernational Home: How Expatriate Women in Kathmandu Labour to Assuage Fear." In Coles and Fechter 2008, 41–61.

Hindman, Heather. 2013. *Mediating the Global: Expatria's Forms and Consequences in Kathmandu*. Stanford: Stanford University Press.

Johanson, Martin, and Heléne Lundberg. 2016. "Why Expatriates' Private Relations Matter." In *Extending the Business Network Approach: New Territories, New Technologies, New Terms*, edited by Peter Thilenius, Cecilia Pahlberg, and Virpi Havila, 99–120. London: Palgrave Macmillan.

Kanter, Rosabeth M. 1995. *World Class: Thriving Locally in the Global Economy*. New York: Simon & Schuster.

Kendall, Gavin, Ian Woodward, and Zlatko Skrbiš. 2009. *The Sociology of Cosmopolitanism: Globalization, Identity, Culture and Government.* London: Palgrave Macmillan UK.

Krause, Kristine. 2011. "Cosmopolitan Charismatics? Transnational Ways of Belonging and Cosmopolitan Moments in the Religious Practice of New Mission Churches." *Ethnic and Racial Studies* 34 (3): 419–35. doi:10.1080/01419870.2 011.537355.

Lefebvre, Henri. 1991. *The Production of Space.* Oxford: Blackwell.

Ley, David. 2004. "Transnational Spaces and Everyday Lives." *Transactions of the Institute of British Geographers* 29 (2): 151–64. doi:10.1111/j.0020-2754.2004.00122.x.

Löw, Martina. 2008. "The Constitution of Space: The Structuration of Spaces Through the Simultaneity of Effect and Perception." *European Journal of Social Theory* 11 (1): 25–49. doi:10.1177/1368431007085286.

Meier, Lars. 2015. "Learning the City by Experiences and Images: German Finance Managers' Encounters in London and Singapore." In *Migrant Professionals in the City: Local Encounters, Identities and Inequalities*, edited by Lars Meier, 59–74. New York: Routledge.

Meier, Lars, and Sybille Frank. 2016. "Dwelling in Mobile Times: Places, Practices and Contestations." *Cultural Studies* 30 (3): 362–75. doi:10.1080/09502386.20 15.1113630.

Sassen, Saskia. 1998. *Globalization and Its Discontents.* New York: New Press.

Schütz, Alfred. 1972. *The Phenomenology of the Social World.* Evanston: Northwestern University Press.

Sklair, Leslie. 2001. *The Transnational Capitalist Class.* Oxford: Blackwell.

Szerszynski, Bronislaw, and John Urry. 2002. "Cultures of Cosmopolitanism." *Sociological Review* 50 (4): 461–82. doi:10.1111/1467-954X.00394

van Bochove, Marianne, and Godfried Engbersen. 2015. "Beyond Cosmopolitanism and Expat Bubbles: Challenging Dominant Representations of Knowledge Workers and Trailing Spouses." Population, Space and Place 21 (4): 295–309. doi:10.1002/psp.1839

6 Gendered Mobilities, Gendered Cosmopolitanism

Male and Female Expatriate Managers and Their Accompanying Spouses

Anna Spiegel

After having analyzed the self-contradictory character of expatriates' cosmopolitanism in the sphere of everyday live, we now turn to the negotiation of the *gendered division of labor* regarding practices of enabling, shaping, and stabilizing mobility and cosmopolitan lifestyles. Both mobility (Urry 2007; Elliott and Urry 2010) and cosmopolitanism (Beck 2006, 2009) have been declared key characteristics of the second modernity. However, there is an ongoing debate about the relationship between mobility and cosmopolitanism (Amit 2015; Amit and Barber 2015) (see Chapter 4). Traditionally, many scholars have conceived of cosmopolitanism as a direct consequence of increased mobility and global connectivity (Kanter 1995; Szerszynski and Urry 2002, 2006; Beck 2009; Elliott and Urry 2010) More recent research, however, specifically from the field of migration and identity research, pleads that this connection cannot be taken for granted, instead encouraging a theoretical deconstruction of "teleological connections among mobility, transnational networks and cosmopolitanism" (Glick Schiller, Darieva, and Gruner-Domic 2011, 414). However, there is still a lack of empirical studies on the everyday junctures and disjunctures of mobility and cosmopolitanism.

In this chapter, we argue that especially the relation between gender, mobility and cosmopolitanism needs further attention. Most of the existing expatriate literature (as discussed in Chapter 3 and 4) has focused primarily on individual, mostly male, expatriates. If gender aspects are addressed at all, these are narrowed down to the following perspectives each of which focuses on individual actors: (1) *accompanying wives*, (2) *female expatriates*, and (3) *accompanying husbands*. First, research on gender relations and mobility of expatriates has concentrated on so-called female "trailing spouses"—that is, women accompanying their husbands on foreign assignments (Coles and Fechter 2008a; Lauring and Selmer 2010; Stadlbauer 2015; Spiegel and Mense-Petermann 2016). These studies have shed light on the diverse contributions of women as accompanying spouses.[1] For example, Hindman (2008) has elaborated that accompanying wives' demonstrative consumption of Western goods hyperbolizes their own and their husbands loyalty to the ethnocentric company approaches (ibid.). The fact that in most cases the accompanying wives do not take up paid employment has been interpreted as contributing to the organization and to the subjectively constructed success of the male professional project (Stadlbauer 2016, 175). The activities of expatriate mothers in national enclave schools abroad have been highlighted as fostering the cosmopolitan outlook of their children (Moore 2008). Studies addressing the traditional expatriate couple as such have also focused on the decrease of conjugal intimacy in expatriate couples in consequence of a polarized gender arrangement (Walsh 2008). Research has also pointed to the fact that in the context of multiple mobilities, such as in diplomatic families, dependency of wives on their husbands might be growing (Coles 2008).

Second, *female expatriate managers* (Harvey and Wiese 1998; Yeoh and Willis 2005; Fechter 2008; Willis and Yeoh 2008; Cole and McNulty 2011) have been addressed as part of nontraditional expatriate gender constellations (McNulty and Hutchings 2015), without, however, taking the male accompanying spouse into account. Also, the question of whether female managers create the same "macho culture" (Coles and Fechter 2008b, 9; Walsh 2008) and gendered division of labor that is cultivated by most male mobile professionals remains open. Coles and Fechter (2008b, 9) suggest the possibility that "this working culture may have the same exhilarating effect of women," without, however, giving much empirical evidence.

Finally, in contrast to this growing body of literature about female expatriates, *accompanying husbands*—with the exception of some studies (Selmer and Leung 2003; McNulty and Byoko 2004; Braseby 2010; Bernard 2014)—remain an under-researched group. These few studies have highlighted the bigger challenges in adapting to the role of accompanying husband (McNulty and Byoko 2004). Braseby (2010, 255) found that male accompanying spouses rejected to taking on a fathering identity, in contrast to female accompanying spouses who easily adopted a mothering identity. McNulty and Byoko found that accompanying husbands do not tend to develop a "sense of ownership" or a supportive identity toward their wives' careers (McNulty and Byoko 2004).

Whereas there is indeed research treating individual female accompanying spouses, female expatriates, and male accompanying spouses as research subjects, research on expatriate couples and the negotiation of *gender relations within these couples* is still rare. If couples are addressed at all, it is done from a perspective of managing and optimizing the couples' adjustment, as in the IHRM literature on dual career couples (Selmer and Leung 2003; Lauring and Selmer 2010). Thus, there is a need for further research on how the gendered division of labor regarding the everyday activities of producing mobility and cosmopolitan lifestyles is negotiated within expatriate couples.

The purpose of this chapter is, thus, to contribute to such a research agenda by examining how the gendered division of labor regarding the everyday activities of producing and stabilizing mobility and cosmopolitan lifestyles is negotiated within expatriate couples and to what extent the mobility and the inconsistent cosmopolitan lifestyles of expatriate managers are based on gender-specific practices. Our main argument is that in order to understand the phenomenon of expatriate managers' mobility and their ways of relating to the host locality, it is not enough to solely look at the managers themselves. Instead, we have to take into account the entire mobile family and specifically the gendered division of labor within the expatriate couple when it comes to the everyday mobility practices (Salaff 2000). It also takes into account the perspective put forward by a number of feminist scholars who argue that couples constitute a central institution where gender relations are negotiated, performed, and stabilized (König 2012) and where specific social positions such as the bourgeois family (Habermas 2000) or contemporary business executive families (Böhnisch 1999) are produced through unequal but reciprocal and entangled gendered practices. To make the gendered dimensions of expatriate mobility and inconsistent cosmopolitanisms visible in the context of expatriate couples, we compare two differently gendered expatriate constellations namely, *male expatriate managers* and their *accompanying wives*, for one, and *female expatriate managers* and their *accompanying husbands*.² For each constellation, we will analyze three sets of activities crucial for enabling, shaping, and stabilizing the entangled mobilities and cosmopolitan lifestyles of mobile managers: (1) activities related to preparing and managing the relocation (*mobility work*), (2) activities related to building up social networks at the new place of residence (*local attachment work*), and (3) activities related to maintaining the ties and networks to family and friends at the place of origin or other places of the family's mobile trajectory (*translocal attachment work*).

We now continue this chapter by presenting the empirical accounts of our analysis focusing on gendered and relational aspects of expatriate mobility and cosmopolitanism for the three different sets of activities. In the final subchapter, we discuss our empirical findings and address the chapter's contributions to the debates on cosmopolitanism and mobility.

Gendered Mobility Work

Being mobile is hard work. In addition to flexibility, the ability to organize projects, and the potential to form and maintain innovative networks, another individual competence demanded of employees, which is ever increasingly decisive for their managerial success, is the successful managing of intensive and spatially extensive mobilities, as Kesselring and Vogl (2010, 27) have put it. People need to be mobilized; they need to be dislocated from one place—their old house, home school, banking, and health system—and relocated to the new place—a new house, new school, banking, and health system. Also, objects need to be mobilized—personal belongings, furniture, etc., some more inert than others. In the following, all activities related to this mobilization of people and objects will be addressed with the concept of *mobility work*. In the case of expatriate managers, the company and professional relocation services certainly take over part of the work (see Chapter 4). However, a significant part of this work is not carried out by the organization but is rather delegated to the private sphere. The question that we want to pose now is whether this kind of *mobility work* is gendered, and if yes, in what sense.

Mobility Work in the Traditional Gender Constellation

In the traditional, most widespread constellation of a male expatriate manager and an accompanying wife, most of the *mobility work* is carried out by the accompanying wives. This includes the preparation of the 'look-and-see-trip' and the house hunting process, the management of the relocation as such, and also the management of 'mobility problems,' especially of the children, such as the transfer from the home country school system to the host country school system and vice versa.

For most of the accompanying wives, being the 'family mobility manager' includes doing primarily activities relating literally and directly to the management of their family's relocation process either from their home country or their previous host locality to the new destination. In the case of the Müllers, a German expatriate couple assigned to the U.S. (see Chapter 5), it was the accompanying wife, Mrs. Müller, who took over the responsibility of looking for a new house and preparing the 'look-and-see-trip' in advance. She had already started an intensive Internet search about houses and prices at their new host locality via Internet while still in Germany. She explains,

> And from that point in time, I started looking at real estate offers in the Internet, so that I would get an idea about what I had to expect. So, which size is equivalent to which price? And once you have followed this for quite a while, you're able to realize: This house is still available. There must be something wrong with it, so that it is not easily to be let. Or some houses are taken immediately, and after a while, you even understand why. And you are able to say, "That's expensive." And then I looked on the whole region on Google maps: Where is the school? Where is the office? Where is the house? What does it mean for all the driving? And then you can calculate the distances. Then you can say, "How long does it really take you?" Sometimes it appears to be very close at the first look, but actually, it takes a long time. In this respect we were less . . . there are people who come here very naively and let themselves to be taken in by the real estate agent. Yes, he has got a list, but I went there and checked all the real estate agents, and I had a list with objects myself (. . .). And then you also get an idea about the different neighborhoods. And with time, you get an idea, which ones are recommendable and which are the ones, where you rather do not want

to live because it could get sort of awkward. So in the end, I was very happy that I had checked these things in advance, because I had reached the point where I could say, "This neighborhood? OK, let's see, this is just around up there. For me, that's too far away. With this house, we don't even have to start with."

Before even arriving at the host locality, Mrs. Müller had already systematically acquired considerable knowledge about different relevant local aspects: adequate prices for houses, the perils and tricks of the local housing market, where their most important everyday places—office, school, shopping facilities—were located and the real distances between them, and, finally, the socio-spatial characteristics of different neighborhoods. This knowledge enabled her to successfully steer the house hunting process in an environment where she had never been before, making it possible for the family to find a suitable house in a very short time. It also provided her with a strong sense of agency, not being naively lost in an unknown place or dependent on others' decisions and judgments.

In addition to organizing the 'look-and-see-trip' and doing the house hunting, the accompanying wives in our sample took over a significant amount of the work related to the relocation as such. The Kletts, a German expatriate couple assigned to the U.S., who in the past 24 years have had eight assignments all over the globe with an average duration of 3 years—five of these assignments taken together with their two sons—are a good example of how mobility affects the gendered division of labor in the family. Mrs. Klett has been solely responsible for managing all of the relocation processes, including packing and unpacking and for managing all bureaucratic procedures—registration, school, insurances—related to the relocation. When asked about the relocation experience, Mr. Klett admits, "Yes, OK, the general relocation manager is my wife. Because we have moved 15 times during the last few years. And so, I would say, of course there is a certain routine with it." Also, Mrs. Klett points to her competences and routines in managing her family's mobility over the past years:

> Experience has shown, with all together 15 times the full monty of packing and unpacking everything for going abroad, that I do the packing all by myself. My husband (. . .), he of course comments "I need this and that," or "I would like to have this and that," but otherwise I am the one doing the packing, and I decide what comes along and what not. This has actually turned out to work quite well over the years, that my husband keeps out of this, because he says, this is something that he does not want to care about on top of all the other things.

The quotation makes clear how this specific gendered division of labor has emerged within the highly mobile couple over the years. While highlighting her autonomy and power in deciding which items are to be taken to the next assignment, in this quotation, Mrs. Klett also adumbrates that this strict gendered division of labor is mainly shaped by her husband's reluctance to take over responsibility for issues not related to his immediate work context. Not being able and willing to take over tasks related to the relocation "on top of all the other things," that is, in addition to the demanding activities immediately connected to his work, is, in most cases, the result of a working process that does not take into account time resources for the expatriate manager to manage his and his family's mobility. Mr. Novak, a German manager assigned to the U.S. who did not participate in the organization of the relocation process at all also explains,

> I have to say, my wife did a terrific job with the relocation. At that moment, I had a very intense job. There was a project which had to be concluded and it was too bad that I was the only one with the relevant knowledge for this specific project. So I really was on full speed to get the thing finished. So, I did not have the time for . . . I really had enough on my mind to care for this relocation hullabaloo, if I may say so. So my wife did run the whole show. Appointments with the moving companies, the moving as such, what goes in which box, what goes to airfreight, what to sea freight, what stays in Germany, and so on. This whole show was run entirely by my wife.

He clarifies that in the preparatory phase just before the relocation his workload increased dramatically because he already had to cope with simultaneous responsibilities in multiple locations of work (Felstead, Jewson, and Walters 2005). This increased workload resulted in a lack of time resources for dealing with matters concerning the relocation. His recognition is highly ambivalent: whereas he indeed praises his wife as having done a "terrific job," his use of the term "hullabaloo" indicates his general disregard for and dis-identification with the everyday activities related to the relocation process.

In addition to preparing and carrying out the relocation process, the accompanying wives took over the work related to managing diverse mobility problems of each family member. Both Mrs. Klett and Mrs. Müller are exclusively responsible for their children's mobility problems. This includes the problems arising from changing between different national schools systems. Both women were constantly comparing host and home country school systems and identifying possible gaps between them. They were constantly looking for possible solutions for buffering their children's language and school problems in interaction with local school authorities by, for example, negotiating special conditions such as additional tutoring or other special arrangements. Mrs. Müller explains why it was so important to first concentrate only on her children:

> In the beginning I did not work for sure, because I said, the problem is that I don't know how it will be going with school. When we arrived

here, my younger son could not even speak a single word in English and my older son had only one and a half years of English. And therefore, it was clear to me, that it would take a lot of time, once they were back from school. Because if you cannot even read the homework, if you do not understand what you have to do, then you are doomed, you know.

Whereas her primary focus was on getting her children integrated into the new school system, she was from the very start also conscious about making the reintegration of their children back into their home school system as easy as possible by, for instance, organizing specific tutoring in subjects central to their home school's curriculum but not included in their host school system. In addition, the accompanying wives were exclusively responsible for the children's transportation to school and various leisure time activities, and they tended to take over all work related to the general organization of everyday life at the new location. Mrs. Müller highlights that it is she who was in charge of organizing family mobility issues:

I went to the doctor's with the kids, I took care of the kids' vaccinations and also all this other authorities stuff and things like that. Someone has to do it. Or banking issues. My husband says now and then, "Do we still have money?" Because I do the whole thing with the bank online, and I also go there, because it is on my way. So I have the time to do all these things; that's what's good about it.

Although they talked about their share in the mobility work for the family very self-consciously, the sense of frustration and the ambition to go beyond the identity of a 'family mobility manager' is evident in many interviews. Referring to the polarized division of labor between she and her husband, Mrs. Müller comments: "So, I am the one who takes care of everything. Being a little bit mean, I would say, that I am a married single mother, yes." Her term of the "married single mother" very strongly illustrates the kind of workload that she has: she is a single mother in the sense that she gets little to no support from her husband in the everyday reproductive and *care work* in the family and, in addition, has to cope with the mobility work emerging from being married to a globally mobile manager. The feeling of being abandoned, which is implicit in the formulation of the "married single mother," and the frustration arising out of this constellation is very evident in the quotation noted earlier.

Mobility Work in the Nontraditional Gender Constellation

We turn now to the couples constituted by a female corporate expatriate and a male accompanying spouse. What does the gendered division of mobility work look like in these couples? Are these accompanying husbands 'married single dads' and family mobility managers in the sense as described earlier for the accompanying wives? Our analysis indicates that this is not the case. The cases of the Williams and the Carters, both U.S.-American expatriate couples living in Germany, illustrate the complexities of the gendered division of mobility work in a couple of a female expatriate manager and an accompanying husband. Mrs. Williams is in her 40s and has held a top management position in a German subsidiary of a large U.S.-American MNC for four years. Mrs. Carter is in her 30s and has been working as a project manager at the headquarters of a large German MNC for two and a half years. Both female managers are married, have two children, and are accompanied by husbands who have taken the role of stay-at-home dad. For both couples, this is already their second assignment to Germany. Both couples indeed practice a new type of gendered division of labor concerning domestic and care work. Mrs. Williams refers to this nontraditional arrangement as a "modern relationship." Mr. Williams takes over many tasks of the domestic work, such as getting the daughter ready for school in the morning and bringing her to the bus stop, picking her up from special school events, supporting the daughter in doing homework, and caring for her, shopping, and cooking, until Mrs. Williams comes home from work. Mr. Carter also takes over domestic responsibilities; he cooks, does the family shopping, brings the children to school and kindergarten and picks them up again in the afternoon, and oversees that the homework has been done. Both stay-at-home dads take their children to sports lessons and to their friends when they want to meet up in the afternoon to play together. However, this new gender arrangement does not lead to the polarization between a 'married single dad' taking over all mobility and family care work and a female manager, who is fully freed from this work, as was the case for the arrangement of a female accompanying spouse and a male corporate expatriate. Although both accompanying husbands take over care work, they do not entirely embrace the role of family mobility managers in the sense of taking full responsibility for the mobility problems of their children. This is partly due to the fact that both stay-at-home dads have only a very limited command of German. Mrs. Carter explains how her husband's lack of language skills increases the workload for her:

> One of the topics I had as well with my bosses was trying to make them understand also what it is to be an expat. And to be the one who speaks German. There is a lot of things that my husband can't do or can't communicate with my kids' schools, for example, and I have to be the one to translate that. The things that you don't quite think about but so many little things I have to do which I really shouldn't need to do but only because of the language, I'm the only one who can do it. So it has to wait for me till I get home, then I have to do that.

Mrs. Carter has to take over parts of the mobility work for her children, especially regarding problems connected with the different school systems, language problems, and also—in some cases—doctor's appointments, etc., because, due to language problems, Mr. Carter is not able to attend consultation hours with his daughter's teachers or events for parents at school or kindergarten, respectively. He also is not able to supervise his daughter's homework or to help her when she has problems with his work. The fact that Mrs. Carter had to discuss this with her bosses indicates that it also interfered to some extent with her professional responsibilities. However, because of her long working hours, she could not adequately solve her daughter's mobility problems:

> But with that again I'm the one working, and I'm the one who speaks German; I can't help her with her homework because by the time I get home it's dinner and bed or it's a bed time already, plus she is tired.

Because neither her husband nor she could assist their daughter in an adequate way, their daughter attends afternoon lessons where there are teachers who can help her in case she needs support. In the case of the Carters, family work has been outsourced because neither Mrs. Carter nor Mr. Carter can act as full family mobility manager. Mrs. Carter lacks the time, and Mr. Carter the skill.

Mrs. Williams, too, specifically addresses the fact that she has to be a more active family manager during her assignment than at home due to her husband's limited language skills:

> I can speak the language, but my husband can't or can't to a certain degree. And I feel that than there are more issues that I have to manage for our family, because there's the language barrier. Because there are the language differences, and because of these language barriers, sometimes things are put on me to manage. Normally, he would be able to handle it things like doctor's appointments or other personal appointments, stuff like that.

Other responsibilities that are put on her because of her husband's limited language skills include, for example, taking her daughter to the hairdresser and to the doctor. One definite reason for the involvement of the female expatriate managers in this mobility work is their husbands' limited German language skills. However, the interesting thing is the husbands' continuing resistance against learning the local language, although it was already each of the accompanying husbands' second stay in Germany. The fact that the two husbands do not speak German has to be regarded as an indicator for their reluctance to embrace the position of family manager and to assume the same position as an accompanying wife.

The same picture emerges when looking at the gendered division of labor concerning the management of the relocation. This part of mobility work, too, is not polarized between the corporate expatriate and the accompanying

spouse in the same way as in the couples of a male manager and an accompanying wife, despite the same formal division of labor. Mobility work is partly,
but not exclusively, carried out by the accompanying husbands. Mr. Carter
was indeed responsible for the hands-on part of moving, for tasks necessitat-
ing craftsmanship. For example, when they moved into their new house in
Germany, he went to buy the lights and fixed them. He also took responsibility
for selling the lights, wardrobes, and cupboards that they bought in Germany
to an expatriate family who was going to rent their house when they returned
to the U.S. Mrs. Carter described the work of her husband as follows:

> He had to do most of it. I was busy working, so he was going to all the
> furniture stores and the lighting stores having to put up all the lights in
> the house and those things that we're not used to in the States as well.

However, Mr. Carter does not act as the full 'family mobility manager'
as most of the accompanying wives did, as becomes clear in the following
quotation. Mrs. Carter explains why she had insisted, against her prior decisions, on having the whole household packed and shipped in a container
instead of only taking a few things and arranging everything locally at the
new domicile:

> I think one of the interesting things with this trip was that after our
> last assignment with x-brand we said we would never again take all
> our furniture and pack up a whole sea container and ship everything
> back and forth across the Atlantic. And when it came time for this
> one, we just decided, you know what, it is the easier way to just take
> everything. So we brought everything again; all our furniture again,
> packed up a sea container. We have it all to take back with us again,
> and that was a big consideration because I knew coming into this job
> that it would be a very busy job, and the idea of trying to figure out
> where to go, what to buy, how to set up your house, what things to
> hang on the wall, you know, all of that, I just thought that it's too
> much for me.

At first sight, Mrs. Carter explains that because of the very heavy workload
of her new job, she tried to minimize the work and time resources related
to the relocation—deciding which items to take along and which to leave
behind as well as the time-consuming acquisition of new furniture—by just
taking everything. When she says, "I thought that it's too much for me," she
is implying that, in addition to the "very busy job," this work would have
been placed on her shoulders and not on her husband's. In contrast to the
male expatriate managers, who were able to delegate everything related to
the relocation to their wives, Mrs. Carter cannot rely on her husband being
the main family mobility manager to the same extent. As a consequence, she
has to redefine how their mobility is organized in a way that she expects to
be generally less work intensive.

Throughout the interview, it became clear that it was Mrs. Carter who had been responsible for solving several everyday problems related to the relocation, during prior assignments and also during this current assignment. For instance, when they had difficulties in finding a suitable apartment during her first assignment to Germany, it was she who 'pushed' her colleagues, as she says, to support her in finding an apartment. Solving other problems, like installing and setting up the Internet and phone in the new apartment, for example, was clearly her responsibility. This specific gendered division of labor has to be interpreted as a sign of the enduring double sociation (Doppelte Vergesellschaftung) of women with all its inherent contradictions and ambivalences (Becker-Schmidt 2010) and an intensification of the sociation in the private sphere for female managers through the process of mobility. In contrast to the male managers who took their dispensation from the family mobility work for granted, the female managers explicitly worked on integrating both spheres. Mrs. Williams explicitly frames her tensions regarding the integration of both work and domestic sphere with her position as an expatriate:

> For me, the biggest challenge is . . . how would I say that? . . . is trying to balance. But I think this is also the struggle of being a working mother. There is so much you want to be involved in, on the personal side, especially with your family, but that work sometimes takes precedence. And I think that this is the case no matter where you are, but being an expatriate . . . it compounds. (. . .) There are some expectations that the company has, you know. You know as an individual that your company is spending quite a lot of money for the fact that you were living overseas. And so you feel you have an obligation for the company. And in some ways for me, what's necessary for the company comes first. And knowing all that, whether that's right or wrong, it's just, it's there. (. . .) So, you know, again, it's the obligation that you feel, because you are an expatriate. And that it sometimes takes precedence, and has impact even if you want to manage just something very simple in your life, whether it's a weekend or an evening.

Mrs. Carter also describes her decreased participation in domestic work as very frustrating and unsettling, for example, in doing parts of the family shopping:

> To me one of the frustrating points, is (. . .) I often find with the hours that I have to work and the shop hours here, it, um, makes me feel very non-contributing to the home cause I can't even go buy shampoo.

Being an expatriate intensifies the double sociation for women, creating double and contradictory, real and imagined responsibilities in both the work and the private sphere, as indicated in the quotation noted earlier. The perceived investment of the company in the expatriate intensifies the sociation and thus the workload in the sphere of paid work and at the same time creates a sense of loss on the private side. The lacking sociation of the husband in the domestic sphere creates a relative intensification of the female managers' workload in the private sphere and at the same time a sense of insufficiency within the work sphere. Becker-Schmidt has emphasized that the combination of the two spheres does not lead to a combination of the positive features, but to a constant tension between two contrasting logics: "And yet nothing whole results from the combination of private work and gainful employment. The result is not an addition of a positive feature to another positive one" (Becker-Schmidt 2003, 13, translated from German original). Especially in the private sphere, this leads to tensions in the couple's relationship, as the following quotation from the interview with Mrs. Williams indicates,

> I think this is one of the toughest things for me as a working mom. I so want to do more things with her [her daughter] with respect to school, but I can't. And so I rely on my husband and I think sometimes that there is a bit of a tension between him and I, we now have a routine, where school work is done and he, my husband also does all the cooking, so I'm very fortunate with that. So he, many times they will have eaten way before I got home, so, you know, by the time I get home, . . . hopefully I don't have calls, but most of the time I do have some work I usually do. So I still try to connect with my daughter, but when I come back at nine o'clock, there's not so much time. And then when my daughter is at school, you know, very different thing: He could be painting, he could be playing music, or he could be working doing something, you know, so it's kind of fair deal?

The discussed cases indicate that in the arrangement of the *female expatriate manager and an accompanying husband*, despite its formal parallelism to the male manager/accompanying wife arrangement, a full-time working manager and a nonworking spouse, the actual division of labor in mobility work is not mirrored in the same way. Whereas male expatriate managers self-consciously disregard the mobility work of their wives as something "on top" or as "hullabaloo," which is not worth their involvement, their female accompanying spouses do most of the mobility work. In contrast, the male accompanying spouses do not assume the role of a family mobility manager to the same extent, and the female managers' struggle with their double workload and, in addition, regret their lack of opportunity to be involved more equally in the mobility work.

Gendered Local Attachment Work

As strangers (Schütz 1944), expatriates need to acquire practical knowledge about how to carry on their lives at the host locality. Much of such practical knowledge about the new place of residence is transmitted through informal networks, be it to locals or other expatriates. We suggest calling the work of building up such networks and of looking for information that is relevant for the everyday life of the whole mobile family *local attachment work*. The question that we want to pose now is whether this kind of *local attachment work* is gendered, and if yes, in what sense.

Local Attachment Work in the Traditional Gender Constellation

When asked where they got their information on everyday life issues and how they established friendships, most male expatriate managers highlighted the importance of contacts established by their accompanying wives to other expatriates, especially other expatriate mothers. The prime sites for building up these networks were the schools their children attended (Moore 2008). In the case of the Müllers, the parking lot of the school most German expatriate children attend is the central meeting point for German mothers. Whereas local U.S.-American parents prefer to just quickly pick up their children from school and not get out of the car, the German mothers meet at the school's parking lot and always stick around for a little while to chat and exchange information with the other German mothers. Meeting on the school's parking lot is of such importance to the German mothers with middle school children that even though, according to the school regulations, they are not supposed to get out of their cars anymore when picking up their children but instead should drive through in order to avoid congestion, these mothers have pressed the local school authorities to give them the special right to continue using it. The school's parking lot has thus become a "very German issue," as Mr. and Mrs. Müller report. Mr. Müller talks about how important the contacts that his wife has established were for the whole family in the beginning of their stay in the U.S.:

> All of the German mothers pick up their grade-school children from the parking lot. This means there is communication, exchange. You can just ask each other, "Hey, how's that going? How do you guys do it?" and so on. (. . .) Overall, the school was a tremendous help, at least in the first months, like in getting integrated into this arrangement. And then maybe a friendship might develop from these contacts. Or after meeting at school, you go somewhere together afterwards. What we did is, we had one mother who had two children in the same grades as my sons (. . .). And she explained a lot to us. So this is another way I was able to find my bearings.

Mrs. Müller also reports of getting important information about the local school system, recommended pediatricians, and general physicians through the informal support structures of the 'German mothers' at school:

> There's always someone who has arrived earlier and who can tell you: "Well, listen, this and that you better do it this way. And you have to

go there to get this and that, and this you get there and that there, and the pediatrician is there etc., etc." This helps a lot. When I arrived here, there was another German lady (. . .), who came to school and talked to me briefly. And she told me: "Listen, once you have arrived, go and take a private French teacher, because if not, it's going to fade away." So these are the kind of things that you would never figure out by yourself. Or you get it with time, but then it is too late. So that's helpful.

Through these networks, the accompanying wives have built up meaningful sociabilities for their families and have acquired necessary knowledge for the organization of their families' everyday life. For other accompanying wives, company organized spaces, such as a German Ladies Regulars' Table (*Stammtisch*), or residence based spaces, such as the playground at their compound, were central places to establish networks and get practical everyday knowledge, as Mrs. Zacher, a U.S.-American accompanying wife based in China, reported,

> And you take your kids (. . .) to the playground, you meet other moms and other kids and this becomes your support group. And your network. They've been here longer than I have, so they knew where to go. There is this place called Jenny Lou's—supermarket that has a lot of Western goods. So I have never heard about of Jenny Lou's. So my friend Holly said "You've never heard of Jenny Lou's?" and I said, "No, how else would I know about Jenny Lou's unless you're going to tell me." I mean, we moved here in December, my son's birthday was in January—how do I make him a cake? (. . .) I get it in Jenny Lou's. So that's how you survive. It's from this network of other expats that have been here longer than you. And they help you and then you're there to help the next ones, because they'll all leave and then you're the one who is on the playground saying "What, you've never heard of Jenny Lou's?! Let me tell you where Jenny Lou's is." So it kind of works that way.

In this quotation, besides highlighting the importance of the networks between expatriate mothers for the 'survival' of her family, Mrs. Zacher describes the process of turning from a newcomer into an active mentor for newcomers herself, a process nearly all accompanying wives emphasized. For instance, Mrs. Klett reports of "Newcomer Committees" organized mostly by mothers at the different German schools her children attended on their several assignments. In the beginning of each assignment, Mrs. Klett received support from these groups, but then after a while, she herself started volunteering in all of these "Newcomer Committees," offering support and counseling to newly arrived German expatriates. Mrs. Müller had embraced her role as mentor for expatriate newcomers to such an extent that even we, as researchers, immediately benefited from her support und knowledge. Mrs. Müller was extremely committed to our well-being and immediately gave us information on what to do on our free days; she provided us with maps of the recommended destinations and was also keen to suggest the best places to buy maternity fashion and baby clothes to one of the female researchers who was pregnant at the time of the research.

So far, the data has shown that the accompanying wives not only stabilized the everyday life of their own families but also supported other expatriate families in organizing the practicalities of their everyday life. What also became clear is that this kind of attachment work as mentors for newcomers is clearly directed at their own national expatriate community. They did not approach locals for support and advice, but instead primarily approached other expatriates. In addition, they saw themselves as mentors and knowledge brokers for other newly arrived expatriate families.

The interaction of the male corporate expatriates with these local institutions outside of their direct work context, contrastingly, is very weak. Mr. Müller explains,

> My attachment to the school is relatively low. (. . .) so, as I said, it is rather my wife who is very active and I have more of a passive role concerning school issues and activities. Once in a while, I accompany them or go there once in a while. But when you go there every single day, then after a short while, everybody knows you and it's different. So when she goes there . . . she has volunteered at the library and has done this and that.

In China, some of the accompanying wives took over an even more basic form of attachment work—namely, communication and translation work. The expatriate managers, in most cases, did not speak Chinese. In fact, English or German were the main languages used in their daily work routines and most of them said that due to their high workload, they did not have the time to enhance their Chinese language skills. Their accompanying wives, however, in many cases did indeed have the time to attend Chinese classes. For instance, Mrs. Winkelmann can successfully communicate in Chinese on an everyday level. We could clearly observe Mrs. Winkelmann assuming the role of a translator and broker, speaking Chinese with security guards at their compound, with cab drivers, salespeople, and waiters at restaurants, whereas Mr. Winkelmann did not take up any interaction with them in such situations. In the case of Mr. and Mrs. Simon, a German expatriate couple in China, it was especially through Mrs. Simon's constant attachment work that they made acquaintances outside the expatriate community during their assignment. This was part of Mrs. Simon's overall social orientation of explicitly avoiding the typical gatherings of the expatriate community, such as "charity events and coffee mornings for expatriate wives." Mrs. Simon explains that she declared it explicitly her aim to "only meet with Chinese in the first years and to talk with them about everything, about China, about the government, even about sexuality. This has helped me to understand the country and the culture, to understand why people are how they are." Through this constant *local attachment work*, especially by Mrs. Simon, the Simons have been able to build up an extended network especially to local Chinese artists and other international expatriate friends with whom they frequently meet for cooking or dining. These networks are based on the joint identity of "art lovers."

The cases of the Kletts, the Müllers, the Winkelmanns, and the Simons reveal that in the arrangement of the *male expatriate manager and an accompanying wife*, there is a clear gendered division of labor regarding the creation of everyday sociabilities at the host locality (Willis and Yeoh 2002). Whereas the corporate expatriates are absorbed by their immediate work environment and do not possess over time resources to engage with the locality outside their workplace, the accompanying wives interact with a diversity of local actors and take over a significant amount of building up social networks at the new place of residence, in most cases to other expatriates, but in some cases, they also acted as cultural and even linguistic brokers. Depending on the local context, that is, whether the children attended a national enclave school, an international school, or a local school, the volunteering created sociabilities to conationals, to nationally mixed expatriate communities, and to locals. Thus, women's social networks often form the basis of their husbands' social lives and are therefore key in the development of communities of transnationals and also the operation of transnational capital, as social contacts can be key for developing business links, and also for making the overseas posting comfortable and more likely to succeed.

Local Attachment Work in the Nontraditional Gender Constellation

We now again turn to the couples comprised of a female expatriate manager and a male accompanying spouse. What does the gendered division of local attachment work look like in these couples? Do the accompanying husbands create meaningful sociabilities for their families, either within the expatriate community or to the host country in the sense as described earlier for the accompanying wives? Drawing on our case studies, the answer, again, is no. Mr. Carter repeatedly tells about his difficulties to get in contact with people, both in the expatriate community and with Germans. Because of his lacking language skills, he says it has been extremely hard for him to establish contact to Germans. This made it especially difficult and time-consuming for him to "find out where to get things and how to organize everything," because he always has to look for people who can speak English. Moreover, as accompanying husbands tended to be excluded from the mostly female networks of mothers and 'expatriate wives' at the host locality also their position in the community was very liminal. Mr. Carter, for example, indicates that he never met any other stay-at-home dad since arriving in Germany and that it has been very difficult for him to relate to the mothers and other expatriate wives. He speaks of a situation where he took his daughter to her best friend's because the girls wanted to play together. As his daughter was still very young and new in that school, he stayed at her friend's house and, together with that friend's mother, he was playing with the children. Then, later in the afternoon, when the father of his daughter's friend came home from work, he realized that that was a "very odd situation." Mrs. Carter also talks about her husband's difficulties blending in to the activities normally shared by accompanying wives:

> Same thing as being home in the States too, there is not a natural support group for men who are home with kids like there is for women. You know, if you're a woman home with the kids you can meet several other women for coffee if you want, and baby is playing, kids are playing, whatever and that's just not a natural way that men interact and the way they work. So having the male side not able to work and me being an expat it's also challenging because he has to find his way around without really being able to find good male friends. And he has some now but that took probably longer than it would normally. (. . .) I mean I've known women who've come over here with their husbands, and they have literally taken basket-weaving class. And you know, classes are fun and it's a good time for your leisure time and then a good break for them or they could go and take classes that maybe lead them to something different when they go back to the States. But there is you know, I don't know many men who want to go to basket weaving or want to learn crochet. You know, those things that you do as a women you can do on the side like hobby-wise. But for men hobbies tend to be more sports oriented and you know woodworking or something. (. . .) And sport-wise, there is not much you can do when you have to stay home with your kids. So that's definitely a different aspect of it as being the female expat.

In this quotation, Mrs. Carter alludes to the rareness of accompanying husbands and the incongruence of gendered interests and activities resulting in difficulties for accompanying husbands to build up meaningful sociabilities. Another German female expatriate manager assigned to China, Mrs. Frank, also acknowledges that expatriate communities to a large extent are communities of housewives and that even for a working mother, it was nearly impossible to become part of that community, because most of the activities take place during the morning or in the early afternoon. This shows how the expatriate community is gendered in a sense that it only privileges same-sex networks and is additionally based on specific images of women as nonworking, which makes it difficult both for nonworking expatriate fathers, not being female, and working expatriate mothers, as not having the same daily routine, to be part of that community (see also McNulty and Byoko 2004). This disciplining feature of gendered expatriate communities has also been discussed by Lauring and Selmer (2009, 1458), who found that women who started working during the assignment and no longer fit into the expected role of a nonworking 'trailing spouse' were systematically excluded from community activities by the other women. For expatriate families comprised of a female corporate expatriate and an accompanying husband, this means that the husbands are excluded from networks that could provide them with a sense of community and belonging. Because of these difficulties, Mr. Carter, for example, indicates that he engages mostly in sports and other activities that he can do on his own, like playing golf, running, playing guitar, or going to the gym. Mr. Williams, too, spends his day on his own, painting or making music. This focus on solitary activities of accompanying husbands has been also reported by Braseby (2010, 143). This created very serious emotional problems not only for themselves. Both accompanying husbands said that their lack of social contacts was the most challenging problem connected to this specific expatriate arrangement and reported emotional instabilities and tensions in their couple's relationship. It also made it more difficult for them to create meaningful sociabilities for their families and to acquire practical everyday knowledge for their own and for other expatriate families.

The fact the Mr. Carter does not speak German has also shaped his family's sociabilities and friendships to a vast extent. Although he knows many of the German parents, mostly mothers from school and kindergarten, he has not been able to turn some of them into family friends due to his limited German language skills. Mrs. Carter explains how their different command of German made it nearly impossible to have local German friends:

> So the majority of our friends are either non-Germans living here or they're Americans or we have a couple of friends who are Germans but they've lived in the States and they all speak English very well (. . .). I was thinking who do we have as friends and after all is it a little bit limiting (. . .) if you're both in the same place, then even if you find people who don't speak very good English you just kinda work through it together, but I think I'm fluent in German and he is definitely not and so, if we start to speak German the conversation can quickly go away from where he can even follow it at all anymore and then so we go back to English, but then somebody else might have trouble with it.

However, despite the liminal position of the accompanying husband in the expatriate community, the family is not socially isolated. They have managed to build up friendships through their participation in an English-speaking non-denominational church in their town, which is led by an U.S.-American pastor and has an Anglophone congregation. Every Sunday, the whole family attends the church services. These friendships are, thus, not based solely on Mr. Carter's individual but also on the whole family's local attachment work. However, because of Mrs. Carter's heavy workload during the week, once these connections have been established, it is Mr. Carter who manages the contacts and organizes appointments and meetings.

In the case of the Williams, because they send their children to an international school, Mr. Williams' lacking German skills are not as much of a problem for the establishment of family friendships. However, many of the friendships that are important for the whole family locally are Mrs. Carter's friendships, which she established through her work during her long internationally mobile career with an MNC. This group consists of four other families: one Swedish, one British, one binational German-Italian, and another U.S.-American couple who have been living in Germany for nearly 20 years. This group is characterized by their polyglot everyday practices connecting to the German locality beyond a segregated expatriate 'bubble,' as the following quotation from the interview with Mrs. Williams indicates,

> Everybody can speak; we all speak English with each other. That's the common language, but my friend that's Swedish speaks five, six, seven languages. And so there's given time that you're hearing her talk to my friends' husband in Italian and then along with another girlfriend who grew up with an Italian mother. So it's interesting. And then there is German going on at the same time. So, for the most parts we're all speaking English, but then if there are others that are with us that are, you know, there's other, there's different languages that are going on at different times. So it's very international. It's funny, because then if we all go out to dinner or to brunch or something, we all be chatting in English across the big table but then when the waiters come, we all switch to German.

The cases of the Carters and the Williams show that the division of labor in local attachment work in the arrangement of the *female expatriate manager and an accompanying husband* is not the same as in the male manager/accompanying wife arrangement. Accompanying husbands do not take over the role of building up meaningful sociabilities for their families and of stabilizing their families' everyday life to the same extent as the accompanying wives. The female managers, thus, are much more active in this respect than their male counterparts in acquiring expatriate-life-specific information, and in establishing and maintaining family friendships.

Gendered Translocal Attachment Work

Being mobile not only requires attachment work to the host locality but also requires maintaining ties and networks to family and friends at their home country or to other places that were part of the family's mobile trajectory. In the following, we will refer to these activities as *translocal attachment work*. This type of work is relevant for corporate expatriates as it facilitates the easy and fluid moving between different spaces and places. The analysis of our data of male and female expatriate managers and their accompanying spouses regarding the translocal attachment work uncovers the gendered dimensions also of this translocal attachment work.

Translocal Attachment Work in the Traditional Gender Constellation

As a first mode of maintaining translocal ties and networks, the accompanying wives in our sample took over the role of hosts and tourist guides for visitors; they spent a significant amount of time caring for visitors from home—family members or friends—showing them around and arranging tourism programs for them. When we talked about the question of whether she had been able to take up an employment during the current assignment in the U.S., Mrs. Klett answered, "No, not during this assignment. We had just too much visits to work (laughs). Last year, we had around 185 overnight stays." She continued,

> Yes, this is substantial (laughs). I would have never calculated it, but another friend here, also a mother I know from school, said, "You have to." Because I was complaining "Visitors again!" And then she said, "You have to beat me. I had 302 overnight stays in a year." And then I said, "No, (laughs) I did not reach your level."

In addition to this role as host and tourist guide for visitors, they have also put much effort in organizing a system of gift exchange when traveling: Mrs. Müller, for example, has become an expert in transnationally optimizing price differences between Germany and the U.S. She is an expert in strolling through the aisles of regional wholesale markets, immediately recognizing attractive souvenirs to take to Germany. Whenever they travel back to Germany, they buy huge amounts of pharmaceutical, drugstore, and cosmetic products, as well as clothes in the U.S. on behalf of their friends and family in Germany. Mrs. Müller says that with one full suitcase packed with drugstore products, she often feels like a "detail man." When arriving in Germany, these items are delivered to family and friends.

However, most of the time, accompanying wives are not traveling and are not being visited by their friends and family, and translocal attachment work is carried out under conditions of physical distance. In the following quotations, Mrs. Klett and Mrs. Müller talk at length about how they maintained relationships with their family and friends at home from a distance:

> To stay in touch with the family today with Internet and stuff is much easier than it was during our stay in Japan where we had indeed a PC but email did not exist. (. . .) And I talk a lot over the phone with my parents so that I know what's going on at home. When I call my Grandma it's the same, she tells me what is happening there. And my friends tell me about what is going on in the village. So we stay very

close to each other. And when I talk with someone on the phone, it happens that I sometimes know things that this person does not even know yet, because he lives on the other side of the village. So it's quite easy to really stay in touch.

(Mrs. Klett)

I do not talk over the phone a lot, but I do use Skype a lot. And this is really great. When I am sitting at the table with my friend and we're having a coffee, then I can just say, "Can you give me a refill, please?" So, it's sooo much closer than talking on the phone. I mean, phone is OK; we have a flatrate, so I do not care sitting there for an hour or two. So sometimes I spend the whole morning with maintaining my relationships. And then my husband asks, "What have you actually done the whole morning?" So, at the final count actually not much, but what I did was very important. Because I had not talked with X and Y for a long time, and today I was just lucky to get hold of them.

(Mrs. Müller)

Although they use different technologies, Mrs. Klett talks on the phone and Mrs. Müller uses Skype, they both stress the irrelevance of actual physical distance for the quality of their social relationships with friends and family. Talking via Skype, Mrs. Müller feels so close to her physically distant friends that she perceives nearly no difference from a situation of sitting together around the kitchen table, having coffee together and giving each other a real 'refill.' Mrs. Klett is so much embedded into her networks at home that she, being thousands of miles away, gets information and news earlier then some of her friends who still live in the same village. Mr. Müller also confirms this irrelevance of physical space for the quality and intensity of his wife's friendship relations. "So, my wife is obviously at home during the day. And this of course gives her the possibility to talk with her female friends at home. (. . .) One friend tells her what kind of trouble she had with the other friend and so on. So, sometimes it gets a bit difficult." At the same time, he points to a very important gendered dimension in the translocal attachment work, as the following quotation reveals:

But in my case, when I go for a business trip to Germany, and I go at least three to four times a year, so every three months, then I am just there. As if I had never been away. So, I see the people, be it friends, colleagues from work or family, really more frequently than my wife does.

Mr. Müller can use professional resources for maintaining family and friendship relations. He also highlights this when he talks about how he will be maintaining his friendships in the U.S. once he has returned to Germany:

Mr. Müller:	I think in the future, when we will be back home in Germany, and I will be coming here on business trips, I will definitely pack my tennis racket [to play tennis with his friends from the country club] (laughs).
Researcher:	Oh, yes, you will be able to come here regularly on business trips!
Mr Müller:	Exactly!
Researcher:	But your family not, right?
Mr. Müller:	Exactly. This is the same as when I go to my hometown now. Then every Friday night there is a party at our neighbors' house (laughs).

In contrast to the wives who communicate virtually, the corporate expatriates who often travel can practice forms of bodily mediated sociabilities, such as having a beer and celebrating parties together, which evoke stronger feelings of togetherness and community.

The cases of the Kletts and the Müllers show that in the arrangement of the *male expatriate manager and an accompanying wife*, there is a specific and complex gendered division of labor regarding the translocal attachment work. Because of their bigger time resources during the day, the everyday translocal attachment work of the accompanying wives is based on nearly daily virtual mobility and modern communication technology and not so much on actual physical mobility. The translocal attachment work of the male expatriate managers instead is mainly based on actual physical mobility that occasionally produces not only imagined—as in Mrs. Müllers case—but real physical co-presence with their family members and friends. However, whereas new gossip and other local news from their hometowns reach the accompanying wives immediately, male expatriate managers are not connected to family and friends back home on a day-to-day basis, and local news does not reach them directly but instead only through the spouses as networkers. Male corporate expatriates are able to use their professional resources, such as business trips, to meet their family members and friends at home. And they very much emphasize this positive side effect of their professional mobility.

Translocal Attachment Work in the Nontraditional Gender Constellation

We turn again now to the couples comprised of a female expatriate manager and a male accompanying spouse. What does the gendered division of translocal attachment work look like in these couples and how is mobility addressed? For the female managers with nonworking husbands, the gendered division of translocal attachment work again looks quite different from for the male managers with accompanying wives. Indeed, the accompanying husbands take over some parts of the translocal attachment work.

For example, when Mrs. Carter's father, who lived in Italy, passed away, Mr. Carter drove there and picked up the furniture and their children's toys the family had stored there. It is, however, Mrs. Carter who keeps the contact with her mother and other family members via Skype and Facebook. She explains,

> With Facebook you can quickly check what the rest of your family is doing. And it's not really time-consuming to get the feeling that you really participate in their life. And Skype is really a good way for my mother to actually see how her grandchildren are growing.

Mrs. Carter takes complete responsibility for keeping in touch with her family in the U.S., whereas her husband seems to have lost contact with his family. This supports findings on gender-specific relevance and communication with family members abroad (Braseby, 2010, 219). However, it seems that for both of them, maintaining a close relationship to their families has lost importance. Mrs. Carter mentions that whereas she used to call her family on U.S. public holidays, now, working in an international context, it is increasingly difficult to maintain this tradition and remember U.S.-American holidays because U.S. holidays do not coincide with German holidays. Not remembering the national holidays and breaking with the family ritual of calling on these holidays can be seen as an indicator of a weakening relevance of relations to the family in particular and the home country in general. Once again, for the translocal attachment work, the female manager/accompanying husband couple does not mirror the division of labor of the more traditional expatriate couple, but the intensity of translocal attachment work is reduced.

However, what is most striking with regard to physical mobility, is that in contrast to the male managers, who emphasized the possibility to maintain relationships with friends and family at home as a positive side effect of their professional mobility, the female managers highlight the problems that arise from their professional mobility for their families, especially for their children. For example, Mrs. Carter explains,

> Being a female expat has very different challenges especially I think being a mother, having children, it's, it's much different. (. . .) Um, it is somehow just easier for men to, to leave for a week or two weeks and then come back. It's harder on the family but it's easier for the men to somehow deal with it and adjust back in and out. There is a difference to how children react to mothers and fathers. And for me to be gone on my business trips for a week, two weeks at a time, it's, it's been very hard and it's been something I've had to, had to put into consideration. How do I work with this? Because it's not the same as my male colleagues who can just go and do it and I have a different response when I come back as well from the kids. How long does it take my son to adjust again cause he's glued to my hip the first two days I'm back. He

would come into my bed about a week after I had come back. He would keep coming back in and then he'd settle down and be fine again. And I'm sure that on the male colleagues side there's that as well, but I think probably not as much as, as there is for me.

The inner-family division of labor notwithstanding, with Mr. Carter being a stay-at-home dad, responsible for the household and the children, Mrs. Carter still is engaged in those tasks more than male expatriate managers. The female expatriate managers in our sample, in contrast to their male counterparts, did not escape the double sociation (Becker-Schmidt 2010). They did not unambiguously focus on the professional sphere, celebrating professional mobility as a means for maintaining ties with their peers in their home country, but instead saw their professional mobility as competing with their local domestic responsibilities, which in the end seems to have led to diminishing translocal ties to their home country.

Conclusion

In the beginning of this chapter, we argued that there was a need for analyzing the relationship between mobility and cosmopolitanism through a relational perspective, highlighting the reciprocities and mutual repercussions between male and female identities, practices, and social positioning. The aim of this chapter was, thus, to reassess the image of the expatriate manager as a mobile and cosmopolitan professional by introducing a gendered and relational perspective on this specific form of mobility and engagement with the Other. In order to analyze the gendered and relational aspects of expatriate everyday life, we introduced three different sets of activities—mobility work, local attachment work, and translocal attachment work—which played crucial roles in enabling, shaping, and stabilizing the entangled mobilities and supposedly cosmopolitan lifestyles of corporate expatriates. Our research clearly confirms the existence of gender-specific systems of responsibility (Stadlbauer 2016, 171) regarding the stabilization of mobility and a transnational, mobile lifestyle.

In the *male expatriate manager/accompanying wife* arrangement, it is the accompanying spouses who in almost all of our cases completely take over the mobility work, local attachment work, and most of the translocal attachment work. In this arrangement, we could observe a polarization of a gendered division of labor, leaving this work in the female domain and liberating the male manager from reproductive work. As their families' 'mobility managers,' these women take over a significant amount of work related to their families' mobility. They thus make possible and stabilize the practical preconditions for global mobility. Engaging in the local support structures of the expatriate community, the accompanying wives build up meaningful sociabilities for their families. In addition, they acquire practical, experience-based knowledge that has been accumulated by other expatriate families, and once they themselves have complemented this knowledge with their own experiences, they recirculate it into the community. They thus stabilize not only their own families,' but also other expatriate families' mobility. As translocal consumption scouts, hosts, and tourist guides for visitors, the accompanying wives do most of the translocal attachment work and thus facilitate easy and fluid movement between different spaces and places. The data thus showed that women as accompanying spouses form an "intrinsic part of such a capitalist class" (Coles and Fechter 2008b, 18).

For the *female expatriate manager/male accompanying spouse* arrangement, the picture is significantly different. As our empirical cases indicate, the accompanying husbands did not take over mobility work, local attachment work, and translocal attachment work to the same extent as the accompanying wives (see also Selmer and Leung 2003). In this gender arrangement, the gendered division of labor in mobility work, local attachment work, and translocal attachment work was indeed reshaped and not so extremely polarized between the working and the nonworking spouse. Despite their heavy workload and their role as main breadwinner, the female managers were themselves responsible for specific parts of this essential work, because accompanying husbands were symbolically excluded from the predominantly female support networks in the expatriate community as well as from local institutions that expected mothers to be principal communication partners. Accompanying husbands did not build up sociabilities for their families, whereas the female managers had to cope with the burdens of being simultaneously embedded in their translocal workscape and the local space. Despite their heavy workload, the female managers had to act as brokers to the local context and manage a significant amount of family and local attachment work. The female managers perceived this double sociation as an extremely challenging situation. The accompanying husbands were also under a lot of pressure and felt isolated—both female managers commented on their husbands' emotional stress—as the formal division of labor within the couple's relationship did not fit the broader societal gender conceptions. Additionally, in the couples with a female manager and an accompanying husband, we could witness a transformation of certain parts of mobility and family practices, such as redefining the organization of mobility in a way that it is expected to be generally less work-intensive, delegating care work to educational institutions, or reducing the intensity of translocal attachment work.

In addition to emphasizing the gendered dimension of mobility management, this chapter has highlighted the paradox relation of mobility and cosmopolitanism (Beck 2009). For the couples comprised of a male manager and an accompanying wife, our cases indicate rather clear, gender-specific systems of responsibility (see also Stadlbauer 2016, 171) with regard to mobility work and local and translocal attachment work. However, with regard to cosmopolitanism, the picture is not so clear. Although the work of building up sociabilities for the mobile families turned out to be a rather female domain, these sociabilities in most cases did not include locals. Some of the spheres, that accompanying wives were responsible for, tended to direct them to other expatriates of their own nationality. As their families' mobility managers, accompanying wives did not focus so much on their children's integration into the host country school system, but instead focused mainly on the question of how they could smoothly reintegrate into their old home country school system. As their families' local networkers, they did not initially approach locals for acquiring practical knowledge on the everyday life at the host locality, but instead looked for advice from others like them who had gone through the same experiences. As their families' transnational networkers, they indeed showed a great amount of hospitality, which has been identified as a gendered dimension of cosmopolitanism (Høy-Petersen, Woodward, and Skrbis 2016). However, this hospitality was confined to friends and family from home, whereas hospitality to local Others was rather neglected. In sum, instead of building up inclusive cosmopolitan sociabilities (Glick Schiller, Darieva, and Gruner-Domic 2011), they rather contributed to the stabilization of a national expatriate 'bubble.'[3] Amit had argued that for many contemporary mobile people, mobility did not "entail a learning of how to be 'local' but how to be a particular kind of visitor." (Amit, 2015, 564) For most of the accompanying wives, their complex mobility work did emphasis this transient identity of a visitor. Only in a few cases did the local attachment work of the accompanying wives also create cosmopolitan sociabilities for the whole couple or family.

In contrast, the sociabilities of the couples comprised of a female manager and an accompanying husband reflect a higher, however still limited degree of openness. Both families had a dense network of friends transcending at least their own national 'bubble.' Both cultivated sociabilities including mainly other international expatriates, and also—although to a very limited extent—locals. This relatively larger openness was achieved either by friendships from the female manager's work context or by spaces such as the church group, where both partners were involved in networking. Thus, the participation of the female managers in establishing family friendships played a significant role. Despite the social isolation of the accompanying husbands, the less polarized gender-specific systems of responsibility (Stadlbauer 2016, 171) with regard to mobility work and local and translocal attachment apparently led to more open sociabilities.

The findings that we have presented suggest that mobility and mobility work do not automatically lead to cosmopolitan sociabilities (Glick Schiller, Darieva, and Gruner-Domic 2011, 404), but paradoxically also lead to new "stoppages and fixities," as Beck (2009, 33) has argued. What became clear is that both closure and openness were related to the mobile lives of the expatriate managers and their families. We will take up these inherent contradictions in the conclusion (Chapter 10), by introducing the concept of 'paradoxical cosmopolitanisms.'

Notes

1 These contributions have been theorized by feminist scholars with the concept of the "incorporated wife" (Callan and Ardener 1984). They argue that modern organizations exercise power over the private and domestic domains (see Chapter 4) and that this transcendence dismantles the ideological dimension of the private-public divide. The concept has been in the context of expatriate mobility (Coles and Fechter 2008a) in order to shed light on how the invisible work of the accompanying wives is related to their husbands' formal work.

2 We do not focus on dual career couples, because we are interested how the formal division of labor within the couple is transformed and negotiated due to specific gendered practices, expectations, and ideologies.

3 In the cases presented here, the expatriate 'bubble' was also stabilized by the relatively large MNCs and their specific institutions for expatriates.

Bibliography

Amit, Vered. 2015. "Circumscribed Cosmopolitanism: Travel Aspirations and Experiences." *Identities* 22 (5): 551–68. doi:10.1080/1070289X.2014.975709.

Amit, Vered, and Pauline G. Barber. 2015. "Mobility and Cosmopolitanism: Complicating the Interaction Between Aspiration and Practice." *Identities* 22 (5): 543–50. doi:10.1080/1070289X.2014.975714.

Beck, Ulrich. 2006. *The Cosmopolitan Vision*. Cambridge: Polity Press.

Beck, Ulrich. 2009. "Mobility and the Cosmopolitan Perspective." In *Tracing Mobilities: Towards a Cosmopolitan Perspective*, edited by Weert Canzler, Vincent Kaufmann, and Sven Kesselring, 25–35. Farnham, Burlington: Ashgate.

Becker-Schmidt, Regina. 2003. "Zur doppelten Vergesellschaftung von Frauen. Soziologische Grundlegung, empirische Rekonstruktion." *Gender . . . politik . . . online*, 1–18. http://www.fu-berlin.de/sites/gpo/soz_eth/Geschlecht_als_Kategorie/Die_doppelte_Vergesellschaftung_von_Frauen/becker_schmidt_ohne.pdf. Accessed June 2, 2017.

Becker-Schmidt, Regina. 2010. "Doppelte Vergesellschaftung von Frauen: Divergenzen und Brückenschläge zwischen Privat- und Erwerbsleben." In *Handbuch Frauen- und Geschlechterforschung*, edited by Ruth Becker and Renate Kortendiek, 65–74. Wiesbaden: VS Verlag für Sozialwissenschaften.

Bernard, Donald J. 2014. "A Narrative Study of Male Accompanying Partners: Adaptation to a Nontraditional Role in Dyadic Partnerships." UNLV Theses/Dissertations/Professional Papers/Capstones Paper 2245. Las Vegas: University of Nevada. Accessed June 28, 2016.

Böhnisch, Tomke. 1999. *Gattinnen—die Frauen der Elite*. Kritische Theorie und Kulturforschung. Münster: Westfälisches Dampfboot.

Braseby, Anne M. 2010. "Adaptation of Trailing Spouses: Does Gender Matter?" FIU Electronic Theses and Dissertations Paper 153. Florida: Florida International University. Accessed June 28, 2016.

Callan, Hilary, and Shirley Ardener. 1984. *The Incorporated Wife*. London: Croom Helm.

Cole, Nina, and Yvonne McNulty. 2011. "Why Do Female Expatriates "Fit-in" Better than Males?" *Cross Cultural Management: An International Journal* 18 (2): 144–64. doi:10.1108/13527601111125996.

Coles, Anne. 2008. "Making Multiple Migrations: The Life of British Diplomatic Families Overseas." In Coles and Fechter 2008a, 125–48.

Coles, Anne, and Anne-Meike Fechter, eds. 2008a. *Gender and Family Among Transnational Professionals.* London and New York: Routledge.

Coles, Anne, and Anne-Meike Fechter. 2008b. "Introduction." In Coles and Fechter 2008a, 1–20.

Elliott, Anthony, and John Urry. 2010. *Mobile Lives.* London and New York: Routledge.

Fechter, Anne-Meike. 2008. "From 'Incorporated Wives' to 'Expat Girls': A New Generation of Expatriate Women." In Coles and Fechter 2008a, 193–209.

Felstead, Alan, Nick Jewson, and Sally Walters. 2005. *Changing Places of Work.* Basingstoke: Palgrave Macmillan.

Glick Schiller, Nina, Tsypylma Darieva, and Sandra Gruner-Domic. 2011. "Defining Cosmopolitan Sociability in a Transnational Age: An Introduction." *Ethnic and Racial Studies* 34 (3): 399–418. doi:10.1080/01419870.2011.533781.

Habermas, Rebekka. 2000. *Frauen und Männer des Bürgertums: Eine Familiengeschichte (1750–1850).* Göttingen: Vandenhoeck & Ruprecht.

Harvey, Michael, and Danielle Wiese. 1998. "The Dual-Career Couple: Female Expatriates and Male Trailing Spouses." *Thunderbird International Business Review* 40 (4): 359–88. doi:10.1002/tie.4270400404.

Hindman, Heather. 2008. "Shopping for a Hypernational Home: How Expatriate Women in Kathmandu Labour to Assuage Fear." In Coles and Fechter 2008a, 41–61.

Høy-Petersen, Nina, Ian Woodward, and Zlatko Skrbis. 2016. "Gender Performance and Cosmopolitan Practice: Exploring Gendered Frames of Ppenness and Hospitality." The Sociological Review 64 (4): 970–86. doi:10.1111/1467-954X.12390.

Kanter, Rosabeth M. 1995. *World Class: Thriving Locally in the Global Economy.* New York: Simon & Schuster.

Kesselring, Sven, and Gerlinde Vogl. 2010. *Betriebliche Mobilitätsregime: Die sozialen Kosten mobiler Arbeit.* Berlin: edition sigma.

König, Tomke. 2012. *Familie heisst Arbeit teilen: Transformationen der symbolischen Geschlechterordnung.* Konstanz: UVK.

Lauring, Jakob, and Jan Selmer. 2009. "Expatriate Compound Living: An Ethnographic Field Study." *The International Journal of Human Resource Management* 20 (7): 1451–67. doi:10.1080/09585190902983215.

Lauring, Jakob, and Jan Selmer. 2010. "The Supportive Expatriate Spouse: An Ethnographic Study of Spouse Involvement in Expatriate Careers." *International Business Review* 19 (1): 59–69. doi:10.1016/j.ibusrev.2009.09.006.

McNulty, Yvonne, and Val Byoko. 2004. "Understanding a New Phenomenon: The Male Trailing Spouse." http://www1.expatica.com/hr/story/understanding-a-newphenomenon-. Accessed May 31, 2017

McNulty, Yvonne, and Kate Hutchings. 2015. "Looking for Global Talent in all the Right Places: A Critical Literature Review of Non-Traditional Expatriates." *The International Journal of Human Resource Management* 27 (7): 699–728. doi:10.1080/09585192.2016.1148756.

Moore, Fiona. 2008. "The German School in London, UK: Fostering the Next Generation of National Cosmopolitans?" In Coles and Fechter 2008a, 85–102.

Salaff, Janet W. 2000. "The Gendered Social Organization of Migration as Work." In *Gender and Migration*, edited by Katie Willis and Brenda Yeoh, 153–74. Northampton: Edward Elgar.

Schütz, Alfred. 1944. "The Stranger: An Essay in Social Psychology." *American Journal of Sociology* 49 (6): 499–507. doi:10.1086/219472

Selmer, Jan, and Alicia S. Leung. 2003. "Provision and Adequacy of Corporate Support to Male Expatriate Spouses." *Personnel Review* 32 (1): 9–21. doi:10.1108/00483480310454691.

Spiegel, Anna, and Ursula Mense-Petermann. 2016. "Verflochtene Mobilitäten und ihr Management: Mobilitätspraktiken von Expatriate-Managern und ihren ‚trailing spouses' im Auslandseinsatz." *Österreichische Zeitschrift für Soziologie* 41: 15–31. doi:10.1007/s11614-016-0188-8

Stadlbauer, Johanna. 2015. *Mobile Gattinnen: Privilegierte Migration und Geschlechterverhältnisse*. Münster: Westfälisches Dampfboot.

Stadlbauer, Johanna. 2016. "Privilegierte Migration und Geschlechterverhältnisse: Expatriate Spouses in Österreich." In *Migration und Integration – wissenschaftliche Perspektiven aus Österreich*, edited by Jennifer Carvill Schellenbacher, Julia Dahlvik, Heinz Fassmann, and Christoph Reinprecht, 167–82. Vienna: Vienna University Press.

Szerszynski, Bronislaw, and John Urry. 2002. "Cultures of Cosmopolitanism." *Sociological Review* 50 (4): 461–82. doi:10.1111/1467-954X.00394

Szerszynski, Bronislaw, and John Urry. 2006. "Visuality, Mobility and the Cosmopolitan: Inhabiting the World from Afar." *The British Journal of Sociology* 57 (1): 113–31. doi:10.1111/j.1468-4446.2006.00096.x.

Urry, John. 2007. *Mobilities*. Cambridge: Polity Press.

Walsh, Katie. 2008. "Travelling Together? Work, Intimacy, and Home Amongst British Expatriate Couples in Dubai." In Coles and Fechter 2008a, 63–84.

Willis, Katie, and Brenda Yeoh. 2002. "Gendering Transnational Communities: A Comparison of Singaporean and British Migrants in China." *Geoforum* 33 (4): 533–65. doi: 10.1016/S0016-7185(02)00039-8

Willis, Katie, and Brenda Yeoh. 2008. " 'Coming to China Changed My Life': Gender Roles and Relations Among Single British Migrants." In Coles and Fechter 2008a, 211–32.

Yeoh, Brenda, and Katie Willis. 2005. "Singaporeans in China: Transnational Women Elites and the Negotiation of Gendered Identities." *Geoforum* 36 (2): 211–22. doi:10.1016/j.geoforum.2003.07.004.

Part III

Negotiating Difference in the Professional Sphere

Part III empirically investigates how expatriate managers negotiate difference *in the professional sphere* by focusing on everyday management practices within the MNC.

Chapter 7 aims at contributing to a deeper understanding of the intraorganizational boundary spanning work of expatriate managers. Going beyond the different boundary-spanning functions as identified in the expatriate literature, we reconstruct different modes of dealing with the challenges and complexities of boundary spanning roles, and important dimensions of the context that reconfigure these modes.

Chapter 8 explores the subsidiary office as a cultural contact zone and analyzes (1) expatriates' interactions with local colleagues, (2) their strategies in dealing with the different work practices with which they are confronted, and (3) the cultural identity they display in the setup of their office space. We identify different types of symbolic management ranging from attempts to displace host country work and cultural practices from the office space to visions of creating cosmopolitan office spaces that integrate diverse cultural meanings.

Part III, thus, probes into expatriate managers' cosmopolitan or anti-cosmopolitan practices in the organizational context of the host subsidiary and the identities and orientations displayed in these practices.

7 Role-Taking and Role-Making

Expatriates as Creative Organizational Boundary Spanners in MNCs

Bastian Bredenkötter

As we have developed in Chapters 2 and 3, the expatriate manager can be conceived of as an actor who contributes to the construction of the MNC as a transnational social space by acting as a *boundary spanner*. Dominant parts of the expatriate literature discussed in Chapter 3 conceptualize expatriates as role incumbents at organizational and, at the same time, cultural boundaries, and it is their central function to exert influence and process information across these boundaries. Expatriate managers are sent abroad by the headquarters with a set of more or less specific tasks. Accentuating the primary direction of desired activities and flows of information and influence, we suggest to analytically differentiate three ideal-typical intraorganizational boundary roles: (1) As *controller and transfer agent* the expatriate can be appointed to transfer organizational models, programs, technology, work processes, best practices, knowledge, and other information from the headquarters to the subsidiary and to influence and control the subsidiary according to the headquarters' interests and standards. Here, a clearly hierarchical relationship between the expatriate manager and local employees can be assumed. (2) As *coordinator and negotiator* the expatriate manager can be used to coordinate tasks, mediate conflicts, and generally resolve problems between headquarters and the subsidiary or to jointly develop projects and strategies. It is therefore about bidirectional flows of information and influence. In this case, expatriates and local employees can be expected to meet more at eye level. (3) It is conceivable that a manager is sent abroad as *learner and information seeker* to observe the subsidiary, gain local knowledge and intelligence, pass it on, and thereby help the headquarters to learn about and adapt to its organizational environment. In this case, we can speak of a focus on unidirectional flows of information and influence from the subsidiary to the headquarters. Here, the subsidiary has something the headquarters are interested in, and the local staff can be expected to have at least a higher position in the knowledge hierarchy than the expatriate.

These ideal-typical roles position expatriate managers in the subsidiary in a specific way that decisively prestructures their work. Nevertheless, we argue that it is not enough to look at roles and functions to understand expatriate boundary spanning and the stabilization of MNCs as transnational social spaces (see Chapter 3). In contrast to approaches that suffer from a structuralist bias, we posit that in order to act as boundary spanners, expatriates must actively and creatively 'make' their roles. At least two aspects of role-*making* must be considered: For one, our actor-centered approach emphasizes that differing individual orientations, interpretive schemes, micropolitical interests, and resources influence how expatriates enact their roles. For another, we stress that there is not only a "transnationalism from above" but also a "transnationalism from below" (Smith and Guarnizo 1998; Morgan 2001) in MNCs; boundary spanning always takes place in interaction and negotiation with local (and headquarter) employees who have their own interests and dispose over their own micropolitical power resources and who can either contribute to and complete or counter, change, and resist the expatriate managers' initiatives (Dörrenbächer and Geppert 2006; Mense-Petermann 2006; Minssen 2009; Mense-Petermann 2013; Mense-Petermann and Spiegel 2016). Hence, to act successfully as boundary spanners, expatriate managers always rely on the (at least partial consensus-driven) cooperation of the local employees.

Against this background, the question, to be answered empirically, arises: How do expatriates practice their boundary roles in their everyday work—and how are they able to practice them in face of the hard to meet challenges and the micropolitical constellations of the subsidiary (and of the overall organization). Other than in the literature on expatriate functions and assignment purposes, which solely focuses on the 'official' boundary roles and takes role-taking by the expatriates for granted, the focus of this chapter is on the creative role-making of expatriates. Therefore, in this chapter, we examine expatriates' boundary spanning practices and possibilities in-depth and identify typical, empirically observable *modes of 'making' boundary roles*.

The chapter is structured as follows: In a first step, we identify two different modes of boundary spanning in the controller and transfer agent role that can be typified as those of a *teacher* and an *entrepreneur*. With the *service provider* and the *chameleon* we then identify two modes of boundary spanning in the coordinator and negotiator role. Note, that the ideal-typical role of the learner and information seeker is not at all represented in our empirical cases. In the conclusion, we discuss how our research enhances the understanding of the structured and structuring features of expatriate boundary spanning. Our findings indicate that images of the host country as well as the willingness of local employees to accept specific practices impact the modes in which expatriates are able to 'make' their boundary role. They also show that personal backgrounds, career orientations, life plans, and even ascriptive characteristics like ethnicity can encroach the intensity with which expatriates want to and can immerse themselves into the social environment of the subsidiary and thereby shape their boundary spanning.[1] Finally, we relate to our overarching question: Considering that relevant parts of the literature conceptualize expatriates as cosmopolitans and take cosmopolitanism as given (see Chapters 1 and 4), we discuss in how far expatriates become visible as cosmopolitans in their role-making in the sphere of work.

Boundary Spanning in the Controller and Transfer Agent Role

In the *controller and transfer agent* role, expatriate managers are sent abroad to transfer organizational models, programs, work processes, knowledge, and other information from the headquarters to the subsidiary and to influence and control the subsidiary according to the headquarters' interests and standards. The general challenge of this role is that models, programs, and processes developed at the headquarters cannot be easily implemented without problems and frictions in a foreign context. Expatriates are confronted especially with the problem of having formal authority but not necessarily the necessary power resources to put through headquarter objectives against the will and habits of the local employees. Therefore, they must mobilize 'willingness to cooperate' for initiatives the subsidiary had no influence over and which may deviate from usual local practices and ways of doing things (see Mense-Petermann 2017, 183–4), a problem discussed in the literature as the 'not invented here' problem. In this subchapter, we investigate how expatriate managers enact the controller and transfer agent role and deal with its challenges. We discuss two selected cases, which are exemplary for two modes of boundary spanning we can identify in our data.

Mr. Barnett and Mr. Schwarz are two expatriate managers who are responsible for setting up departments at newly established production sites of their MNCs. Whereas Mr. Barnett is responsible for the quality management at the plant in China, Mr. Schwarz is building up a department within logistics at a production site in the U.S. As controllers and transfer agents, both managers have the task of establishing and monitoring company standards and building up local teams at the new plants. Which different modes of 'making' the controller and transfer agent role and dealing with its challenges do Mr. Barnett and Mr. Schwarz develop?

The Expatriate Manager as Teacher

Mr. Barnett is an U.S.-American manager in his 40s working for a large U.S.-American MNC in China. As head of quality management, he is responsible for establishing and controlling the quality standards of his company at the new plant. MNCs seem to fill this position, at least in new subsidiaries in China, specifically with Western managers: According to Mr. Barnett's Austrian friend, who heads the quality control of another Western MNC, Western managers serve as a kind of "eye of the Western customer" in China. They are to ensure that products meet the quality requirements of Western customers. Regarding his role-making as a controller and transfer agent, Mr. Barnett describes himself as a *"teacher."* We take up this emic term[2] to elaborate on his specific mode of boundary spanning.

Mr. Barnett stands as an example for several German and U.S.-American managers in China who assume there are significant differences in both professional competence and culture between home and host country employees and therefore develop specific management practices (see also Chapter 8). He reports that the professional skills of Chinese employees are usually not enough to enable them to complete their tasks independently from the outset with the required quality. He therefore assumes that he cannot simply direct the execution of tasks, but instead first has to enable the local employees before they can adequately fulfill the tasks. Furthermore, Mr. Barnett explains that there is one cultural property of particular importance for working together with the local workforce: "The fear of Chinese employees 'to lose face.'" According to him, Chinese employees, "to save face," tend to confirm delivery dates to the headquarters that are from the beginning unrealistic of being met. For the same reason, they do not report any mistakes or problems and cover them up at the last minute. Against this background, Mr. Barnett sees it as a challenge to plan, carry out, and monitor projects:

> If you agree with someone that something is to be finished in three weeks, you can't really be sure that it will actually get done by then. Instead, it's more likely that a bigger problem has arisen that you won't find out about until after the deadline, and then you're suddenly in a position where you have to justify this to the headquarters.

Mr. Barnett and some other expatriate managers in China share the expectation and/or experience of certain difficulties in working together with Chinese employees. Thus, the managers construct clearly asymmetrical relationships with their Chinese employees. Nevertheless, they differ in their subsequent analyses and in their views of the local Other: Whereas some managers view Chinese employees as interculturally inflexible and unable to develop, others stress the legitimacy of their deficits and their capacity and willingness to learn. Hence, they develop different modes of boundary spanning.

Mr. Barnett expresses this by stating, "Here in China, I'm some kind of teacher, not a general." He uses the term "general" to characterize the practices of "many other expatriates" as authoritarian, not empathetic and virtually colonialist. Hence, he clearly describes them as anti-cosmopolitan. He distances himself from this way of role-making not only for moral but also for functional reasons. He argues that shouting at Chinese employees, criticizing them too harshly, and telling them all the time that everything they do is wrong inevitably leads to the local employees feeling they have "lost face" and damages the basis for working together almost irrevocably.

Mr. Barnett, thus, describes the basis for cooperation as relatively fragile and the execution of power in an aggressive, escalating, or even uninhibited manner as dysfunctional in light of the prominent significance of "saving face."

Especially in order to set himself apart from those "other expatriates," he interprets his role as that of a *teacher*. Although he views his employees as being deficient, he takes those deficiencies to be legitimate and of no fault of their own. Rather, he blames the Chinese education system, which becomes clear in statements like "How should they know, they've never learned it." Furthermore, he stresses the possibility for overcoming this deficient status by underlining their ability and enormous willingness to learn. Against the backdrop of this interpretation of his employees as 'students,' he presents himself as "some kind of teacher" in three ways: He first takes the role of a patient subject teacher. He discusses the time he takes to sit down with his employees to show them step-by-step and as often as necessary how to do specific work tasks correctly. Second, he sees himself as not only a broker of technical and practical knowledge but also as teacher in Western corporate culture. He describes a video conference which can be downright characterized as a 'school lesson.' Participating in this conference were Mr. Barnett, superiors from the headquarters, and several Chinese employees. The conversation deals with the completion of a larger technical system, and the headquarters is asking whether the system can be completed by the end of that month. The Chinese employees confirm the date, but Mr. Barnett senses some uncertainty and doubt in their facial expressions. He pauses the video transmission to the headquarters and asks the employees what is wrong. He explains to them that in a Western company it would be acceptable to tell superiors if it is not possible to keep a certain date, but that if a date is confirmed, it is expected that the deadline will be met. Then, he asks his employees to describe the situation to the headquarters, restarts the transmission, and the Chinese employees agree on a realistic date with the headquarters. He describes another 'lesson' regarding the communication practices inside the company in which he explains to the Chinese employees that it is normal in Western companies to criticize one another and to explicitly show that one is dissatisfied or frustrated about something without this meaning that one loses respect for someone even if he personally made a mistake—"everyone makes mistakes." Like a teacher, third, he views his 'students' as protégés. He goes on to elaborate that he does not report mistakes to the headquarters if they can be corrected on-site. According to him, in this way, he was able to slowly gain the trust and respect of his employees, which is central to cooperation. Thus, he uses his room for maneuver, which he has on the basis of the spatial distance from the headquarters, to protect his employees and thus gain their trust.

To sum up, several expatriates in our sample have an image of the local employees as deficient, which is a result of expectations of and/or experiences with significant cultural differences and lacking professional skills. Drawing on the case of Mr. Barnett, we have reconstructed the teacher as one specific mode of boundary spanning in the controller and transfer agent role. The teacher-way of 'making' this role represents a paternalistic-benevolent mode of dealing with the local Other which is based on a self-distancing from authoritarian and aggressive ones. Paradoxically, on the one hand, it indeed establishes an asymmetrical relationship between the expatriate and the local employees. On the other hand, however, the expatriate's behavior is very supportive and builds on an image of the local employees as both able and willing to learn. In the next subchapter, we will explore a mode of how the controller and transfer agent role is made that is not built off a deficient image of the local employees.

The Expatriate Manager as Start-Up Entrepreneur

Mr. Schwarz is a German manager in his 40s who works for a large German MNC in the U.S. He is one among many other expatriates who have been sent abroad by the company to transfer know-how to the subsidiary, define and establish working processes, and to build local teams who can later on replace the expatriates. As head of a subunit, Mr. Schwarz is responsible for building up a department within logistics. His boundary-spanning mode can best be characterized as that of a *"start-up" entrepreneur.*

The basis for this role-making is the interplay between two aspects that (individually or combined) also shape the boundary spanning of other expatriates in our sample: First, for Mr. Schwarz, the assignment is accompanied by a gain in responsibility and scope of decision making. This gain in autonomy and the excitement to help build up a "young company" are of significant importance for his interpretation of his role. In his work, he sees the chance to build something big and meaningful:

> To build up a plant. I'd say that's a professional challenge that almost no one else has (. . .) It's unique and isn't comparable with an ordinary job. And my guys are always saying that I'm exhausting myself here, but there's just so incredibly much to do, but there are also so many possibilities. The creative possibility to go in here and to say, I get to shape this now. Of course we have standards and of course there are processes. OK, yeah, so this is in addition. I'd say, this is terrific, this chance.

Second, in addition to this perception of extraordinary efficacy and room for maneuver, there are specific expectations and images regarding the cultural characteristics and professional skills of the local employees that Mr. Schwarz shares with several German expatriates in the U.S. and U.S.-American managers in Germany: Although he certainly expects differences between German and U.S.-American employees, he—at least initially—assumes equal professional skills and largely compatible cultural characteristics.

How, then, does he create his controller and transfer agent role under the condition of a perceived symmetrical relationship? He interprets his role not as that of a teacher but instead develops a boundary-spanning mode that can be characterized as that of a start-up entrepreneur who wants to "build" something new and innovative with his "team": First, he enacts his role in an extremely motivated, dynamic, and performance-oriented manner. At the same time, he maintains a casual, chummy, and only slightly hierarchical tone with his "team." This is not only observed by the researchers on-site. His (overly) intense working pace and dedication is addressed by his subordinates in the researchers' and also his presence jokingly on several occasions. Second, he constructs the local employees as capable and competent actors and as valuable resources rather than conceiving of them as deficient, incomplete, and dependent 'students.' He reports how he used highly participative management methods during the training phase: "Then people's self-assessment, I was working a lot with that, self-assessment: 'What do you think, in your perception, how ready are you for the job?'" Beyond that, in the beginning, he says, he was planning to "really integrate" the experiences of his employees, most of whom had college and university degrees and had worked for other manufacturers and suppliers in the same industry. By doing so, he wants to "generate" a "best-of-breed," the "best of the best." Thus, Mr. Schwarz constructs a clearly symmetrical and non-paternalistic relationship with his U.S.-American employees. Third, his self-perception as a start-up entrepreneur is shown by his strong identification with the new plant and his team. When asked about his role between headquarters and subsidiary, he answers that he is "first and foremost (. . .) an employee of this plant" and that he represents "the interests of the plant over the headquarters, against company and brand committees." He underlines his independence from the headquarters performatively by referencing that prior to his assignment he did not hold a position at headquarters but instead at one of the productions sites in Germany. Fourth, Mr. Schwarz's entrepreneurial orientation becomes clear in his strong interest in a rapid growth of the subsidiary. We could observe this at a meeting during which a very sensitive issue concerning the production volume was discussed. Despite delivery problems with a supplier and doubts in other even more senior local managers, Mr. Schwarz tries to push through an increase in the planned production in order to keep the plant growing and ensure the employment of the newly established third shift. In this negotiation process, he can capitalize on his strong ties to the German CEO of the subsidiary, whom he is able to convince to support his position over that of the local managers.[3]

It is noteworthy that Mr. Schwarz does not (or cannot) switch into the teacher mode of 'making' the boundary role even at a point when his expectations and experiences regarding the U.S.-American employees fall apart. Mr. Schwarz reports that he is used to working with well-trained employees and working students in Germany who complete their tasks largely independently after only a few instructions and explanations. In accordance with his initially positive image of the skills and competencies of the U.S.-American employees, in the beginning, Mr. Schwarz let them also do their jobs largely independently with minimal supervision after giving them brief instructions. However, in his opinion, this management strategy failed. He is disappointed that many local employees were incapable of fulfilling tasks with the required quality from the beginning:

> And especially German students working [in the headquarters] towards their diplomas, you tell them, "Hey, here is an assignment for your studies, let's try to streamline the topic together (. . .)." But from that point on, the students pretty much work on their own. When I look at the people I have here [in the U.S.]—and they all have college degrees—you notice that this is different here (. . .). You notice that when you get the work back and look at it and think "Hm, but this isn't what I had expected."

Thus, Mr. Schwarz sees himself confronted with the same problems Mr. Barnett had and, somewhat reluctantly, decides to adapt his management style to involve "a bit more micromanagement." Nonetheless, he cannot switch into the teacher mode in the way Mr. Barnett did, because a prerequisite of this mode of boundary spanning, a shared notion of a fundamental knowledge asymmetry, is not given. The local employees do not take such an asymmetry as given and, accordingly, do not accept subordinated complementary roles.

> Generally, everyone says, "Freedom, we're in the land of the free (. . .) We're in the land of the free and (. . .) You can't boss me around, because I'm a free citizen and you can't," you know, that was always the first thing everyone said.

Therefore, Mr. Schwarz has to find a way of giving more instructions and supervising in greater detail without, however, enacting the controller and transfer agent role in a hierarchical way (e.g., like a teacher or even a general). Instead, he develops a strategy that goes with his role-making as a start-up entrepreneur, and sticks with the participatory culture of a start-up on the level of communication. To legitimize his new practices, he deliberately puts his subordinates in a position where they have to ask for support rather than him just giving them straightforward instructions:

> And when I, specifically related to work, asked, "Regarding your task, do you need more detail?" Then one by one they all actually came back and said "Well, a little bit more detail."

Hence, it becomes clear that Mr. Schwarz's role-making is still restricted by the necessity to address the local employees as sovereign and competent actors. The jointly constructed image of the U.S.-American employees remains effective, even as Mr. Schwarz's expectations and experiences fall apart.

Teacher and Start-Up Entrepreneur: Two Modes of 'Making' the Controller and Transfer Agent Role

In the *controller and transfer agent* role, expatriate managers are assigned to transfer organizational models, work processes, knowledge, and other information from the headquarters to the subsidiary and to influence and monitor the subsidiary according to headquarter interests and standards. While they enact the role, expatriate managers see themselves confronted especially with the challenges of integrating the local staff both professionally and culturally into the overall MNC and mobilizing their willingness to cooperate and adapt to headquarter procedures.

We have identified two modes of 'making' this role with the *teacher* and the *start-up entrepreneur*. It became clear that the perception of one's own influence as well as the expectations and experiences regarding the professional skills and cultural properties of the local employees shape how expatriate managers interpret and enact their roles. Whereas the teacher is a paternalistic-benevolent mode of boundary spanning that conceptualizes the local Other as in need but capable of learning, the start-up entrepreneur is a collegial-demanding mode that conceptualizes the local Other as equal and competent but in need of motivation (for the headquarters' objectives). Therefore, both modes differ with respect to the asymmetrical or symmetrical relationship the expatriate manager constructs with the local employees. In contrast to authoritarian-aggressive modes of boundary spanning, like the general, the modes are equal in their generally positive view of the local employees.

It is interesting that we find the teacher mode of boundary role-making only in China, even though expatriates in the controller and transfer agent role are confronted with similar problems across the different host countries. Our case studies indicate that this can be explained, for one, by widespread, pre-existing images expatriates have of local employees in different host countries and, two, by differences in the willingness of local employees from different host countries to accept certain management practices. It is striking that we find modes of boundary role-making built off of expectations of significant cultural differences and professional deficits especially in the cases of German and U.S.-American expatriates in China and a role-making based on notions of professional competence and cultural similarity primarily in the cases of German expatriates in the U.S. and U.S.-American expatriates in Germany. However, the cause for the development of specific boundary-spanning modes cannot be solely found in different expectations and images expatriates have of local employees. Role-making also relies on the willingness of local employees to accept certain practices and complementary roles. The teacher role, namely, relies on a mutually shared notion of a fundamental knowledge asymmetry. In this respect, we find indications that local employees in China seem to be more willing to take fundamental knowledge asymmetries as given and accept inferior roles compared to those in the U.S.—at least for a limited time. Several managers in our sample report that they are especially respected by Chinese employees for their competencies and knowledge. One German manager even received a Chinese name from his Chinese employees that refers to his age, sophistication, and wisdom. Regarding his ascriptive characteristics, another German manager tells us that "gray hair" is interpreted positively as a sign of experience and authority in China, whereas it is interpreted negatively as a sign of decreasing abilities in the West. With an U.S.-American manager, who characterizes himself as a "mentor," we can observe how even Chinese employees with academic degrees willingly let him 'lecture' them. This compliance is not least a result of the fact that through their 'holistic' (professional and cultural) schooling, the teachers/mentors aim to make the local employees ready for an 'independent life' in a Western corporation and therefore open up future prospects and career aspirations. For example, the mentor has chosen a Chinese employee as his successor, and he takes a lot of time to prepare him for his tasks.[4] We find opposite indications regarding the willingness of local staff to accept asymmetrical relationships and lecturing practices in the U.S. In addition to Mr. Schwarz, this is also clearly apparent in the case of another experienced German manager who was sent to the U.S. after two postings in China. He reports,

> And in the perception of non-Germans, we Germans are often seen in this one way: "They come along and tell us how to do everything and act very teacher-like and very self-confident." And that's not how you're going to get an American to buy into it. Americans are a very proud people—the Americans, they've built up this country over the last 300 years. Before that, there were just a few buffalos and Indians running around here. And Americans are very proud of what they are and who they are and also of their pragmatism and economic success. In their own perception, Americans can do everything themselves; they don't need a German square-headed engineer to come and tell them how it's done.

In summary, our data show that expatriate managers inhabiting the same boundary role 'make' that role quite differently depending on where they are: in China or in the U.S./Germany. This points to the importance of specific conditions of the socio-cultural context for expatriates' boundary spanning. We will systematically investigate and compare the impact of different host countries and host localities on expatriates' orientations and everyday practices in Chapter 9.

Boundary Spanning in the Coordinator and Negotiator Role

In the *coordinator and negotiator role*, expatriate managers are posted to exchange knowledge, coordinate tasks, mediate conflicts, and generally resolve problems between head and subsidiary offices or to jointly develop projects and strategies with the subsidiary. In this role, expatriates still come to the subsidiary as outsiders, but they do not come as 'missionaries' of the headquarters. Rather, it is intended that they help to develop solutions that pick up local perspectives, practices, and interests, but still are compatible with the rationalities and standards of the headquarters and the overall organization (Mense-Petermann 2017, 184–5). Unlike the controller and transfer agent role, the coordinator and negotiator role is about bidirectional flows of information and influence. The general and tense challenge of the role lies in the necessity to balance dual membership (or rather, "dual citizenship"; Black and Gregersen 1992): To enact the role successfully, expatriates must integrate and become accepted members of the subsidiary to gather required local knowledge and support for their objectives. At the same time, they must remain accepted members of the headquarters and maintain their networks there in order to be able to collect the latest headquarter information and exert influence on that side of the boundary. Therefore, the modes and possibilities of boundary spanning in the coordinator and negotiator role are shaped by resources and restrictions that enable or disable expatriates to 'switch roles' and credibly perform their belonging to both organizational units and, thereby, to remain as invisible as possible in each unit as loyal members of the other unit. In this subchapter, we investigate the role-making of expatriates in the coordinator and negotiator role by discussing two selected cases which exemplify two modes of boundary spanning we can identify in our data.

Mr. Scheffer and Mr. Rossi are two German managers working as product managers in the marketing units in the U.S. subsidiaries of two large German MNCs. The product management is an "interface" (Mr. Scheffer) between the local market (customers, dealers, competition) and the headquarters in Germany. The boundary-spanning tasks of product managers include identifying relevant developments and requirements in the local market and communicating them to the headquarters in order to influence the production and development of the products they are responsible for in the direction of the local market needs. Additionally, another task is to define different "configuration packages" for the "raw products" given by the headquarters (Mr. Scheffer), to organize the entire market launch in the host country and to develop strategies for reaching the planned "numbers" and "market shares" (Mr. Rossi).

Headquarters and subsidiaries share the hope that in filling this position with expatriates they can—in the midst of the tense relationship that is sometimes shaped by "misunderstandings"—"clean up and mediate a little" (Mr. Scheffer) between both organizational units. The product management, thus, has a bidirectional boundary spanning function. Which modes of 'making' the coordinator and negotiator role do Mr. Scheffer and Mr. Rossi develop in the face of the specific resources they have at their disposal and their restrictions to balance dual membership?

The Expatriate Manager as Service Provider

Mr. Scheffer is a product manager in his 30s who works for a large German MNC in the U.S. He stands as an example for a number of traditional expatriate managers[5] who have limited resources for immersing into the social environment of the subsidiary and whose possibilities of 'making' the coordinator and negotiator role are especially restricted by their home country focused career orientations and therefore have been termed "fast-trackers" or "tourists" by Loveridge (2005). These expatriates display headquarter-oriented allegiance patterns and have been labeled "hearts at home"-expatriates by Black and Gregersen (1992). Mr. Scheffer's limited mode of boundary spanning can best be characterized as that of a *service provider*.

Like several other managers in the coordinator and negotiator role, especially German managers in the U.S., Mr. Scheffer stresses his intention to "integrate and become a part of the local team." This intent is not only based on his general wish to increase his well-being during his assignment and "not to remain the outsider for three years." It also relates to the particular challenges of the role: Mr. Scheffer states that he does not have enough knowledge about the local market. To become capable of acting and making decisions, he is therefore not only dependent on a general cooperativeness on the side of local employees, like an expatriate in the controller and transfer agent role, but also on their active support and willingness to share their local knowledge. Becoming a part of the local team is, thus, a prerequisite for successfully enacting the coordinator and negotiator role. How, then, does Mr. Scheffer try to immerse into the local work environment and culture? Which resources does he have to become an accepted member of the subsidiary?

Mr. Scheffer is making several efforts to immerse into the subsidiary work environment and especially to not appear as an authoritarian boss from the headquarters. Like several other managers, he reports how he, in the beginning, adjusts his general management style by demonstratively deferring his formal authority and claim to leadership. He tries to appear as "careful and quiet" as possible and particularly not as "the big guy from headquarters who knows it all and who's going to tell everyone how to do their jobs." He instead positions himself as a learner who observes and asks questions "to learn as much as possible about the customers and the most important challenges and processes in the company in the shortest amount of time" and to get accustomed to the local working and management practices. Furthermore, Mr. Scheffer uses language as a resource for 'undoing'[6] the perception of him being the "guy from headquarters." Although he does not like it, he adapts to the local language practices regarding the headquarters to increase his acceptance in the subsidiary:

> Talking about the headquarters just like the employees here do. For example, I'll say "headquarters wants," "they want," although I've actually always inwardly, I think it's a shame, because actually, in that way of talking, a kind of thinking in terms of fronts happens, that we say "they" and "we" (. . .) you just automatically fall into this behavior pattern, and maybe it's also important for being accepted (. . .) to clearly position yourself as a product manager in the market.

Other efforts Mr. Scheffer makes to immerse into the local environment and culture are to meet with local employees and colleagues over a beer after work and to adopt local standards of dress: He stops wearing business suits when he realizes that no one else in the subsidiary wears them. What becomes clear is that Mr. Scheffer must actively perform his belonging to the subsidiary and also a distance to the headquarters to successfully 'make' his coordinator and negotiator role.

Nevertheless, it becomes clear that his belonging to the subsidiary remains incomplete both from his side but also from the side of the U.S.-American employees. Like in most cases of traditional expatriates, Mr. Scheffer's life plans are focused on his home country and, as is especially characteristic for the German cases, a career in the headquarters. As a 'fast-tracker,' he clearly sees his assignment as a temporary break from his work in the headquarters and as a development opportunity.[7] He "cannot imagine to stay here" and is a 'heart at home'- expatriate in the way that his loyalty is ultimately with the headquarters. These career orientations, including his focus on the repatriation and his allegiance pattern, restrict his immersion into the social environment of the subsidiary. His statement that he does not invest as much in social relationships as he would on a permanent stay indicates that 'doing' a local colleague position remains superficial and instrumental. He generally does not feel like "a part of this society but rather (. . .) like an observer or kind of like an outsider." Furthermore, his actions for and loyalty to the subsidiary are limited in that they must never cause major conflicts with the headquarters or otherwise damage his relationship with the headquarters in Germany. This does not escape the local employees either: Despite his effort to appear "as part of the market," Mr. Scheffer states, "Everyone knows (. . .) that I'm from the headquarters." 'Undoing' his position as the "guy from headquarters" remains inevitably incomplete. He does not become a full member or 'citizen' of the subsidiary and stays a 'tourist' instead.

However, like several other expatriates, Mr. Scheffer does not just report of challenges to become accepted in the subsidiary. Additionally, as there are no detailed repatriation plans or programs in his company, he tells us about the necessity to actively keep his relationships to Germany "alive" to stay a full member of the headquarters. He works "on being present" in the headquarters by scheduling a lot of (informal) extra meetings when he is on a business trip to Germany. Besides 'doing' his position as a headquarters colleague he also 'undoes' being the 'guy from the subsidiary' by talking badly about the subsidiary with his German colleagues on the phone.

Becoming a 'dual citizen,' in the sense of becoming an accepted member of the subsidiary and staying a member of the headquarters, is a prerequisite for successful boundary spanning in the coordinator and negotiator role. So far, we have shown that Mr. Scheffer makes several efforts to become such a dual member by strategically performing local belonging and distance to the headquarters in the subsidiary and, at the same time, performing allegiance to the headquarters and distance to the subsidiary in the headquarters. However, it becomes clear that Mr. Scheffer—as a traditional expatriate—has only a few resources at his disposal to really immerse into the subsidiary work environment and that his possibilities to integrate are at the very least limited by his career orientations as a 'fast-tracker' and 'heart at home'-expatriate. How, then, can Mr. Scheffer carry out his concrete boundary spanning work of processing information and exerting influence in face of these restrictions.

Mr. Scheffer's limited mode of 'making' the coordinator and negotiator role can, as mentioned earlier, best be characterized as that of a service provider. He can (offer to) "add value" by using his networks to and his knowledge about the processes in the headquarters but has difficulties making his "own marks" in the subsidiary. He reports that his local employees actively ask him to explain the headquarters' processes and rationalities or to check whether they fulfilled tasks up to the headquarters' wishes and standards. Thus, he can use his knowledge to act as a translator of the headquarters' logics and demands and as a facilitator between local work practices and global standards. Furthermore, his superior in the U.S. asks him to take over communication with an unfavorable colleague in the headquarters. In this regard, he can utilize his headquarter networks to avoid conflicts and ensure smooth information flows between subsidiary and headquarters. This respected mode of acting as a service provider notwithstanding, the knowledge of the local employees about his primary loyalty to the headquarters restricts the way he can act as a coordinator and negotiator: On the one hand, he notices that although the subsidiary is using him to gain information from the headquarters, it does not even try to use him to influence the headquarters in its interest. The subsidiary also sends an U.S.-American product manager to a meeting in Germany to represent its interests. On the other hand, the limits to his boundary spanning are particularly obvious when he wants to break out of the service provider mode and tries to make his "own marks" by influencing the subsidiary from his headquarter perspective. He recalls an instance of conflict regarding the data-saving structure on the shared drive as an example for failing in pushing through headquarter standards against local practices in the subsidiary:

> This structure is an absolute mess; this totally contradicts my German sense of order. But those are things where at some point you have to say, "OK, don't overdo it with your German virtues, you can't force

those on everyone here." That's why I then started, it really is frustrating when you notice that in some respects, you're just not going to get anywhere, and then I just started to build my own drive.

The quotation shows that Mr. Scheffer accepts this failure in order not to jeopardize his partial integration and starts to build up a parallel structure according to the headquarter standards on his local drive. Against this background, it is doubtful that Mr. Scheffer can succeed smoothly in making "strategic marks" from his headquarter perspective.

To sum up, Mr. Scheffer's case exemplifies how the return orientation of traditional expatriates can shape their boundary spanning in the coordinator and negotiator role. His headquarter-oriented and Germany-oriented life and career plans limit his engagement and his possibilities for immersing into the subsidiary environment. His only partial integration into the subsidiary restricts his local influence and constrains his boundary spanning capacities to providing specific mediating services that do not come into conflict with subsidiary interests.

The Expatriate Manager as Chameleon

Mr. Rossi is an Italian-German product manager in his 40s who works for a large German MNC in the U.S. In contrast to traditional expatriates, he located to the U.S. ten years ago for private reasons and has no concrete plans to repatriate to Germany. His case shows that specific orientations of localized managers and experiences and ascriptive characteristics of bicultural managers can be utilized as resources for easing the necessary integration into the subsidiary environment and even maintaining headquarter networks. They can help in overcoming complications traditional expatriates experience when having to become 'dual citizens' and thereby open up possibilities for adopting other modes of boundary spanning. Regarding his role-making as a coordinator and negotiator, Mr. Rossi describes himself as a "*chameleon.*" We, again, take up this emic term to elaborate on his specific mode of 'making' this boundary role.

As mentioned earlier, the key challenge of the coordinator and negotiator role lies in the necessity to balance dual membership. Which resources does Mr. Rossi have to become a 'dual citizen' and which modes of 'making' the boundary role does he develop?

With the case of the 'fast-tracker' Mr. Scheffer we previously showed that immersion into the subsidiary work environment may remain incomplete from both the side of the manager and the side of the local employees due to expatriates' home country–oriented or headquarter-focused career orientations. In contrast to traditional expatriates, Mr. Rossi's life plan and career orientations are not focused on a career in the home country: After two stays in the U.S. during his university studies and getting engaged to his Italian-American wife, Mr. Rossi, who at the time worked at the company's headquarters, decided to move to the U.S. He found a position on the MNC's

internal job market and located to the U.S. without concrete return plans—
he only agreed with his wife that "in case I don't like it anymore after a few
years, we'll move to Germany." His career orientation can thus be labeled
as that of a "local" (Loveridge 2005) who married a local partner and, after
ten years in the subsidiary, still has no plans to repatriate. Due to this career
orientation and his strong private ties to the host country, Mr. Rossi does
not report on any limitations regarding his will to invest in social relationships. He also does not refer to any feelings of not being a part of society or
problems of being accepted by the local employees. It is interesting that this
career orientation and the duration of his stay, for one, and also his ascriptive
characteristics stemming from his migration background can be regarded
as resources helping Mr. Rossi to successfully immerse into the subsidiary
environment. He reports that some of his colleagues do not even know that
he was born and raised in Germany and comes from the headquarters. Others are, at the very least, not constantly drawing a connection between him
and the headquarters in Germany. Mr. Rossi is certain that subsidiary colleagues trust him more than other German managers because they perceive
him to be American or rather as "non-German" because of his Italian name
and appearance. Consequently, U.S.-American employees would include him
more in informal conversations and local networks than other Germans who
would often be suspected of loyalty to the headquarters. For example, they
would talk more openly about differences between the subsidiary and headquarters and would criticize them more directly in his presence:

> But you do notice that there's a bit of "Ah yeah, and then Germany
> comes and then Germany tells us what to do, but they don't under-
> stand the U.S." (. . .) And they wouldn't say that that way to a German
> employee or to a German boss, there it's more sugar coated, but that's
> what they say to each other if they're talking to an American, and two
> Americans would talk like this, and when I'm standing there, then I'm
> the American, or rather, the non-German.

In other words, Mr. Rossi does not have to make many efforts to 'undo'
his headquarter belonging and perform being a local colleague to become
an accepted member of the subsidiary and gather local knowledge. Because
of his "non-German" look and his career pattern, the local employees
do not see him as a 'guy from the headquarters' or as a 'heart at home'-
expatriate. But how is it with Mr. Rossi's networks and acceptance within
the headquarters?

Contrary to what the literature suggests (Black and Gregersen 1992; Loveridge 2005), the long-term presence and substantial integration into the
subsidiary environment seem not to have damaged his relationship to the
headquarters. This can, for one, be explained with an interesting interplay:
Because of his private relationships in the U.S. and professional communication with local employees and customers, Mr. Rossi speaks "almost no

German anymore." Therefore, he consciously uses every opportunity to speak German with other German expatriates and colleagues in the headquarters so that he "doesn't completely lose hold over the language." At the very least, this communication practice has led to Mr. Rossi's building strong relationships to other German expatriates, who remain reachable and approachable for him after their return to Germany. Combined with his old contacts, these people make up his translocal network of German managers, which enables him to circumvent formal communication channels and access information more quickly from the headquarters:

> I have to say (. . .) because I come from corporate, I have had very, very strong ties to Germany. And I also used them here (. . .) when something was going too slowly for me here at the U.S.-subsidiary, then I would go directly to Germany and got the information for myself directly from Germany, because some of the colleagues who were delegates here returned to Germany.

For another, the shared background and socialization in the same work culture seem to be resources for gaining trust, collecting information and remaining an accepted member of the headquarters. According to Mr. Rossi, German colleagues express their views more plainly and frankly to him than to U.S.-American managers and associate him with specific German work values and practices:

> But I just feel that there is trust there, because the colleagues know that I have those German values or the German way of thinking business, that I get it, and that I'm not, you know, trying to do the American thing, which of course an American can't help but doing, I mean, he can do the American thing, so he does. And when I say, "OK, this has happened," then they know that, "OK, this is the German this-has-happened" and not the American version, which is when two days later you hear, "Wow, something came up" and so on. This is, I believe, what helps me on both sides.

It becomes clear that Mr. Rossi does not have to exert too much effort for 'undoing' his 'guy from the subsidiary' status and for performing his allegiance to the headquarters in order to stay accepted there and gather information. His headquarter networks have not vanished. On the contrary, they have constantly been renewed through his 'speaking German' to various traditional German expatriates during their assignments in the U.S. Although his career orientations are that of the 'local,' the headquarter employees do not see him as someone who has "gone native" (Black and Gregersen 1992) in the sense of only being loyal to the subsidiary—and the quotation indicates that they might be right: Mr. Rossi still identifies with "German" work values and practices.

It is against the background of this easy and almost automatic adaptation to the subsidiary and to the headquarters environment that Mr. Rossi's extended boundary spanning mode, as mentioned earlier, can best be characterized as that of a chameleon. However, his mode of 'making' the coordinator and negotiator role is not limited to generating trust and gathering information in both environments. Especially because of growing up biculturally, Mr. Rossi sees himself as able to precisely identify cultural differences, to alternate and translate between different communication practices and rationalities, and, thereby, to mediate and buffer conflicts between the German headquarters and the U.S. subsidiary. Going beyond the possibilities of Mr. Scheffer, who complains of his limited influence, Mr. Rossi sees himself also as able to exert influence on both sides of the boundary because he knows "how to position things."

Service Provider and Chameleon: Two Modes of 'Making' the Coordinator and Negotiator Role

In the *coordinator and negotiator* role, expatriate managers are assigned to coordinate tasks, mediate conflicts, and generally resolve problems between headquarters and the subsidiary or to jointly develop projects and strategies. Our case studies show that while enacting the role, expatriate managers see themselves especially confronted with the need to immerse into the subsidiary work environment and culture to gather local knowledge and support, which can potentially turn out to be a tense challenge, as they have to simultaneously maintain their networks to the headquarters.

With the *service provider* and the *chameleon*, we have identified two modes of 'making' the role. It has become clear that we must consider personal orientations and attributes of the expatriate managers to understand these modes and their limits: On the one hand, the case of Mr. Scheffer shows that career and life plans that have a strong focus on the home country can limit the managers' dedication and their chances for immersing into the social environment of the subsidiary. This partial integration then limits the possibilities for enacting the coordinator and negotiator role. Despite the fact that his standards for himself go beyond that, Mr. Scheffer's boundary spanning seems to be restricted to providing specific mediating 'services' that match with the subsidiary's interests. On the other hand, the case of Mr. Rossi shows that a career and life plan focused on the host country and also a migration background and an ethnicity different from that of typical headquarter/home country nationals can increase the managers' chances for immersing into the subsidiary—seemingly without damaging the relationship with the headquarters. This increases his room for maneuver for 'making' the coordinator and negotiator role. Thus, Mr. Rossi can adapt "chameleon-like" to nationally shaped intraorganizational environments and thereby gather information and exert influence in the subsidiary and the headquarters. Hence, the findings show that personal experiences or a bicultural socialization, career orientations and life plans, and individual attributes like ethnicity can influence the intensity with which expatriates want to and can immerse themselves into the local environment and thereby shape their boundary spanning modes and possibilities (see also Park and Mense-Petermann 2014).

Conclusion

In this chapter, we have analyzed how expatriate managers 'make' their roles as *controllers and transfer agents* and as *coordinators and negotiators*. It was shown that managers in each boundary role are confronted with two challenges: Managers in the controller and transfer agent role primarily are concerned with implementing headquarters' strategies and standards while at the same time displacing local practices. In the case of managers in the coordinator and negotiator role, the necessity for them to immerse into the subsidiary environment and culture while at the same time maintaining the connection to the headquarters has shown to be a potentially tense challenge.

We have identified specific modes of role-making for both types of roles. In doing so, different structured and structuring features of expatriate boundary spanning have emerged: In the context of the identified modes of enacting the controller and transfer agent role—i.e., the *teacher* and the *start-up entrepreneur*—it became clear that they are, on the one hand, shaped by the image and the expectations the managers have regarding the local employees' professional skills, cultural properties and abilities to learn; on the other hand, they are shaped by the willingness of local employees to accept specific practices. The identified modes of 'making' the coordinator and negotiator role, the *service provider* and the *chameleon*, have shown to be dependent on the life plans, career orientations, and the associated intensity with which expatriates want to and are able to immerse themselves into the local work environment and culture.

Beyond specific types of roles, it is an important insight that for expatriates, rather different possibilities for demonstrating 'distance to the headquarters' constitute resources for building trust in the subsidiary: Mr. Schwarz, for example, refers to the fact that he is not from headquarters but instead from one of the productions sites in Germany. Mr. Barnett, when possible, does not report local mistakes to and even stops videos conferences with the headquarters in order to avoid problems for the subsidiary and to demonstrate loyalty. Mr. Scheffer tries to use polarizing talking practices to show distance to the headquarters. For Mr. Rossi, his ethnicity, which does not match that of a typical headquarter/home country national, is a resource for being identified less with the headquarters. It becomes clear that it is paramount for the expatriates to performatively build a local belonging in order to increase their acceptance and to mobilize the willingness on the side of the local employees to cooperate. 'Distance to the headquarters' is a resource for immersion into the subsidiary environment.

If we consider our findings in light of this book's general question of whether expatriates are cosmopolitans, i.e., being open for local Others and generally appreciating difference (see Chapter 1), it is, first of all, interesting to consider the ways they do *not* enact their roles—or at least claim not to. The type of role and the home and host country notwithstanding, numerous expatriates from our sample express their rejection of anti-cosmopolitan modes of enacting roles by distancing themselves from the practices of other expatriates. They characterize them either as authoritarian, direct, and strict by using militaristic terms such as "general" and "tank" or as coarse, martial, and uninhibited by using terms such as "big guy," "King Kong," and "like a bull in a China shop." What is striking is how they explain the rejection of these practices. On the one hand, they do it from a moral standpoint. The respective practices are seen as morally objectionable. This points to the fact that in the field a cosmopolitan orientation is taken at least as a standard of value. On the other hand, the managers distance themselves from anti-cosmopolitan practices for functional reasons. They are presented as being less promising for reaching one's goals. This shows that local employees control their own working practices and have power resources at their disposal which can hardly be ignored by expatriate managers. Rather, the managers have to find ways of dealing with these practices that simultaneously secure the necessary willingness to comply, cooperate, and support, which authoritarian and aggressive modes of boundary spanning seem largely unable to do. For successful boundary spanning, a minimum level of consideration for local customs turns out to be of importance.

At the same time, the identified boundary spanning modes cannot clearly be described as cosmopolitan. For example, although the teacher's boundary spanning is based on the image of Chinese employees as willing and able to learn, underneath that image lies an inferior view of them, which is the basis for his building an asymmetrical-paternalistic relationship with them. Even though the start-up entrepreneur at first displays an interest in the local knowledge stock and practices, he rejects them rigorously when they come in conflict with his own practices. Even though the service provider in principle is interested in integrating into the host organization and in inclusive sociabilities, his primary orientation toward headquarters for career reasons just allows for a limited social integration. Whereas the chameleon seems especially interculturally competent, his self-perception, however, is shaped by the assumption of clearly distinguishable and unchangeable nationally and culturally determined working and communication practices. Hence, regarding the boundary spanning of expatriates, inconsistent and to some extent contradictory or even paradoxical cosmopolitanisms can be assumed.

Notes

1 We do not purport the presented types of boundary spanning modes to be a comprehensive typology. They were consciously chosen because they, on the one hand, clearly show that managers in the same boundary role develop specific modes of 'making' their respective role and, on the other hand, allow us to also elaborate on specific structured and structuring features of expatriate boundary spanning.
2 Emic terms are terms used by the informants themselves that researchers take up due to their analytical capacity to theorize empirical phenomena.
3 See for the role of nationalized networks in the subsidiary, Mense-Petermann and Spiegel (2016).
4 Here it becomes clear that it might only be an acceptance of inferior roles for a limited time. We expect an increasing self-confidence of Chinese employees if they are rewarded with a promotion and an increasing frustration if they are not promoted after some time. We posit both scenarios to decrease the willingness of Chinese employees to take inferior roles.
5 Traditional expatriates are managers originating from the home country of the MNC who have been delegated by headquarters to a foreign subsidiary for a limited period of time.
6 We borrow the terms 'doing' and 'undoing' from gender studies (West and Zimmerman 1987) in order to stress that membership and allegiance cannot be taken for granted but need to be actively performed or invisibilized, respectively.
7 He only strives to "get into the market," "make some experiences," and "live in an exciting city" with a "good quality and standard of living" for a limited period of time.

Bibliography

Black, Stewart, and Hal B. Gregersen. 1992. "Serving Two Masters: Managing the Dual Allegiance of Expatriate Employees." *Sloan Management Review* 33 (4): 61–71.

Dörrenbächer, Christoph, and Mike Geppert. 2006. "Micro-Politics and Conflicts in Multinational Corporations: Current Debates, Re-Framing, and Contributions of this Special Issue." *Journal of International Management* 12 (3): 251–65. doi:10.1016/j.intman.2006.07.001.

Loveridge, Ray. 2005. "Embedding the Multinational: Bridging Internal and External Networks in Transitional Institutional Contexts." *Asian Business and Management* 4 (4): 389–409. doi:10.1057/palgrave.abm.9200143.

Mense-Petermann, Ursula. 2006. "Micro-Political or Inter-Cultural Conflicts? An Integrating Approach." *Journal of International Management* 12 (3): 302–17. doi:10.1016/j.intman.2006.07.002.

Mense-Petermann, Ursula. 2013. "Expatriates as Micro-Political Actors: Power Resources and Strategizing on Global Assignments." *Gazdasági élet és társa dalom (Economy and Society)* 1–2: 44–73.

Mense-Petermann, Ursula. 2017. "Die Arbeit des 'boundary-spanning – Der Expatriate als Protagonist transnationalen Arbeitens? In Globalisierung als Auto-Kapitalismus. Studien zur Globaliät moderner Gesellschaften, edited by Philipp Hessinger, and Markus Pohlmann, 179–95. Wiesbaden: Springer VS.

Mense-Petermann, Ursula, and Anna Spiegel. 2016. "Global Mobility Policies, Social Positioning and Boundary Spanning Work of Expatriate Managers." *Bielefelder*

Beiträge zur Wirtschafts- und Arbeitssoziologie (bi.WAS Working Paper) 1. Bielefeld: Faculty of Sociology, Bielefeld University.

Minssen, Heiner. 2009. *Bindung und Entgrenzung: Eine Soziologie international tätiger Manager.* München and Mering: Rainer Hampp Verlag.

Morgan, Glenn. 2001. "Transnational Communities and Business Systems." *Global Networks* 1 (2): 113–30. doi:10.1111/1471-0374.00008.

Park, Kathleen, and Ursula Mense-Petermann. 2014. "Managing Across Borders: Global Integration and Knowledge Exchange in MNCs." *Competition & Change* 18 (3): 265–79. doi:10.1179/1024529414Z.00000000060.

Smith, Michael P., and Luis Guarnizo, eds. 1998. *Transnationalism from Below.* New Brunswick and London: Transaction Publishers.

West, Candace, and Don H. Zimmerman. 1987. "Doing Gender." *Gender and Society* 1 (2): 125–51. doi: 10.1177/0891243287001002002.

8 Expatriate Managers as Cosmopolitan Professionals?

Dealing with Difference at the Workplace

Anna Spiegel

In this chapter, we will continue the analysis of expatriate managers practices of dealing with difference in the professional sphere. Whereas Chapter 7 has reconstructed the differentiated modes of 'making' and negotiating boundary roles, this chapter concentrates on the negotiations of the cultural identity of the company and its individual members by exploring the MNC as a transnational space, and, specifically, the intercultural office as a cultural contact zone (Pratt 1991; Yeoh and Willis 2005).

As the detailed literature discussions in the introduction and the chapters in Part I of this book have shown, expatriate managers have been addressed in the mainstream management literature as core protagonists of economic globalization, management, and knowledge exchange in MNCs. They have been celebrated as interculturally adept 'global managers,' members of a 'cosmopolitan business elite,' and as successful 'boundary spanners.' On the other hand, studies in critical management and anthropology instead have drawn a picture of expatriate managers as engaged in multiple practices of *boundary making* and highlighted the existence of neocolonial power structures in MNCs. "The colonial imaginary permits—and legitimizes even—the persistence of race-based hierarchical structures within today's transnational organizations" (Leggett 2012, 88). The aim of this chapter is thus to reassess these polarized images by focusing on expatriate managers everyday practices of dealing with difference in concrete workplaces as well as the expatriate managers' interpretive schemes and material practices regarding the cultural identity of the office space. The chapter thus asks whether expatriates can be described as cosmopolitans regarding the way they deal with cultural difference in their professional lives.

As in Chapter 5, sociability and spatiality will be the central analytical dimensions here for researching the practiced cosmopolitanism (Nowicka and Rovisco 2009) of expatriate managers. Besides homes (see Chapter 5), corporate offices are relevant spatial dimensions of expatriates' everyday lives where identity and belonging are negotiated and reshaped through the materiality of the location. Choosing this concrete spatio-temporal setting of the corporate office is based on the idea that the tensions within the transnational social space of an MNC become virulent and materialize in the concrete spatial settings where specific actors have to make sense of them and negotiate them in their everyday practices. Spatial and material arrangements in companies are not only part of the companies' symbolic management, but are also part of the individual managers' symbolic management, given that they have the power to influence the spatial arrangements of their companies (Franzpötter 1997; Dörrenbächer 2007). The chapter analyzes how references to different localities are made through specific artifacts/accessories of the company's internal spaces and the kind of cultural identity that is thereby constructed.

This spatial turn regarding methodology is inspired by authors from different disciplines theorizing on global encounters at different points in history. Mary Louise Pratt had introduced the concept of the "cultural contact zones" for the analysis of literary texts as products of colonial encounters. According to Pratt (1992, 8), the concept of the contact zone

> invokes the space and time where subjects previously separated by geography and history are co-present, the point at which their trajectories now intersect. (. . .) A "contact" perspective emphasizes how subjects get constituted in and by their relations to each other. It treats the relation among colonizers and colonized, or travelers and "travelees," not in terms of separateness, but in terms of co-presence interaction, interlocking understandings and practices and often within radically asymmetrical relations of power.

For our purpose of researching how expatriate managers negotiate the cultural identity of the MNC, we will take the term *cultural contact zones* as defined by Buchanan (2010) as a general term for places where expatriate managers encounter their cultural and sometimes ethnic or racial Other and are transformed by the experience.[1]

The remainder of this chapter is structured as follows: The main empirical part of the chapter explores three specific inconsistent and self-contradictory practices in the professional sphere—defining negotiable and nonnegotiable cultural domains, nationalizing and denationalizing difference, demanding cosmopolitanism from others while rejecting one's own cosmopolitanism—using ideal-typical ethnographic cases studies. Our empirical case studies indicate that also in the professional sphere the managers' modes of dealing with cultural difference go beyond the stereotypical images of expatriates as either cosmopolitan or anti-cosmopolitan. The chapter ends with a conclusion, where the diversity and inconsistencies of corporate expatriates practiced cosmopolitanisms are systematized.

Expatriate Managers' Professional Life Beyond Cosmopolitanism and Colonial Imagination: Ambivalences and Contradictions

The analysis of our data revealed that expatriate managers were simultaneously engaged in practices of boundary spanning and of boundary making. In the following, we systematize three types of such inconsistencies dominant in the practices and narratives of the expatriate managers: They simultaneously distinguished between negotiable and nonnegotiable cultural domains; they nationalized and denationalized difference, and they demanded cosmopolitanism from others while refusing to engage in practices of cosmopolitan translation themselves.

Defining Negotiable and Nonnegotiable Cultural Domains

One typical inconsistency displayed in the narratives and practices of managers from our sample was that they simultaneously made use of contradicting approaches to cultural difference, namely, the cultural superiority of the West, on the one hand, and cultural diversity and cosmopolitanism on the other. This synchronicity of apparently contradictory orientations toward difference was based on a distinction between hierarchical cultural domains with nonnegotiable rules defined by the global organizational culture of the MNCs and dialogic cultural domains with negotiable features. In the domains defined as nonnegotiable, host country practices were not accepted, and local staff was expected to adapt. In the domains defined as negotiable, the managers displayed flexibility and talked about their willingness and openness to adapt to local practices.

These ambivalences and contradictions of dealing with cultural differences in cultural contact zones are specifically pronounced in the case of Mr. Simon. A strong national-cultural Othering characterizes his interpretive schemes. He emphatically engages in a national-cultural comparison where he frames differences in a cultural essentialist juxtaposition between German and Chinese ways of doing things, including work and management practices. In the following, he elaborates on the differences of what he calls German and Chinese ways of thinking:

> Another point that comes to mind is the relation between the task-related functional dimensions and the personal dimension. As you know, *we* believe that the task is independent from the individual employee. So, if something goes wrong, then it is that specific issue that goes wrong, so to speak, and not the person as a whole who fails. So, what *we* do is to distinguish fundamentally between these two. In the Chinese way of thinking regarding responsibility and how to do something, one should start with the person who one can influence so that a task can be fulfilled. This is why the Chinese only know the one-on-one meeting if there is something important to arrange. If *I* want to influence something, I go ahead and conduct a meeting [with several employees], you know, and say, we have to do this and that. *He* instead [the Chinese Joint Venture Manager] talks to a specific person (. . .). For *him*, it is the individual person he needs to influence who comes first. What *we* do is to say, OK, this is our goal; this is the task which we need to fulfill together and then the people are attached to this task. This is the complete opposite.

Mr. Simon's narrative is full of statements like the one earlier. The other quotations, like this one, are also characterized by strong binary oppositions between "us," the Germans, and "them," the Chinese, as two opposing cultural entities. He highlights the categorical quality of these differences by frequently using expressions like "completely, completely opposite," "fundamentally different," or "totally different."

However, Mr. Simon develops a complex way of dealing with these irreconcilable differences between Chinese and German practices in his professional life. On the one hand, he constructs nonnegotiable domains where he clearly hierarchizes German and Chinese practices and thus delegitimizes local practices. On the other hand, he constructs negotiable domains where he conceives of German and Chinese practices as equally valid and thus acknowledges diversity. In the following quotation, he elaborates on the hierarchical domains:

> On the one hand, I think you need to be stubborn. Because our corporate culture is our corporate culture. You cannot debate about such things like this; they are not debatable. And it is not my decision either. It's not my decision whether this is our culture. It's not my decision as to whether we commit to set a limit of X amount for gifts. Not debatable. For me, in my position, culture in that sense is not debatable. In fact, only the implementation is open for debate. And you have to tell people that right away. This is how we are. We are part of that. We take the good parts with us, but we have to take what we don't like as well. This is my philosophy. "Look, then just go somewhere else, you will like many things, and dislike others." But you can't take a part of our German corporate and a part of a typical Chinese corporate, no, doesn't work, impossible.

In this quotation, he clearly identifies the transnational social space of his MNC with the company's headquarter cultural identity and practices and takes a tough stance on the nonnegotiable character of those norms. Here, Mr. Simon as representative of the headquarters is the one who sets the rules, whereas the local staff has to adapt to these rules. And as the quotation indicates, Mr. Simon has the power to enforce this adaptation by threatening local employees with being laid off. He conceives of boundaries between the different working cultures as being non-permeable and thus, the organizational culture as being a holistic package which can either be fully accepted or not at all. He makes a clear emphasis that only one practice is legitimate, whereas the other is not. This practice of hierarchizing German and Chinese practices and of delegitimizing different local practices is associated rather with closure than with cosmopolitan openness.

At the same time, however, Mr. Simon states that there are other domains where dialogical modes of dealing with cultural difference are appropriate:

> For some things, yes, you have to sometimes be a bit more open. What's not important like I said and where you're allowed to be different in

that sense, yeah, then you should be open. Well, if it's our culture, the German corporate and working culture, that in the evening we make a stark distinction between private life and work life, then we just won't do it here. We party, and the devil knows what all else we do, yeah (. . .) But when there's something to celebrate, we invite everyone to dinner. That's just the culture here. Everyone involved is invited to dinner, to have wine or a round of beer, yeah, to eat together. That is certainly not the culture of corporate. That is local culture.

Within these nonhierarchical domains, such as local traditions of conviviality or different communicative practices of how to achieve a goal, Mr. Simon positively acknowledges diversity and is the one who is flexible and willing to adapt. In these domains, Mr. Simon constructs German and Chinese practices as two alternative and equally legitimate versions of how to do things and interpret the world. Mr. Simon establishes the equivalence of the two cultural repertoires by discursively relativizing his own perspective. When talking about these negotiable domains, he frames his explanations on differences with expressions such as "according to us" or "we believe that," indicating that there is no normative superiority in his way of doing things. In addition to this relativistic culture concept, he presents the Chinese way of doing things as indeed different, but as equally rational. When elaborating on the Chinese way, he offers rational explanations of seemingly "weird" Chinese behavior. This taking over of a different perspective is visible in the following quotations:

Just as an example, OK, I'm here at the company for a week and go through the offices around lunchtime. And everyone is sleeping in the offices! What should I do, just let out a scream and say, "This cannot be true that everyone is sleeping here!?" And in this situation, it was then clear to me that I should go ask a colleague. He said, yeah, calm down, yeah. The Chinese, and in Asia, yeah, they are a bit more clever. They use the time here to take a short, a small little nap, yeah. That is normal. And the people are able to do that because, with their social distance and so on or however that is called, intimate distance, because it is handled totally differently. So they just lay down at the keyboard and sleep. So such things are, yeah, naturally very foreign—you learn to be very careful.

He leaves no doubt that he was more than irritated when he first observed his Chinese staff taking a nap in the office. However, the reference to the concept of "intimate distance" referring to distinct cultural definitions of private and public spheres enabled him to reinterpret this initially irritating behavior as indeed being more "clever."[2] This is what makes it even possible for Mr. Simon to reevaluate the initially irritating practice as a positive skill.

One field where Mr. Simon is especially open to local difference is the field of the material-symbolic management of the company. He actively worked on creating an office space with both local and non-local references. Mr. Simon's secretary told us that under his predecessor, there had been many pictures throughout the entire plant with logos, symbols, and images related to the German mother company. Mr. Simon, however, had decided to remove all of these images and replace them with new images referring to a local and personal identity of the employees. Chinese staff participated in working out the design and decoration of the new canteen and the office floors. They were invited to submit self-taken photos of holiday, leisure time, and family scenes. A selection of these photos were enlarged and put up in the canteen. In addition to these photos, employees' children have decorated the canteen with drawings. With these practices, Mr. Simon intends to create an authentic space that provides local staff with multiple possibilities for resonance. In addition to these personal symbols, also objects and symbols alluding to both traditional and modern Chinese cultural identity, such as original sized terracotta warrior figures, Chinese plants, and local pieces of modern art are very prominent in the office space. At Mr. Simon's suggestion, students of the local Academy of Arts decorated the management floor with woodcarving works. The specificity of these reliefs was their hybrid character, as they used a traditional Chinese technique of woodcarving for depicting modern subjects, such as factory work and urban scenes. Mr. Simon's sensitivity for symbolic management also becomes evident when he talks about the negotiations with the local joint venture partner about the symbolic representation of the joint venture—e.g., with images and objects such as logos or company flags. Referring to a conversation with his Chinese joint venture partner, who complained about the fact that there was no visible logo of the joint venture at the company office space, he says,

> I called him and said, we have to think about how to do this [the logo], without generating a stark contrast [between the German and Chinese joint venture partners]. We don't want to put emphasis on contrast. But still it would be interesting to express this in a way. We have not found a good solution yet, but the first thing to do would to have one flag more, not just the German corporate flag but also a Chinese Joint Venture partner flag. (. . .) This is really an issue, so I try to be the German corporate, but I also have to be careful not to be only the German corporate.

So far, there is only a German corporate flag in front of the main building. Mr. Simon's emphasis on giving the Chinese joint venture partner more visibility in the logo and the flags has to be interpreted as a practice to create spaces with both local and non-local references. Also, Mr. Simon's own office is such a space where he displays his connection to the locality. Next to a big panoramic picture of Shanghai's skyline and a little sculpture of a Chinese dragon and Chinese talismans, there is an abstract painting by a befriended Chinese artist who did this painting especially for this purpose. Mr. Simon makes explicit use of objects and images with references to different dimensions of the locality. Instead of trying to displace what he perceives to be a reference to local culture, he integrates them into his symbolic management, and thereby creates a multi-referential space.

To sum up, the simultaneous use of multiple and evidently contradictory orientations toward difference, as explicated here with the case of Mr. Simon, was typical for many managers in our sample. Thus, they cannot be easily labeled either cosmopolitan or anti-cosmopolitan. They distinguished between hierarchical cultural domains with nonnegotiable rules and dialogic cultural domains with negotiable features and developed multiple modes of dealing with difference. This has to be seen as a viable strategy to balance the built-in tensions between 'local adaptation' and 'global integration' as described in Chapter 2 (see also Mense-Petermann 2005, 2012).

Nationalizing and Denationalizing Difference

A second typical inconsistency that emerged out of our data was the simultaneous employment of contradictory interpretive frames to explain differences encountered in everyday work life. On the one hand, as already mentioned for Mr. Simon, they used very strong culturalist language. On the other hand, they used other interpretive schemes beyond the national paradigm, such as organizational-specific culture, and thus contributed to a de-essentialization of difference. We will now work out the synchronicity of divergent interpretive schemes in the exemplary case example of Mr. Novak, a German manager assigned to a subsidiary of a major German MNC in the U.S.

On the one hand, Mr. Novak makes clear use of interpretive schemes based on national-cultural differences. Unexpected differences and mutual irritations between himself and the local coworkers are among the main topics that he brought up in the interview and in his comments during the job shadowing. Among the issues that he frames within the language of national-cultural difference are different time frames for making decisions and different roles of managers within the decision-making process, as the following quotations illustrates:

> When you say, all right, this and that has to be implemented, yeah, then they show up on the next day with a solution. It's a solution that hasn't been thought all the way through, it's only about 75 percent, but they do have a solution. And it is not the culture here to say, OK good, but I need a week for that, and then I can give you a solution that is 100 percent. Yeah, so that, so that's how you notice it. But also the way, the way you get an email, "Can you please deliver this and that?" And if things are not delivered on the next day, then you get a reminder email, "I asked you yesterday, so where is it?" Yeah.

> Whereas in Germany it's the collective that is in the foreground, meaning, for example, the consensus that decisions are made together, here

> it is rather that the individual is in the foreground. The manager should decide. He should make the decision, he should support the decision, and he should also take over responsibility for the decision. So this topic, shared responsibility, shared burden, that's not so strong here in the U.S. as it is in Germany. For this reason, there is always a lot coming at the general manager, because he is the one who then has to decide. Here, I'm much more in a decision-making and representative role than, let's say, in a working role, like I would be in Germany. Yeah, so that's some of the difference, that's how I perceive it.

He explicitly uses national frames in order to explicate experiences of difference. These differences are not put into a hierarchical or asymmetrical order though. Instead, they are constructed as equally legitimate and symmetrical. Yet this interpretive scheme still leads to boundaries being erected between himself and the local Others. This reduces possibilities for a form of sociability based on commonality and shared experiences.

At the same time, Mr. Novak undermines his culturalist interpretive scheme by denationalizing difference and employing various other interpretive schemes for explaining differences between himself and the local coworkers, as well as conflicts between local management and the headquarters.

> Yeah, because they have a different task. They rather have this central task, the task of strategy as a whole. And yeah, so the two worlds just clash, they just slam into each other. That doesn't have anything to do with the fact that some are in Germany and the others are in America. It could be, the warehouse could be in Canada, the central warehouse, yeah, and that would be very similar, I would say. (. . .) There is a difference in business culture when I move from company X to company Y and also within firms themselves; there is always a different culture to which you have to get used to. Even between different divisions, such as aftersales and sales.

In Mr. Novak's perspective, these worlds in conflict are not national-cultural worlds, but different organizational worlds. Besides the national-cultural interpretive schemes, he at the same time also uses other interpretive schemes, such as different organizational logics and rationalities—be it different rationalities of different companies, of headquarters and subsidiaries, or of different divisions within a company—to explain experiences of difference. He thus undermines the perception of fixed boundaries between different cultural blocks and makes room for alternative interpretations based on common grounds of experience. Highlighting the diversity of differences within a complex MNC, Mr. Novak constructs himself as an expert in dealing with difference, regardless of whether these differences are national-culturally or organizational-culturally based.

These contradictory interpretive schemes also lead to contradictory practices regarding difference experienced in the workplace. On the one hand, Mr. Novak has indeed highly valorized the local knowledge of his coworkers and has established dialogic and nonhierarchical relations with his coworkers, instead of only controlling and transforming the local practices. He explicitly used the first months of his assignment to arrange rather informal meetings, such as going for lunch, with local management staff from different departments, as we could observe during our job shadowing. Issues that repeatedly came up during these meetings with local staff were their perceptions on expatriate managers in general and concrete examples of inappropriate behavior by expatriate managers. In these conversations, Mr. Novak learned about locally sensitive issues, such as harassment and discrimination, about how locals expected expatriate managers to behave correctly, and about how they had often indeed behaved inadequately. In the interview, Mr. Novak comments on this attitude of transforming his own work practices:

> You have to adapt. You have to adapt. You have to learn this. You come to another country so that you can make these experiences. I did not come here in order to continue in the same old grind as I did in Germany. So this was a thing [speed], where I said, OK, I have to adapt; this is just the pace here, and I have to adapt to this.

Mr. Novak describes himself as being in a learning position and his first months as difficult yet successful—a process of "learning by doing," as he puts it. He talks about the problems of "getting adjusted to the whole thing" and of "getting things straight," formulations emphasizing his attempts to reconsider his own working practices in the light of the local ones. In the meetings with his employees that we were able to observe during our job shadowing, he openly and repeatedly put himself in the position of 'learner,' asking for his employees' knowledge. For example, in a meeting with his secretary where they discussed his idea of introducing so-called sorry cards for clients who got wrong spare parts, his secretary took over the part of adapting his general idea to the local context. She made suggestions regarding the appropriate formulations and layouts, and pointed out linguistic intricacies for different types of recipients (retailer, end costumers). She led the conversation and made clear local limitations to his idea. Mr. Novak embraced this conversation structure and at the same time valued his secretary as a bearer of locally relevant knowledge, which he himself did not possess at this point in time. During the job shadowing, we also observed that he adopted the local rhythm of work. When he got a request from his local superior, he commented that in Germany he would have had a week for replying to this request, whereas here it is expected of him to answer within two days. In order to be able to fulfill the local time standards, he immediately put his whole team to work on the requested report. He has also adapted to local communication practices, to such an extent that regardless of whether writing somebody in the headquarters or within his local working contexts, he writes all of his emails in English. He explains, "I don't write any emails in German anymore; I educated people in Germany to write to me in English so that I can easily forward emails. I don't have any secrets, and some emails really move quickly." This mode of relating to local knowledge and systematically integrating it is based on a relativization and reflexivity of his own professional and managerial knowledge and competences, which can be associated to cosmopolitan openness. Mr. Novak practices an attitude in which he is situationally able to conceive of his own knowledge as a kind of situated knowledge that cannot just be transferred and used in a new context. He stands for taking over the position of a learner, performing proximity and reducing social distance to local staff.

However, Mr. Novak's identity as a learner—connected to interpreting his own and local work practices as different but equally legitimate and to practices of transforming own work practices—is not consistent. He switches between hierarchizing and dehierarchizing his own work practices and local work practices. In some situations, he explicitly used the cultural language to claim authority for his own practices: "OK, when it's really important to bring more quality into the whole thing then you have to say: 'Wait a second, guys, this time it's different, this time I'm doing it the German way.'" Mr. Novak uses the English expression "the German way" also in the German interview, which indicates that this is a recognizable and legitimate expression in the local context. Other German managers in the U.S. also used this expression in order to enforce and legitimize their management decisions. So far, Mr. Novak has used the argument of the "German way" once when he had postponed a decision until he had all relevant information at hand and clearly felt the irritation of his local staff about this proceeding:

> Like once, in one case with an employee, where I said, "So, now give me some time to make the decision of whether to march left or right until I've gathered all the information." OK, fine, they say it's OK, but I know that it doesn't suit their nature, and I'm certainly arousing some surprise there, but you sometimes have to stay above it (. . .) But in general, I have adjusted myself when it comes to that topic.

There are indeed situations in which Mr. Novak does not adapt to local practices but instead clearly uses national culture as a source of legitimation for the superiority of his own working practices and his enforcement of them. Generally, however, the "American way" seems to be the dominant and legitimate way of doing things at the local subsidiary, and local management and staff expect expatriate managers to adapt to local working practices. When Mr. Novak does not adapt, he has to explicate this exceptional case and claim the right of 'doing it the German way.' Whereas this works, it however runs the risk of being perceived as 'strange' by his local staff.

To sum up, the simultaneous use of nationalizing and denationalizing interpretive schemes, as elaborated here with the case of Mr. Novak, was typical for many managers in our sample. Denationalizing conflicts and interpreting them from an organizational-cultural perspective led to a deconstruction of strong hierarchical and ethnocentric discourses on differences between their own working practices and the ones encountered at the subsidiary and led to creative modes of relating to the coworkers and their local knowledge.

Demanding Cosmopolitanism From Others While Rejecting One's Own Cosmopolitanism

A third typical inconsistency that could be identified in our data was that expatriates demanded cosmopolitanism from their local employees, although they themselves did not practice cosmopolitan openness. Mr. Hoffmann, a German manager assigned to China, is a good example for this asymmetrical cosmopolitanism (Shih 2001, 2002; Cheung 2008). Mr. Hoffmann has strong ethnocentric concepts of the cultural identity of his MNC in general and of the local office space in particular, and talked about how they wanted to make the German identity of the company more visible. Looking at the concrete managerial decisions he has made since his arrival, it becomes clear that he sees his task as being to push back Chinese influences within the company:

> Naturally, we want here (. . .) to be German, right? (. . .) In the last years, though, it was such that this place was 80 percent Chinese and 20 percent German, and some things were just not working anymore, and I don't think that was received well (. . .) We're getting there slowly, that we're making it 80 percent German and 20 percent Chinese again and yeah, that's also, I think, a large, a larger part of the success here.

In this quotation, Mr. Hoffmann first of all makes clear which national identity should be the dominant one in the company—namely, the German one. Furthermore, he constructs a sharp hierarchy between being German and being Chinese. He links the good performance of his company to a German identity and the failure or problems in performance to a Chinese identity. He thus understands his task in China in reducing the local Chinese influences in the subsidiary. Although he does not mention concrete examples, it is clear that being too Chinese threatens the success of the company. In addition, he perceives local working practices as inferior. In the following quotation, Mr. Hoffmann talks about differences between German and local working practices regarding the autonomy and independence expected from the employees:

> Here in China it runs like this, I give the employee the task (. . .) then they just wait the first week (. . .) If I don't ask at all in the next three or

four weeks, then I can be sure that the status on the first of December will be the same as that from two weeks ago when they had initially begun digging into it a bit, and they are totally dismayed that I am all of a sudden coming at them with this (. . .) with such a Chinese employee, I'm driving against the wall here, and I also can't play to my own strengths here.

His criticism of the local practices is apparent when he talks about the differences between his own German practices and the local working practices. He clearly constructs them as being inferior to his own working practices, and he conceives of them as being incompatible with his own managerial practices. From his perspective, meeting other working practices in the cultural contact zone of the office space endangers his very position as expatriate manager.

This interpretive scheme of the office space as being overly influenced by inferior host country practices is related to his specific everyday practices aiming to make the local subsidiary less Chinese. In the following, we will elaborate on two specific practices we found in the data that aim to homogenize the transnational social space of the MNC by strengthening the dominance of the home country culture: First, displacing employees who were perceived as 'too local' from the office space and, second, displacing local practices and aesthetics from the office space. Both practices are characterized by the paradox of his demanding local employees to be cosmopolitan translators, while at the same time refusing to take up such a position himself.

On the one hand, Mr. Hoffmann and his general manager demanded that their local employees be cosmopolitan and take over the role of cultural translators. Other employees who did not fit this scheme were displaced from the office space. Since being in command, Mr. Hoffmann and his fellow German general manager have pursued a specific personnel strategy: they have systematically hired Chinese staff who hold German university degrees—that is, Chinese employees who have been academically trained in Germany, have lived in Germany for a couple of years, and have solid German language skills. Mr. Hoffmann refers to these Chinese employees as "German-shaped employees." We observed this hiring strategy also in other MNCs in our sample. The goal of hiring these so-called German-shaped employees is, however, not one of creating a cosmopolitan working culture but of minimizing irritations for the German expatriate managers by displacing non-German working practices from their everyday working routines. As became clear in one of the previous quotations from the interview with Mr. Hoffmann, he perceived it as impossible to work with regular Chinese employees who had not had international experiences. Working with the "German-shaped employees" is, however, very different, according to Mr. Hoffmann:

So, (. . .) these people (. . .) they just understand this thinking differently, (. . .) they definitely have the thinking and knowledge to understand what is asked for. This is much more comfortable with them, they come to me and say, "Be careful, something isn't working here" or "I need another signature."

Whereas he clearly expects his employees to act as cultural translators and to be equipped with cosmopolitan skills, he himself refuses to take up such a role. The reason why he employs "these people" is that they work in a way that Mr. Hoffmann is used to working, without him needing to intervene, enabling him to continue with his habitualized working routines. What is particularly interesting about Mr. Hoffmann's case is that he does not justify his refusal to work with regular Chinese employees by claiming a lack of knowledge on his own part about local working practices. In contrast, Mr. Hoffmann constructs himself as an expert in elaborating the difference between German and Chinese working practices. Despite this claimed knowledge about the Other, he refuses, however, to assume the role of an active translator mediating between different working practices. The work of translating and adapting is put entirely upon local staff, who are expected to translate between their 'Chinese' working practices and his 'German' working practices. In addition, these "German-shaped employees" are expected to cushion Mr. Hoffmann's knowledge gap regarding local institutions, because they are assumed to have the ability to reflect on the limitations and imperfections of a foreign manager's local knowledge due to their international experience. Mr. Hoffmann explains this expected ability for intercultural reflection:

> The German-shaped employees, or those with international experience, they tell me, though, or they think, "Ah, he is German, he just simply doesn't know that, he is certainly qualified for this position here, (. . .) but I have to tell him now that he should arrange this or should do that." And those are the examples that make working with such people simply unbelievably important, and they also just make me good.

This staffing strategy is connected to two different perceptions of knowledge differences (Lachenmann 1994): whereas knowledge gaps on the side of local staff are labeled as illegitimate ignorance and are not tolerated, for the expatriate manager, knowledge gaps are interpreted as a legitimate form of ignorance. Ignorance thus becomes a privilege of the expatriate manager, and demanding cosmopolitan competences from local employees becomes a powerful tool of maintaining Western hegemony. Actually working with cosmopolitans frees him from the irritations of practicing cosmopolitanism himself.

The presence of the host country's cultural identity in the office is reduced not only by displacing staff defined as purely local from the office but also by displacing local practices and aesthetics from the office space—thus transforming the 'Chinese' company spaces into 'non-Chinese' spaces. Here, the control over local staff's practices at the office became a central instrument of displacing local practices and aesthetics from the office space. During our job shadowing, we observed how he tried to transform the office space into a more German space. One incident where Mr. Hoffmann framed a conflict about the material arrangements of the office space in cultural terms and claimed a superiority of his own material practices and standards was the conflict about new trash cans for the office. As the existing trash cans in the office did not correspond to his idea of a representative office, Mr. Hoffmann had instructed one of his employees to buy new trash cans. However, when he saw the new ones purchased by his employee, he was not satisfied with them at all. He thus called his employee and instructed her to exchange them again, giving her very detailed instructions of what type of trash can he wanted—namely, "closed, not plastic, not cheap looking." In the conversation with his employee, he especially emphasized the price that he considered to be appropriate and told her once again that she was allowed to spend a good amount of money on the trash cans, because it was about making a good impression on the costumers. After she had left the room, he explained to the researchers that Chinese employees did not have the same 'sense of perfection' as he had. He said, "How an office looks is just not taken seriously in China. Chinese people just don't see these things; they don't have an eye for making things perfect. This is why I have to monitor so many things." To prove his argument, he added that at one of the business exhibitions where his company had a booth, he had also had serious problems with the quality of the exhibition booth. All the nails had poked out of the material, and he had to complain about it several times. In the following days of the job shadowing, he repeatedly showed us several other spots in the office that did not correspond to his aesthetics and quality-related standards of how an office should look, adding that he would make orders to change this. There were several product samples that according to him already looked a bit 'shabby' because they had been made very quickly and had not been thought through enough regarding quality and aesthetics. Another incident of displacing local practices from the office space was to prohibit Chinese staff from bringing their own lunch to the office and reheating food in the office. Because of the odor it produced, he and the other German managers in the company perceived this local practice as endangering the quality of the office place, which was also being used for receiving costumers. They decided that the food needed to be kept out of the office. Through the material practices in the office and beyond, he clearly constructs Chinese staff as inferior and his own practices and standards as superior.

Paradoxically, the first impression one gets when entering the office space is one of a truly intercultural office space. Everywhere at the office, arrangements alluding to the two different national cultures—German and Chinese—can be found. The reception desk is decorated with a flag bracket holding two miniature flags, the German flag, and the Chinese flag. The wall behind the reception desk is adorned with the company logo in huge illuminated Latin letters and another one in shiny metal Chinese characters of the same size directly beneath it. This duplication of German and Chinese national and cultural symbols can be found all over the office space: every single room is decorated with the small dual flag brackets. They can be found on the coffee table in the entrance area, in meeting rooms, in individual offices, and also in the office of the German general manager. Huge colorful presentation boards about the history of the company in Chinese characters emphasized the location of the office in China. Other corporate identity material decorating individual offices, large-scale pictures depicting European looking, fair-haired families using the company product, however, clearly highlight the non-local identity of the company and office space. The office space is thus characterized by a mix of artifacts presenting China and Germany in an equal way, in addition to artifacts standing for clear host country and home country references. However, when looking at how Mr. Hoffmann talks about the cultural identity of the company and the office space, this impression of a truly intercultural office space is significantly challenged.

This example makes clear an interesting contradiction: On the level of aesthetic representation of the office space, there are strong symbolic references to the transnational social space of this MNC as being equally constituted by diverse cultural and politic entities. These representations are, however, part of a local marketing strategy and directed toward local costumers visiting the office. They do not correspond to how the managers themselves see the cultural identity of the office space. The general manager's comments about a large scale Chinese calligraphy piece given to him by a Chinese costumer and used for decoration of his office illustrates this rather instrumental and distant relationship to the local culture. He dryly commented, "It's some sort of Chinese wisdom, but I can't read it and I have no idea what it means." For costumers, the office space is constructed as a binational and intercultural space. The everyday work of Mr. Hoffmann and his general manager, in contrast, is characterized by a clear devaluation of host country working practices in comparison to their own working practices and by clear ethnocentric practices of transforming the 'Chinese' office spaces into 'non-Chinese' spaces. One of the "German-shaped employees" (*deutsch geprägte Mitarbeiter*) who had studied in Germany in a university program with English as the main language of instruction comments, "This company is kind of crazy. I could get along well in Germany without knowing German so well, but here I feel kind of discriminated against."

To sum up, many of the managers in our sample talked about a discrepancy between the actual cultural practices at the office space and the kind of office space and work culture they envisioned for their company, as was exemplified by the case of Mr. Hoffmann. Host country practices were deemed as being too dominant and home country practices as not being present enough. The cultural politics they pursued were thus to push back cultural practices related to the host country and to strengthen the home country culture, for example, by employing local staff with international experience. This case highlights an interesting constellation that contradicts the mainstream management literature on 'global mindsets': Whereas the local employees display cosmopolitan orientations and competences, the expatriate managers refuse to assume the position of a cosmopolitan translator themselves. Paradoxically, however, in the management literature, cosmopolitan orientations and practices are exclusively attributed to the expatriate managers while local staff are conceived of as parochial (Kanter 1995). Our ethnographic findings, thus, stress that different groups of actors and not just expatriate managers construct transnational social spaces in MNCs.

Conclusion

Embedded into the debates on expatriate managers as either interculturally competent boundary spanners or neocolonial boundary makers, the aim of this chapter was to investigate expatriate managers' everyday practices of dealing with difference in their workplaces. We examined expatriate managers' interpretive schemes about the cultural identity of their MNCs and the local office spaces, their orientations toward different working practices, and their modes of action regarding spatial and social practices of the employees and coworkers. After already having demonstrated that in the non-work sphere expatriates' lives were ripe with ambivalences and inherent contradictions (see Chapter 5) and that also the ways they 'make' their boundary roles they occupy in the professional sphere (see Chapter 7) were highly ambivalent, this chapter showed that such inconsistencies also characterize expatriates' modes of dealing with difference, symbolic management, and knowledge translation. They range from attempts to displace host country work and cultural practices from the office space to visions of creating cosmopolitan office spaces that integrate diverse cultural meanings and knowledge repertoires.

First, our ethnographic research brought a diversity of interpretive schemes regarding the cultural identity of the office space to the fore. One interpretive scheme was the hierarchization of host and home country practices in such a way that host country practices were perceived as inferior to host country practices. Another contrasting scheme was a symmetrization of different practices, viewing them as equally legitimate and evaluating the cultural diversity of the MNC positively. On the one hand, differences in working practices were perceived as nonnegotiable, with interaction with others seen solely as a one-sided process of transformation. On the other hand, it was also seen as a process of mutual transformation and reciprocal learning. Experiences of differences in working practices during the assignment were on the one hand addressed in highly essentialist national-cultural idioms, and, on the other hand, such national-cultural frames of

interpretation were deconstructed, and alternative interpretations allowing for a construction of other imagined communities (Anderson 1983)
were offered where expatriate managers and local employees would not
be opposed but rather united with a joint identity. The selected case studies
also revealed contrasting modes of dealing with difference and of negotiating the cultural identity of the office space ranging from controlling and
displacing difference to integrating local and non-local references in a mul-
ticultural office space.

These practices of controlling and displacing difference at the office space
are clearly not cosmopolitan, but are instead embedded into distinct hierarchical perceptions of the Other. We argue that the reason why it is at all
important to control local practices and to displace local decorative objects
such as vases from the office space goes way beyond aesthetic concerns. If
the MNC defines itself as a transnational space based on "Western (e.g.,
German or U.S.-American) logics of action and ideologies of control" and
tries to implement an "imposed transfer strategy" (Geppert and Clark 2003,
437), decorative objects such as vases referring to local cultural practices do,
however, become symbols of passive resistance to the incorporation of this
local office into the transnational social space of the MNC. If the cultural
argument is used to legitimate the superiority of some management practices
over others, it is probable that the cultural argument then also encroaches
on domains in the company that are not directly work related. In the end,
it is also the legitimation of the expatriate managers' presence in the subsidiary that is negotiated through the material practices. If the office space
is visibly marked as local, then the legitimacy of the expatriate manager is
also put into question. One significant mechanism through which authority
of knowledge is constructed is thus the material setup of the office space.

Second, and most importantly, different ambivalences and inherent inconsistencies in the everyday lives of expatriate managers, which prevent classi-
fying the individual managers as either cosmopolitan or anti-cosmopolitan,
became visible throughout our ethnographic research. The managers simultaneously made use of contradicting approaches to cultural difference,
namely, cultural superiority of the West, on the one hand, and cultural
diversity and cosmopolitanism on the other. This synchronicity of apparently contradictory orientations toward difference was based on a distinction between hierarchical cultural domains with nonnegotiable rules defined
by the global organizational culture of their MNC and dialogic cultural
domains with negotiable features. They simultaneously demanded local
employees to be cosmopolitan translators while at the same time refusing
to assume such positions themselves. And finally, they simultaneously used
nationalizing and denationalizing interpretive schemes. Each of these different typical modes of dealing with difference aims at balancing the tension
between 'local adaptation' and 'global integration' as elaborated in Chapter 2 (Mense-Petermann 2005, 2012). However, balancing this tension does
not mean that the tensions vanish. Rather, these tensions are transformed

into ambivalences and inherent inconsistencies characterizing the everyday agency in their work spaces. We will further theorize on these inherent inconsistencies in the conclusion (Chapter 10) by introducing the concept of 'paradoxical cosmopolitanisms.'

Notes

1 For the use of the concept of the 'contact zone' in the context of expatriate research, see also Yeoh and Willis (2005)
2 Expatriates often operate with very crude and essentialist concepts of cultural difference based on the concept of 'cultural standards' by Hofstede (1997, 2001), or in this case to the concept of 'intimate distance' by Edward Hall (Hall 1966). 'Cultural standards' is the most prominent approach in intercultural management training. Cranston (2016) argues that the intercultural encounter of expatriates is thus already preconfigured in intercultural training in such a way that they provide expatriates with interpretive schemes of incommensurable cultural blocks.

Bibliography

Anderson, Benedict. 1983. *Imagined Communities: Reflections on the Origins and Spread of Nationalism*. London: Verso.

Buchanan, Ian. 2010. *A Dictionary of Critical Theory*. Oxford: Oxford University Press.

Cheung, Lenis L. 2008. "Let the "Other" Speak for Itself: Understanding Chinese Employees from Their Own Perspectives." *Critical Perspectives on International Business* 4 (2/3): 277–306. doi:10.1108/17422040810870024.

Cranston, Sophie. 2016. "Producing Migrant Encounter: Learning to be a British Expatriate in Singapore Through the Global Mobility Industry." *Environment and Planning D: Society and Space* 34 (4): 655–71. doi:10.1177/0263775816630311.

Dörrenbächer, Christoph. 2007. "Inside the Transnational Social Space: Cross-Border Management and Owner Relationship in a German Subsidiary in Hungary." *Journal for East European Management Studies* 12 (4): 318–39. doi:10.1688/1862-0019_jeems_2007_04_doerrenbaecher Franzpötter, Reiner. 1997. *Organisationskultur: Begriffsverständnis und Analyse aus interpretativ-soziologischer Sicht*. Baden-Baden: Nomos.

Geppert, Mike, and Ed Clark. 2003. "Knowledge and Learning in Transnational Ventures: An Actor-Centred Approach." *Management Decision* 41 (5): 433–42. doi:10.1108/00251740310479287.

Hall, Edward. 1966. *The Hidden Dimension*. New York: Anchor Books.

Hofstede, Geert. 1997. *Cultures and Organizations: Software of the Mind* New York: McGraw-Hill.

Hofstede, Geert. 2001. *Culture's Consequences: Comparing Values Behaviors Institutions and Organizations Across Nations*. Thousand Oaks: Sage.

Kanter, Rosabeth M. 1995. *World class: Thriving locally in the global economy*. New York: Simon & Schuster.

Lachenmann, Gudrun. 1994. "Systeme des Nichtwissens. Alltagsverstand und Expertenbewußtsein im Kulturvergleich." In *Expertenwissen: Die institutionalisierte Kompetenz zur Konstruktion von Wirklichkeit*, edited by Ronald Hitzler, Anne Honer, and Christoph Maeder, 285–305. Opladen: Westdeutscher Verlag.

Leggett, William. 2012. "Institutionalising the Colonial Imagination: Chinese Middlemen and the Transnational Corporate Office in Jakarta, Indonesia." In *The New Expatriates: Postcolonial Approaches to Mobile Professionals*, edited by Anne-Meike Fechter and Katie Walsh, 77–90. London and New York: Routledge.

Mense-Petermann, Ursula. 2005. "Transnationale Kulturalität—Ein konzeptioneller Vorschlag zum Problem der Sozialintegration transnationaler Konzerne am Beispiel der Automobilindustrie." In *Und es fährt und fährt. Automobilindustrie und Automobilkultur am Beginn des 21. Jahrhunderts*, edited by Gert Schmidt, 173–200. Berlin: Edition Sigma.

Mense-Petermann, Ursula. 2012. "Multinationals, Transnationals, Global Players—Zur Besonderheit grenzüberschreitend operierender Organisationen." In *Handbuch Organisationstypen*, edited by Maja Apelt and Veronika Tacke, 43–61. Wiesbaden: VS Verlag für Sozialwissenschaften.

Nowicka, Magdalena, and Maria Rovisco, eds. 2009. *Cosmopolitanism in Practice*. Aldershot, Burlington: Ashgate.

Pratt, Mary L. 1991. "Arts of the Contact Zone." *Profession*, 33–40. New York: MLA

Pratt, Mary L. 1992. *Imperial Eyes: Travel Writing and Transculturation*. London and New York: Routledge.

Shih, Shu-mei. 2001. *The Lure of the Modern: Writing Modernism in Semicolonial China, 1917–1937*. Berkeley: University of California Press.

Shih, Shu-mei. 2002. "Towards an Ethics of Transnational Encounter, or 'When' Does a 'Chinese' Woman Become a 'Feminist'?" *Differences: A Journal of Feminist Cultural Studies* 13 (2): 90–126. doi:10.1215/10407391-13-2-90

Yeoh, Brenda S. A., and Katie Willis. 2005. "Singaporean and British Transmigrants in China and the Cultural Politics of 'Contact Zones.'" *Journal of Ethnic and Migration Studies* 31 (2): 269–85. doi:10.1080/1369183042000339927.

Part IV

Comparative Perspectives and Conclusion

Part IV summarizes and discusses our empirical findings in a *comparative* and *synthesizing* perspective.

Chapter 9 addresses the question of how host locality properties impact practiced cosmopolitanism. We question the universalism presupposed by the thesis of the 'global manager' and the emergence of a transnational business elite. Instead, we reveal typical variations in the setup of orientations, everyday practices, and networks of expatriate managers in different host localities.

Finally, building on the findings presented in Parts II and III, Chapter 10 re-problematizes the relation between increased transnational mobility and a privileged position in the global economy on the one hand, and the emergence of a cosmopolitan business elite on the other. We argue that the undifferentiated images of business elites as either cosmopolitans or anti-cosmopolitans, respectively, fail to account for the ambivalences, frictions, and tensions that characterize expatriates' lives in the professional and in the non-work spheres. To theorize the latter, we propose a typology of 'fragmented cosmopolitanisms'—a concept that highlights the ambivalent quality of expatriate managers' everyday lives and the paradoxical ways in which they deal with difference in the varying spheres of their professional and everyday lives.

9 Host Country Effects?

How Host Locality Properties Impact Practiced Cosmopolitanism

Ursula Mense-Petermann

The previous empirical chapters have investigated specific aspects of expatriates' working and living abroad, drawing on typical cases that best exemplify the phenomenon under scrutiny, without, however, systematically factoring in the different host countries of the expatriates from our sample. Yet a cursory glance already suggests that China, the U.S., and Germany, as respective host countries, may impact the modes of practicing cosmopolitanism in very different ways. Therefore, in this chapter, we adopt a comparative perspective, systematically examining possible impacts of different host countries on expatriates' cosmopolitan practices. We question the universalism presupposed by the thesis of the 'global manager' as regards the emergence of a new global class of cosmopolitan managers. Instead, we reveal the significant differences in the practicing of cosmopolitanism by expatriate managers posted in different host localities. This chapter thus builds on the empirical analyses presented in the previous chapters and puts them into a comparative framework.

A look at the expatriate literature, both from IHRM and IB studies, and from social sciences literature rooted in social geography, social anthropology, and mobility research reveals a striking lack of comparative studies. In fact, the majority of the expatriate literature takes into account either expatriates from different home countries or expatriates posted in different host countries. However, in most cases, these studies do not adopt a systematic comparative approach.[1]

There are, however, some comparative studies, mainly from the IB, IHRM, and institutionalist organization studies camp. Here, one important area of comparative research refers to the question of why MNCs show differing utilization rates of expatriates in different host countries. These studies reveal the importance of home country as well as host country effects on the propensity to staff overseas management positions with expatriates (Boyacigiller 1990; Peterson, Napier, and Shul-Shim 2000; Harzing 2001; Beaverstock 2004; Tungli and Peiperl 2009).[2] None of these comparative studies, however, focuses primarily on the expatriates themselves, including their orientations, logics of action, ways of dealing with the challenges of the assignment, or immersion into the host organization and the wider host society. Instead, they are, first and foremost, interested in organizational and management issues of MNCs—i.e., consider expatriates to solely be part of MNCs' global coordination and control strategies, or with regard to their organizational functions. It is an interesting but open question, though, as to whether these organizational differences translate into different ways of dealing with difference of expatriates on their stints.

The sociological, social anthropological, and human geography expatriate literature explicitly dealing with expatriates' dispositions, social positioning, and everyday practices reveals an even more striking lack of comparative studies.[3] Most of these studies focus on expatriates in one host country or even in one single locality (Glasze and Alkhayyal 2002; Fechter 2007; Stadlbauer 2016)—mainly in the Global South.

A review of the expatriate literature, both from the IB/IHRM and from the social sciences camp, thus, reveals a clear gap regarding comparative studies systematically investigating host country effects on expatriate managers' practicing of cosmopolitanism—both at work and in the private sphere. Our study with its subsamples of expatriate managers delegated to China, to the U.S., and to Germany, respectively, allows for addressing this gap and systematically investigating host country effects.

In the remainder of this chapter, therefore, we analyze possible host country effects on expatriates' practiced cosmopolitanism. We will start by developing our analytical lenses and continue by delivering an empirical reconstruction of those properties of the three host countries and, more specifically, the host localities of the expatriates from our sample that impact expatriates' modes of practicing cosmopolitanism. We summarize our findings in the conclusion.

(To What Extent) Does Host Country Matter? An Analytical Framework for a Host Country Comparison

Host country effects is a highly important theoretical category, especially in the institutionalist camp of scholars in organization studies when it comes to explaining differing MNC structures and strategies (see Chapter 2). Elements of country-specific institutional settings, like the education and vocational training system, the corporate governance system, or the system of industrial relations, are considered to be explanatory variables in these approaches (see Maurice 1991; Sorge 1991; Whitley 1999; for a summary, see Geppert, Matten, and Walgenbach 2006). Yet how can we conceive of possible host country effects on *expatriates' ways of practicing cosmopolitanism?*

The institutionalist approaches have been criticized for neglecting the role of actors and agency in enacting and—possibly—changing these institutions (see Dörrenbächer and Geppert 2006, see Chapter 2). Therefore, following our agency-centered approach, we do not subscribe to theoretical positions adopting an ontological and essentialist perspective on host country properties, like approaches suggesting that institutions determine specific modes of agency. Instead, in our comparison, we adopt a theoretical perspective as has been developed in new sociological theories of *space* (Schroer 2009; Löw 2013). We consider space to be socially (re)constructed by actors. Thus, instead of thinking of host countries as fixed and given structures, or 'containers' with fixed borders containing objects and people,[4] we posit that different actors construct different host countries in processes of 'spacing' and 'synthesis' (Löw, 2013). Martina Löw defines 'spacing' as the process of "locating, constructing or positioning" objects and people (Löw 2013, 714), whereas "the capacity for synthesis" refers to connecting goods and people to space "through the processes of perception, ideation and recall" (Löw 2013, 714). In the social process of producing and reproducing space, however, actors relate to and incorporate objects and (groups of) people at hand in their environment. Hence, following Giddens's theory of structuration, space is not only socially (re)produced by actors but also as a type of resource prestructures social practices (see Nowicka 2006; Schroer 2009; Löw 2013, 721).[5] For our investigation of host country effects, we therefore need to identify those objects and (groups of) people the expatriates from our sample draw upon for constructing the spaces in which cosmopolitan or 'bubble' life practices, respectively, are situated.

Yet adopting this theoretical perspective also implies that the very category of host country itself has to be questioned. It is an open empirical question as to whether expatriates attribute properties they draw upon for cosmopolitan practices to the host country as a whole, or whether it could just as well be the case that they attribute these properties only to certain parts of the host country—like global cities or peripheral regions, respectively, or just to their host city or parts of it. We therefore use the term '(host) locality' instead.

Hence, we consider cosmopolitanism as a practice built on the interaction of properties of specific localities and the ways actors enact these properties in 'spacing' and 'synthesis.' However, whereas Chapters 5 and 8 have reconstructed ambivalences and inherent contradictions in practiced cosmopolitanism in the professional and the non-work spheres from the perspective of viewing expatriates as agents (i.e., concentrated on the actors and their ways of enacting these properties), this chapter takes the perspective recognizing the specific localities where the expatriates from our sample have been posted as sites that are equipped with specific properties. Hence, the focus here is on these properties. We will set out to show that the specifics of these properties systematically shape expatriate managers' cosmopolitan practices.

The analytical category of space in this sense is particularly well suited for conceiving of how the expatriates' host localities effect their modes of practicing cosmopolitanism, because in our understanding, the latter exactly implies *specific modes* of 'spacing'—i.e., of arranging objects and people and tagging them symbolically. This theoretical lens, thus, fits our understanding of cosmopolitan practices very well—i.e., a specific mode of managing and engaging with difference and boundaries (Hannerz 1990, 2011) that can be empirically scrutinized by focusing on (1) the forms of sociabilities, (2) which are enacted in concrete spatial practices, and (3) the forms of belonging displayed in attachments to spatial or social locations.

The question addressed in this chapter, is then: what kinds of properties of the different host localities exist and are used by expatriates for space—making, thus shaping expatriates' ways of practicing cosmopolitanism?

We consider three types of properties to be important for expatriates' cosmopolitan practices or 'bubble' life practices, respectively.

The first property refers to the images the expatriates have of the host country and/or specific localities within it. In his study on residential practices and selection of resident places of German financial managers in London and Singapore, as well as on their identity development and performances, Meier (2015, 2016) has convincingly shown that the images expatriates have of their host localities[6] is a highly important variable that makes a great impact. Meier shows how different localities evoke different images of the place, the social space, and the expatriates' own positions within this space. These images impact the ways in which the expatriates relate to the host locality and its population. Expatriates may position themselves in either a hierarchical manner, as being superior to the host population, or at eye level, i.e., equal with the host population, or even as inferior to the host population, i.e., feeling pressure to adopt to superior host locality practices and expectations.[7] And, as previous chapters have shown, how expatriates relate to the host society population strongly impacts their immersion into the host society and how they practice cosmopolitanism.

The second kind of property is material-symbolic. Different localities offer different material and symbolically charged preconditions and options for selecting and enacting places of residence, leisure activities, consumption, sociabilities, and mobility practices (see Meier 2015, 2016). All of these features of the locality, like the availability of compounds, sightseeing destinations, exclave schools, etc., have been proven to strongly impact the ways in which expatriates immerse themselves into the host society and thus develop (paradoxical) cosmopolitanisms (see Chapter 5).

Thirdly, we pay attention to properties of social structure and spatial arrangement. The composition, social structure, and spatial arrangement of the local population constitutes an opportunity structure at the host locality. They affect the opportunities for expatriates to get into contact with host country, home country, and third country nationals, and, thus, affect the kinds of sociabilities that expatriates engage in.

In the remainder of this chapter, we reconstruct these three types of properties for each of the three host countries where the expatriates from our sample have been posted and, more specifically, for their specific host localities.

Properties of Host Country China and Chinese Host Localities

In this subchapter, we elaborate on the properties of host country China and the Chinese localities enacted in space-making processes by expatriates who were posted there.

With only one exception, the German and U.S.-American expatriates from this subsample were posted in the global cities of Shanghai and Beijing, respectively. Both cities are home to large international expatriate communities. Up until the National Census 2010, Shanghai hosted 209,000 expatriates,[8] whereas Beijing was home to 107,000 expatriates. Only Guangdong hosts more expatriates (235,000), and other first and second-tier cities follow far behind. On the list of the most preferred host localities for expatriates, Shanghai ranks number one, and Beijing ranks number two.[9]

Images of 'China'

When asked about the reasons for deciding to go to China, the U.S., or Germany, the expatriates from our sample disclosed clear-cut and differing images of the possible host countries. Even before they were delegated to their actual host localities, they had an idea of where they would most like to go, ranking potential host countries based on whether they would be acceptable or whether they were to be rejected as a "no-go" (Mr. Pätzold). The—stereotypical—images[10] of different host countries thus also shape expatriates' selections for postings in different countries. On their stints, the expatriates altered these images in some respects. However, the experience-based images of the three host countries also differed in a patterned way.

For the majority of expatriates posted in China, their image of their host country was multifaceted and consisted of different, partly contradictory components: First of all, China was perceived as being very different from the countries in the Global North in terms of culture and everyday practices. Therefore, as a host country, it was perceived to represent an adventure and also a challenge, putting the expatriate to a test. Mr. Winkelmann's pre-assignment perception of China as his prospective host country best exemplifies this image of China: "I wanted to go out there, try new food, make new experiences, and have the feeling that I can make it." At that time, he could have also opted to go to the U.S., but he says that he was not interested in going there. He wanted to "make new experiences and get out because staying always in one place is too boring." He thought that going to the U.S. would be boring because the U.S.-Americans would "be the same as us anyway." Most of the expatriates posted in China shared this image of China as a challenging but very exciting host country and displayed some kind of 'adventurous' attitude toward their stint. The expatriates and their spouses enact the image of a 'most different' Chinese culture during their stints—e.g., when they stroll through traditional neighborhoods (Hutongs) and watch local people practicing strange habits. Mrs. Dittrich, for example, intimated to us her image of China:

> If you go outside, then you'll see old people sitting on the wall who spend their free time outside, entertaining themselves, yeah, chatting with each other, like it was in our village so to say, back in the day, just hanging out in front of the door of the house. You see people who take their birds for walks, people doing gymnastic exercises in the park, there are choirs in the parks that spontaneously meet up, so there are definitely some ancient Chinese behaviors, stuff about everyday communication that you can still experience relatively quickly and often here in the city (. . .) The street scene of several Hutongs that you can still find here, and the many lanterns hung up everywhere, too.

Linked to this image of China as a most different, exotic, and challenging social environment is the image of China as one of the ancient high civilizations, relics of which can be experienced in sightseeing tours to the Great Wall, the Forbidden Palace, the terracotta warrior exhibition in Xi'an, and other such places. Hence, China is regarded as a tourist site on account of its ancient empire history.

Another trait of the pre-assignment image of China is, contrastingly, negative. Mr. Dittrich and his spouse, who were very reluctant to go to China when they were first asked, present it to us. They paint an image of China as a gray and dull socialist country. Others emphasize the backwardness of a "developing country" and the shortcomings in terms of living standards for and civilized behavior of the people. Some of the other traits of the image of China brought up by several expatriates and their spouses were: pollution of the air and of the environment, doubts about the quality of groceries and other products, doubts about the quality of housing, insufficient supply of everyday needs, 'unbearable' habits like spitting and snorting in the streets, dirt, and chaotic and loud traffic.[11]

Those expatriates who did decide to go to China despite this negative image, however, had partially corrected it upon their arrival. For example, upon his arrival in the global city he has been assigned to, Mr. Dittrich was very positively surprised to find himself not in a gray and dull socialist city, but in a vivid and exciting global city with millions of twinkling lights and utterly capitalist in appearance. Mrs. Frank, too, describes her first impression of her host locality, another Chinese global city, as being overwhelming, very exciting, and as a vivid city, a city that is always in motion and never sleeps.

This image, however, only refers to the global cities of Beijing and Shanghai. Therefore, Mrs. Frank differentiates between these global cities—here especially the "urban glamour zones" (Sassen 2001)—and other cities. For her, Shanghai and Beijing "are not China," while the more remote city where she had been posted earlier in her career "is China":[12]

You know, you experience that when you walk through the streets. When you walk through the streets in that remote city, and when you walk through the streets in Beijing or Shanghai. In Beijing, for example, you are surrounded by many Europeans. Thus, you do not always realize that you are in China. In some districts, you meet more foreigners than Chinese. And in that other city, you only see Chinese in the streets, Chinese who are spitting—it's extreme! You know, that is really extreme there in that city. I have never experienced something like this before, not in Shanghai or Beijing. There it has been (. . .) It is just more civilized in the big cities. And here, the people do also speak English, like in restaurants or shops. You know, in that other city nobody speaks English, only very rarely. And you only get Chinese menus, you just get nothing but Chinese things. You get nothing else, and they don't have such a choice of supermarkets and stuff, compared with Beijing or Shanghai.

Hence, 'China' is linked to the negative image elaborated earlier, whereas the positively perceived, exciting places are termed 'not China.'

The same distinction between the global cities and the provincial areas in China is presented to us by Mr. Weber, whom we visited on his stint in the U.S., but who had previously been posted in China. He tells us,

Yeah, China had me excited from day one. But I should clarify that when I talk about China and South-East Asia, I'm referring to the big cities there. I definitely would not accept anything anywhere in the Chinese province. But I would in the Asian metropolises. Why? Because there are a few things that come together for me there. The mix between South-Eastern Asian exoticism and culture and international flair and the possibilities. The unbelievable growth that's taking place there. During my time in Shanghai, as I was in Shanghai, Shanghai was, the GDP, the total domestic product of Shanghai was growing by 16–20 percent each year. These are things that, that you just can't imagine anywhere else in the world, and someone who has themselves never experienced that in person can't even begin to conceive what that means. This whole atmosphere there in the city, this, this, this eruption, this excitement, that was simply extremely invigorating, inspiring, and I still get the chills when I begin to talk about it, when I look at a few photos at home. It was simply unbelievably inspiring.

In this quote, Mr. Weber touches upon a further trait of the image of China as a host country: the incredibly dynamic economy. Other expatriates, too, underline the importance of China as a huge and dynamically developing market. The appreciation of the dynamic, vivid, and exciting traits of China connects to the adventurous attitude and openness for challenges and alien environments the expatriates posted in China generally display.

To sum up, the picture expatriates paint of China as a host country is multifaceted and consists of (1) the image of a most different, even alien, and therefore challenging culture; (2) the image of a tourist site for ancient empire history; (3) the image of a backward and uncivilized developing country; (4) the image of global cities making the pace for global developments; and (5) the image of an incredibly dynamic and capitalist economy. These different, partly contradictory elements of the image of China as a host country are synthetized into a coherent image by differentiating Chinese and non-Chinese spaces within the country and also within single localities. The 'Chinese' spaces, again, are subdivided into exotic and historic spaces on the one hand, and into backward and uncivilized spaces on the other. Whereas the latter are negatively connoted, the former two are considered spaces for experiencing the cultural difference sought after by the expatriates on their stints. As we will see in the remainder of this subchapter, this differentiation of spaces is not only constitutive for the image of China as a host country displayed by expatriates, but is also enacted in their concrete space-making practices and the ways in which they draw on specific material-symbolic and social-structural properties of their host localities in this process.

Material-Symbolic Properties

Having reconstructed the image expatriates have of their host country China and specific host localities, we will now investigate the ways in which they draw upon material-symbolic properties at hand in their host locality and define exactly which properties they make use of in their space-making practices. With regard to our understanding of cosmopolitan practices (see Chapters 1, 5, and 8), we concentrate on how dwelling spaces, leisure and consumption spaces, work spaces, and public and mobility spaces are enacted to this end.

We show that the expatriates from this subsample use different material-symbolic properties at hand in their host localities or in China, more generally, in order to enact the three different spaces represented in their image of China: non-Chinese spaces, exotic and historic Chinese spaces, and backward and uncivilized Chinese spaces. They construct their spaces in such a way that they live 'outside China' most of the time and are able to keep 'China' at a distance. In this way, they either control their exposition to Chinese spaces, like in the case of exotic or historic sites, or completely avoid it in the case of the 'uncivilized' Chinese spaces. Whereas it is the expatriates who select exactly which properties to enact in this space-making process, their practices are shaped by and restricted to the material-symbolic properties in place which themselves suggest specific space-making practices.

With regard to dwelling spaces, as Chapter 5 has revealed, the vast majority of expatriate managers from our sample live in spatially segregated *compounds* restricted to expatriates or embassy staff. As we have shown in Chapter 5, these compounds are designed to meet the expectations of

Western expatriates in terms of quality standards of housing and of the surroundings as well as regarding leisure, sports, and consumption facilities. They are spatially and socially secluded from the local surroundings and the host population to such an extent that they are perceived as not being 'China.'[13] Instead, they are perceived as being safe and comfortable exclaves in an otherwise chaotic, loud, and dirty 'Chinese' environment. The compound, thus, is a most important material-symbolic property used by expatriates to enact 'non-Chinese' dwelling—and also leisure and consumption spaces.

Housing in China is state-regulated[14] and has segmented 'markets' for locals and a specific segment for expatriates only, consisting of houses and flats in exactly the kinds of compounds described earlier. These can be traced on English-language Internet pages and are offered by specialized English-speaking real estate agents. Thus, expatriates depend on these kinds of pre-selected residential offers and the agents offering them. There were expatriate compounds that met the expectations of expatriates regarding housing standards and quality and regarding security, tidiness, and privacy (as hideaways where the expatriates could 'escape China'), as well as residential agents who helped expatriates to find such accommodations in all localities where expatriate communities in China are found. They represent an opportunity structure that makes it easy for expatriates to find residential places that meet their expectations without having to spend too much time and effort on searching. Additionally, the global mobility policies of MNCs take this up and prestructure residential decisions even more by defining housing budgets correlating to what is on offer in the compounds in the localities where they delegate expatriates, by contracting specific residential agents, preselecting specific compounds these agents are to offer their expatriates, and sometimes even by building compounds for their expatriates themselves (in more remote cities) (see Chapter 4).

As we have already shown in Chapter 5, the decision of where to reside to a large extent prestructures the forms of experiencing difference and of developing openness for the Other, or—alternatively—for a separation and sealing off from the host locality and its population. Such decisions, however, cannot be conceived of as rational choices following the individual preferences of the expatriates. Instead, they are largely prestructured by the specific forms of socio-spatial segregation of cities in the different host countries, by the collective images connected to these forms of segregation, by the specifics of the housing market and state regulations,[15] and, last but not least, by the global mobility policies of the employing MNCs and their expatriate packages (see Chapter 4), which again incorporate the specific features and images of the host countries.

In addition to the spatial segregation of housing for indigenous and foreign populations, as featured in Chinese cities with larger expatriate communities, Central State or federal and regional authority legislation regarding controlling the indigenous population and keeping Chinese citizens and foreigners apart also impact expatriates' cosmopolitan practices in a more general sense: *Christian congregations* and *international schools* also represent spaces institutionalized as 'exclaves' that exclude Chinese passport holders and cater only to expatriates. These therefore represent further material-symbolic properties drawn upon by expatriates in their space making. All family expatriates from our sample sent their children to 'exclave schools.'

With regard to leisure time activities at their host localities, the expatriates in this subsample seek to experience especially that which is most different from their home settings but is at the same time connected to positive elements of the image of China—e.g., either the 'non-Chinese' spaces or the exotic and historic sites.

Most of the expatriates from this subsample have been posted in the global cities of Beijing and Shanghai, and most at least of the German expatriates originate from small villages or rather remote hometowns. The things they appreciate most about their host localities are the scale and scope of *world-class* cultural events and fine art exhibitions, the stylish bars, and the large variety of restaurants in the urban glamour zones offering all kinds of national cuisines—i.e., the *leisure facilities of these global cities*. Many international restaurants and shopping malls offering all of the well-known Western luxury brands, international hotels, and many foreigners in the streets—expatriate managers and diplomatic staff—make up the Western appearance of these areas of the respective cities. Hence, in these global cities, it is possible to enact a disembedded cosmopolitan urban lifestyle by consuming products from all over the world, practicing urban leisure activities, participating in the vivid, multifaceted, and exciting nightlife, and meeting people from all over the world.

Whereas one dimension of 'difference' enacted by our sample expatriates at their host localities is the features of a global city, we have identified a second dimension of 'difference' relating to Chinese culture. This is what the expatriates refer to as the 'real' or 'traditional' Chinese culture, as represented in *ancient emperors' palaces, temples, Chinese tea houses, and traditional urban districts (Hutongs)*. These host country features are closely linked to the image of an ancient empire history and of a strange but peculiar and exotic culture. The expatriates posted in China experience these features in a 'tourist' manner. For example, Mrs. Winkelmann regularly took "city walks" with her group of expatriate spouses in order to try and get a glimpse into "real Chinese life" (see Chapter 5). Most of the expatriates also took weekend trips to tourist destinations, such as the Great Wall or Xi'an, with its terracotta warrior exhibition. As pointed out in Chapter 5, however, this 'tourist' mode of immersing into the host society only produces distanced, ephemeral, and nonreciprocal relationships to Chinese Others and represents an observational mode of attachment.

The expatriate managers posted in China not only tend to practice a disembedded cosmopolitan urban lifestyle in 'non-Chinese' spaces and an observational mode of experiencing touristic sites but also—regarding groceries, clothes, media, etc.—tend to predominantly consume 'Western' products. Most of the compounds feature *Western shops and supermarkets*, with a product range that reflects the home countries of the expatriates living in that compound. When we visited Mrs. Frank in late November, for example, the supermarket in the basement of her high rise had a large variety of products in stock typically bought in Germany in the holiday season, such as chocolate Advent calendars and Christmas cookies. Even beyond the compounds, the global cities of Beijing and Shanghai feature a variety of Western supermarket chains catering to expatriates' desire to obtain home country or Western products. These also form part of the 'non-Chinese' spaces made by expatriates in the private sphere of their lives on the stint. Most of the expatriates and expatriate spouses we met were skeptical about the quality of Chinese groceries, especially meat and clothing. What they could not obtain in their compounds or in Western supermarkets they would bring from home, or they would ask visiting family and friends to bring these things with them. Hence, they practice a lifestyle that—with regard to consumption patterns—in many respects resembles their lifestyles back home and evokes a strong perception of home country belonging.[16]

As Chapter 8 has revealed by drawing on the cases of Mr. Hoffmann and Mr. Winkelmann, the *company offices*—i.e., the workspaces of expatriates posted in China are to a large extent also made into 'non-Chinese' spaces. Many MNCs give their globally spread subsidiaries a uniform design with far-reaching directives regarding the appearance of the buildings and their interiors. And, as shown in Chapter 8, expatriates posted in China tend to actively push back against Chinese practices (such as spitting, deposing tea leaves in the toilet, eating in the office) and symbolic-material features (such as feng shui) from the office space. As we have argued in Chapter 8, these practices of transforming the office space into 'non-Chinese' spaces are rooted in perceptions of the Chinese working practices and material culture as deficient and inferior, or as at least not compatible with the expectations of headquarters and/or Western customers regarding how a company should look and how work should be done. Different modes of relating to the perceived differences in working and space-making practices elaborated in Chapter 8 notwithstanding, except Mr. Simon, all expatriates from our sample posted in China worked on making their office space a 'non-Chinese,' or at least a not *so* Chinese space, reflecting a clear hierarchical and ethnocentric—if not neocolonial—attitude regarding Chineseness in most of the cases. MNCs' policies regarding uniform architecture and layout of their globally spread subsidiaries, hence, produce material-symbolic properties in the host localities which also allow for 'escaping China' at work.

The *company car* and the *personal driver* represent other material-symbolic properties introduced by MNCs' global mobility policies (see Chapter 4) at the host localities. In granting the expatriates a company car and a personal driver, and with expatriates expecting this to be part of their 'expat package,' MNCs and expatriates work together to enact the image of the streets and the traffic in China as being part of the backward, uncivilized, and, therefore, unbearable 'China.' The personal driver allows the expatriate to segregate themselves from the locality and the local population even when having to travel outside of the compound or the company premises, as the company car also represents a calm and comfortable, isolated island in the midst of the Chinese surrounding, which is perceived as hectic, loud, dirty, and even dangerous. With Mr. Hoffmann and the Kellys being the only exceptions, all expatriates from our sample who were posted in China disposed over a company car and refused to use other forms of transportation that would expose them to the local ways of moving in the streets and to the local population. And even Mr. Hoffmann, who used to drive an electric scooter and has developed a considerable competence in participating in the Chinese traffic, refused to use the subway because of people having to squeeze together and the risk of infections (see Chapter 5). Hence, the expatriates avoid public transportation and being exposed to the local population in the streets, in buses, and in the underground, whereas enacting a non-Chinese mobility space by using their company cars and their drivers.

To sum up, as has been shown for other host countries in the Global South, the expatriates posted in China also tend to construct a 'bubble' (Fechter 2007, 17; van Bochove and Engbersen 2013) that is detached from the spaces of the local population (see Glasze and Alkhayyal 2002; Fechter 2007) and their local coworkers and subordinates. Hence, the lifeworlds of expatriates posted in China are in many respects very much similar to those of expatriates delegated to other countries in the Global South, as has been shown, for example, in Indonesia (Fechter 2007), Lebanon, and Saudi Arabia (Glasze and Alkhayyal 2002).

Dwelling and working spaces and practices of expatriates in China are, thus, shaped by the images expatriates have of their host countries and localities. Expatriates are first and foremost prompted by a negative image, the image of backwardness, uncivilized and unbearable behavior of the indigenous population, dirtiness, loudness, and chaos, to actively create 'non-Chinese' spaces for dwelling, leisure, consumption, mobility, and working. These 'non-Chinese' spaces can then be enacted by the expatriates, allowing them to 'escape China' at work and in the private sphere.

Social Structure and Its Spatial Arrangement

Having discussed how the expatriates posted in China select, locate, and position *objects* like compounds, supermarkets, means of transportation, etc. in processes of spacing, we will now analyze how they select, locate, and position *people*, especially Others in their space-making practices with regard to practicing cosmopolitanism. We will take a closer look at the sociabilities and the kinds of networks these expatriate managers establish, drawing on the composition, structure, and spatial arrangement of Others who are present at their host localities. The question addressed is about the kinds of Others expatriates co-opt in their spaces and their sociabilities, in terms of nationality and ethnicity of these Others.

As we have seen in the preceding subchapter, expatriates posted in China mainly move within 'non-Chinese' spaces, such as the compounds, the urban glamour zones of Beijing and Shanghai, and their workplaces. These are the spaces where they are most likely to meet the Others with whom they enact sociabilities. Chinese spaces, on the contrary, are to a large extent either avoided or experienced in a touristic manner, a mode of immersing into the host society that only produces distanced, ephemeral, and nonreciprocal relationships with Others. Hence, by drawing on the material-symbolic properties of their host country and host localities, expatriates enact spaces which also prestructure the composition and structure of Others with whom they potentially socialize and establish networks.

In this regard, we can identify three different spaces populated with differently composed and structured groups of Others, and related to these different opportunity structures, we are also able to identify three different types of networks from the cases of this subsample:

(1) Large MNCs maintaining huge production facilities in China with country and even regional headquarters usually located in Beijing or Shanghai generally delegate large numbers of expatriates to these cities. In one extreme case, at the regional headquarters of a large German MNC, we even had the impression that half of the office staff was German. It is mainly these expatriate managers who are employed with such large MNCs who maintain *nationally/ethnically homogenous* networks solely with their expatriate peers. These large MNCs also often organize expatriate 'round tables,' 'spouse lunches,' and leisure activities, like one MNC, for example, that had its own expatriate football team. These expatriates restrict their contacts to colleagues from within their company and neither take part in activities of the wider 'expat community' nor look for opportunities to meet and befriend members of the indigenous population—e.g., with colleagues from work. Mr. Dittrich and Mrs. Frank are such case examples. Notwithstanding the fact that they live in high-rises with international inhabitants, all of their friends and acquaintances are colleagues from the company. In some of its plant locations, their employer company even maintains its own firm-specific compound reserved for its expatriates. One example is described in the following quote:

> In that city, we really have a 'German village.' (. . .) The government has built a compound there for German expatriates only. They have their own mayor there, their own municipal council, their own soccer

club, their own choir; they organize like a German municipality. And they are not at all integrated in the city; they are really secluded; they build their own tight-knit exclusive community.

By living in gated communities and sharing in a homogenous lifestyle in addition to their connectedness through sharing common problems at work and in private life and strong social segregation from the local population, these conditions suggest a strong sociability in nationally and ethnically homogenous expatriate communities.

(2) A second type of network is the *transnational network including members of the wider expatriate community of different national (and sometimes also ethnical) origin* but no members of the indigenous population. Some of the expatriates from our sample, such as the Winkelmanns and the Zachers have deliberately opted for an international compound and have befriended their neighbors originating from a broad range of different home countries. Hence, their sociabilities include Others of different nationalities and ethnicities.

This kind of transnational network builds on specific properties of the host localities, namely, the compounds, the international school, international congregations,[17] the expatriate community in general, and the spaces they make use of and that tend to exclude members of the indigenous population—i.e., the urban glamour zones and their facilities. They can, therefore, be characterized as 'bubble' communities in the same way as the networks of the first type in the sense that they are secluded expatriate spaces which cluster around expatriate-typical lifestyle and activities. However, differently than the networks of the first type, they bring about opportunities to be in contact with cultural Others and experience and learn to deal with cultural difference. In Chapter 5, we have termed this type of sociability a 'global bubble.' Note, however, that these properties are only in place in the large metropolises with large international expatriate communities, like Shanghai and Beijing, whereas expatriate life in more remote, third-tier cities tends to take place in more nationally secluded 'bubbles,' as we could observe during our visit to an expatriate manager posted in one such city. Hence, here, again, it is not a host *country* effect but a *locality* effect that matters.

(3) Contrary to the first two types of networks that did not include locals, the third type of network also embraces members of the local host society—i.e., the Chinese. The sociabilities of Mr. Simon and his wife represent an example of this case: They have befriended a group of Chinese artists with whom they meet for dinner or for a drink on a regular basis. Whereas none of the other expatriates in this subsample speak more than a few words and phrases of Chinese, the Simons both speak Chinese and are able to communicate about a considerable variety of topics.[18] This is important to note: As a result of English not being taught as a foreign language in Chinese schools, there is a lack of English-language skills

among the Chinese population. This kind of network, again, builds on the social structure typical for a global city. The global city where the Simons live is not only home to a large international expatriate community but also to a globally oriented group of indigenous artists who are open for international contacts and sociabilities.

It has to be clearly noted, however, that this third type of network is not very current. Very few of the other expatriates of this subsample have contacts to the Chinese going beyond ephemeral encounters, and in all these cases these expatriates had been living in China already for an extraordinarily long time going far beyond the usual expatriation period of three to five years.

Hence, what we can see from analyzing the forms of sociabilities and types of networks the expatriates posted in China predominantly maintain, their sociabilities are strongly impacted by the composition, structure, and spatial arrangement of the Others who populate the spaces that they enact in their dwelling, leisure, consumption, and working practices. With regard to the indigenous population, what we observe here is a neocolonial, ethnicity-based distancing and hierarchical positioning that conceives of the local Other only as servants and subordinates. With the exception of some expatriates who try to counter this mode of relating to the indigenous Others, this concept of the local Other represents the predominant mode of relating to the Chinese population.

Space-Making and Practicing Cosmopolitanism in China

As we have seen, expatriates construct different types of spaces in their space-making practices: non-Chinese spaces, exotic and historic Chinese spaces, and backward and uncivilized Chinese spaces. The Chinese spaces are either experienced in an observational, tourist mode or—if possible—completely avoided.

Hence, the 'difference' that expatriates seek on their stints in China is experienced either in non-Chinese but urban glamour spaces or in Chinese touristic spaces enacted in expatriates' spacing and synthesizing practices. The former refers to 'difference' in terms of 'global-cosmopolitan' versus 'local-remote' and of 'vivid, dynamic, and exciting' versus 'saturated and boring.' The cosmopolitan practices in these non-Chinese, urban glamour spaces are those of a *disembedded* urban cosmopolitanism that use 'global' spaces (Sassen 2001), and this could be practiced in global cities in other countries than China as well. The latter refers to 'difference' in terms of 'alien—exotic' versus 'familiar.' The mode of practicing cosmopolitanism in this case is one of observing instead of immersing into the different culture. Both modes allow for experiencing difference without establishing sociabilities with members of the Chinese population.

This is not to say that China as a host country and the host localities *determine* specific sociabilities, spatial practices, and kinds of belonging. As earlier chapters have shown, some of the expatriates tried to 'undo' these properties and to develop countering practices (see Chapter 5). But the specifics of China as a host country and of specific localities within it *suggest* that expatriates construct social spaces using material properties that are symbolically charged with notions of the home country or of the Global North and that they very firmly stick to the expatriate community, often to an expatriate community exclusively consisting of home country nationals.

What becomes clear from this analysis is that China as host country and the localities where these expatriate managers have been posted—similar to other host countries in the Global South—strongly reinforce expatriate 'bubble' building and often also a reproduction of the home country lifestyle by offering the respective symbolic-material properties and social and spatial structure of the population. If cosmopolitan practices are at all supported by these properties of the host localities, then they represent either a *disembedded* urban cosmopolitanism practiced in the non-Chinese global spaces or a *touristic* cosmopolitanism practiced in an observational, instead of immersing, mode.

Properties of the U.S. as Host Country and U.S. Host Localities

So far, we have elaborated on how the expatriates posted in China enact segmented images of their host country and localities, and relatedly, also enact segmented spaces strongly supporting expatriate 'bubble' life and a tourist, ephemeral mode of attachment to the host country and localities. We will now comparatively investigate which properties of the U.S. as a host country and the localities where the expatriates from our sample have been posted are drawn upon by these expatriates in their space-making practices.

The German expatriates posted in the U.S. from our sample were stationed either in the larger New York area or in one of the middle-size cities in the Southern States of the U.S. that have emerged as new economic hubs due to investments by large MNCs. Larger expatriate communities were in place in all of these host localities.[19]

Images of 'the U.S.'

We start our investigation of the properties of the U.S. as a host country and the respective host localities enacted by the German expatriates posted there in their space-making practices by again elaborating on the image of the U.S. as a host country, as presented to us by the expatriates posted there. Contrary to the image of China as being most different to the home country, prior to their assignment, the expatriates have an overall conception of the U.S. as being a host country not very different from their home country. Mr. Gruber, for example, tells us that he would never have gone to China, because for him, it is not possible to participate in everyday life there because of language and cultural barriers. In China, expatriates would have to follow a lot of specific rules, and they would only be able to observe the host locality as a foreigner at a distance. In the U.S., contrastingly, expatriates and their families would be able to participate in everyday life because they could use English as a shared language and they could move and behave freely. An alternative host country for Mr. Gruber would have been the United Kingdom, where his company also has a subsidiary. The same is true for Mr. Pätzold, who cares a great deal about having a decent living standard and would not at all be willing to accept a delegation to a host locality that does not meet his standards in terms of security, tidiness, 'civilization,' and nice ambiance. And Mr. Jäger also says, "There are countries where you just don't have a language barrier, where you can very easily get in." For all of these expatriates, European countries, especially the United Kingdom, would have been alternatives. This stresses the point that expatriates who opt for being delegated to the U.S. are not seeking big challenges, adventures, and great cultural difference but are rather seeking a 'small difference,' enough to make a difference compared with the home country but similar enough to allow for continuing one's familiar everyday life. What they enact here could be termed a Global North space that draws on those properties that are similar in the countries of the Global North.

Mr. Klett, who had been posted in seven different countries all over the world prior to his delegation to the U.S., however, presents an image of the U.S. as a host country that markedly differentiates the U.S. from European countries and that refers to 'freedom' as represented in cigarette advertisements and road movies and symbolized, for example, by riding a Harley Davidson motorcycle. He concedes, however, that this image dates back to the time when he was 21 years old and could not really conceive of the big, wide world. At that time, the U.S. represented the utmost difference to his home country for him. Yet the idea of a specific U.S.-American culture of freedom as well as of fun and leisure orientation also forms part of the image of the U.S. as a host country disclosed by other German expatriates posted there. Hence, the expatriates enact a second kind of space here—namely, a U.S.-American tourist space that incorporates properties symbolizing freedom, fun, and leisure activities. Same as their counterparts in China, they undertake extensive tourist programs with shorter weekend trips and longer family holidays to such destinations as the Grand Canyon; Las Vegas, Nevada; Colorado; and local beaches.

It can thus be concluded that the image of the U.S. as a host country is also one that is segmented, which on the one hand builds on the idea of the U.S. being part of the Global North and thus sharing a large number of features with home country Germany. On the other hand, the image is based on the idea of a specific U.S.-American leisure culture: It is an image that incorporates iconographic pictures well known from movies, like driving the Route 66 on a Harley Davidson, California beaches, or the idea of 'endless opportunities' as represented in the notion of the 'American Dream.' These are traits that are specifically connected to the U.S. but that are well known in Germany, too, and thereby not at all seen as 'alien.' In the next subchapter, we will investigate how this image connects to the material-symbolic properties of the host localities.

Material-Symbolic Properties

In the case of the Chinese localities, we have identified the compound to be a highly important property enacted by the expatriates to construct non-Chinese dwelling, leisure, and consumption spaces. Such compounds are not in place in the U.S.-American localities where our expatriates were posted. Instead, all expatriates from our sample assigned to the U.S. were living in very wealthy, *upper-class subdivisions*. In most cases, the large mansions were equipped with private pools, and living spaces were—in the view of the expatriate families themselves—oversized. As the global mobility policies of MNCs include housing allowances in addition to basic incomes and hardship allowances, expatriates can afford such luxurious residential places on their stints abroad (see Chapter 4). Hence, contrary to their counterparts in China, the expatriates posted in the U.S. do not live in compounds reserved only for expatriates and diplomats, but instead live among the local population in U.S.-American neighborhoods. Note, however, that these are elite neighborhoods that are clearly more wealthy and luxurious than their own dwelling places at home (see Chapter 5).

The wealthy subdivision with large, luxurious residences is, thus, a property of the U.S. localities upon which the German expatriates drew to enact a third kind of space—next to the Global North space and the U.S.-specific leisure space: an elite space that is differentiated from 'white trash'[20] and 'black' spaces,[21] hence using class and race categories to construct this space. In addition to the material-symbolic properties, like the mansions, nice landscapes, private pools, and entry gates, members of the local, indigenous elite also form part of these elite spaces. We will come back to this issue in the next subchapter.

The expatriate children attended *local private schools*, as opposed to the German, U.S.-American, and international schools typically attended in China. Mr. Jäger's company, for example, has contracted a very prestigious and expensive Christian private school to cater to all of its expatriate children, and the expatriation package also contains a budget for schooling and childcare. But again, these schools are not—as the German, the U.S.-American, or the international schools that the children of the expatriates delegated to China were attending—restricted to expatriate children. They are, instead, the schools where local elite children are sent.

Another important kind of property of the U.S. localities is the *country club* as leisure and sports facility; whereas expatriates in China typically spent most of their leisure time in their compounds using the facilities they offer, expatriates in the U.S. use local public facilities. The Jägers, to mention just one example, are members of a local country club where they play tennis and their children participate in swim classes every weekend. The country club is a property that—just like the subdivision and the private school—is used to enact an elite space, but that at the same time, however, is also used to enact the U.S.-specific leisure space.

With regard to their consumption patterns, in the cases of the expatriates posted in the U.S., and in Germany, too, we could not observe the same reservation regarding local products and services as was the case for the expatriates in China. Instead, expatriates obtained their groceries and other needs from *local shops and supermarkets* and visited *'local' restaurants and bars*. Note, however, that these 'local' shops, bars, and restaurants are themselves globalized to a large extent, with supermarket shelves filled with products from all over the world and restaurants offering Italian, Greek, Indian and many other cuisines. And in the case of the U.S.—and this is also true for Germany (see next subchapter)—this not only applies to global cities but also to the smaller cities or fringe areas of large cities where the expatriates of this subsample where posted. Thus, in this case, consumption patterns incorporating 'global' products and services do not reflect disembedded cosmopolitan lifestyles, but instead form part of the ordinary, everyday cosmopolitanism (which is not even perceived as such) that characterizes consumption patterns in countries of the Global North.

The company offices—i.e., the workplaces of the expatriates in the U.S.— were also drawn upon in space-making practices in a much different way compared with those observed in China. As elaborated in Chapter 8, expatriates posted here did not convert their working places into non-American spaces but instead were, in their working and managing practices, (re)producing them as U.S.-American or global spaces, respectively, by adapting their own practices to those already common there. With regard to 'spacing,' they thus positioned themselves within the existing material-symbolic and social arrangement. This can be explained by the fact that the workplaces in the U.S.-American subsidiaries did not deviate much from what the expatriates knew from home and considered to be appropriate. Hence, they were synthesizing a space defined as 'Western' or 'Global North' office space.

Hence, the most important properties these expatriates drew upon for space making, namely, the wealthy subdivisions, local private schools, country clubs, and workplaces, do not—as we have witnessed for Chinese locality properties—support 'undoing Americanness' and making non-American spaces. Instead, at least in the non-work sphere, they support seclusion in elite spaces, and hence, suggest class (and racial) categories for space making.

Social Structure and Its Spatial Arrangement

As discussed earlier for the expatriate managers posted in China, the majority restrict their contacts to members of the expatriate community, often to those of their own national origin. We now ask how this is for expatriate managers posted in the U.S. Which kinds of Others do they co-opt into the spaces they construct? And how do they arrange and relate to these Others?

As we have seen, the dwelling and leisure spaces of the expatriates posted in the U.S. are not spatially segregated from the indigenous population, and their working spaces are not made into non-host country spaces, as was the case for China.

Yet astonishingly, the expatriates posted in the U.S. still mainly draw on peer expatriates, mainly those originating from their own home country of Germany, in their space-making practices. U.S.-American neighbors, coworkers, and country club peers do indeed form part of their dwelling, working, and leisure spaces. However, they are placed in peripheral positions with regard to inclusion into their sociabilities.

There are three reasons that can explain this finding: The first reason is that there is a *social* distance keeping expatriates and their local neighbors apart, even despite spatial closeness. As we have done in Chapter 5, for an example case, we now turn again to the Jägers, who emphasize the closed character of the local elite milieus. They are well aware of the fact that while they may fit into this neighborhood in terms of ethnicity and income, they do not fit classwise. Their elite lifestyle depends on their expatriate package and, therefore, is limited to the period of their assignment. They are also well aware of their neighbors' reservation with regard to this temporal character of their elite status. Hence, in constructing these elite spaces, the expatriates do not situate themselves at the center of these spaces, but in the periphery. As members of a transitory elite, they only inhabit the fringes of these elite spaces.

Secondly, the same applies to the work space. Here again, the expatriates position themselves and are perceived by their coworkers as transitory colleagues. Hence, notwithstanding their powerful hierarchical positions in the formal organization structure, they position themselves on the fringes of their work spaces, as visiting guests who in fact belong to a different work space—namely, the headquarters—and will return there after their stint.

The third reason refers back to a topic that we have already discussed with regard to the Chinese localities and their social structure. In the U.S. localities, we also witnessed large MNCs, employers of the expatriates, delegating larger numbers of expatriates and organizing socializing events and leisure activities exclusively for 'their' expatriates. So, in these cases, too, an opportunity structure was in place that supported restricting sociabilities to expatriate colleagues from one's own employer company and their families. Note that we witness an organizational rather than a host country or locality effect here.[22] Hence, the local expatriate community, even in this subsample, again represents the most important reference group and pool of people with whom to establish contacts and even friendships.

On the other hand, the spatial proximities, day-to-day encounters with locals, and certainly English as a common language still allow for—at least selectively—establishing contacts with locals, even though they do not go beyond loose acquaintances for the most part. Hence, the third type of network developed earlier—i.e., the network comprising locals, which we could only observe in one exceptional case in China—is much more common in the U.S. The perception of not belonging into the local elite milieus and the reservation of their neighbors in the case of the German expatriates in the U.S. notwithstanding, their social networks were restricted neither to a national German nor to an expatriate community. The Jägers, for example, with their children as brokers, were indeed able to establish closer contact to some of their local U.S.-American subdivision neighbors who also had children. And through membership with the tennis team of their country club, Mr. Jäger has befriended some fellow local U.S.-American players.

Hence, differently than in China, in the U.S. localities where expatriates from our sample were posted, we witness spaces that are differentiated class-wise (and race-wise), but not in terms of nationality. Thus, these spaces include host country nationals and, hence, support different forms of sociabilities than witnessed in China, even despite the internal structure and disparities of these spaces.

Space Making and Practicing Cosmopolitanism in the U.S

Compared to the Chinese host localities, the properties of the U.S.-American localities as reconstructed above do not support spatial segregation from the host population to the same extent with regard to dwelling and leisure spaces. On the contrary, the class-wise and ethnicity-wise structured housing market, combined with well-equipped expatriate packages allows for selecting residences within wealthy U.S.-American neighborhoods. Additionally, English as a common language allows expatriates to participate in the everyday life of their host society. However, the properties of the U.S. as a host country and of U.S. host localities suggest a kind of space-making in which the expatriates position themselves on the fringes. Given that cities in the U.S. are characterized by strong income-based and ethnicity-based spatial segregation of neighborhoods, expatriates orientate themselves along these divides when looking for suitable places of residence and try to fit into their new neighborhoods in terms of income and ethnicity. At the same time, they try to avoid unsafe and threatening areas.[23] Yet dwelling, leisure, and working spaces are 'contaminated' by the notion of temporary residence and temporary elite status (see Chapter 5). In this case, the expatriates did not feel that they really belonged where they lived class-wise or in terms of social structure. This constellation entails sociabilities that only selectively include host country nationals and mainly build on peer expatriates, mostly from the same home country. However, compared with the secludedness and often national/ethnical exclusiveness of the expatriate 'bubbles' in China, sociabilities of expatriates from Germany delegated to the U.S. are more open.

The same applies to the working spaces as constructed by the expatriates. The images they have of their host country, its population, and the design and outlook of the subsidiary offices do not support hierarchical or—as witnessed in China—even neocolonial distancing. Instead, the expatriates also position themselves as visiting guests in their working spaces—and hence refrain from establishing close sociabilities with their local colleagues.

As regards the forms of attachment and belonging resulting from the peripheral positioning, most of the German expatriates and their spouses delegated to the U.S. take up positions as 'long-term tourists.' All in all, their lifestyle is oriented along leisure time more than it was in Germany. Hence, in the case of German expatriates in the U.S., there is also a search for experiencing 'difference' in a tourist manner. However, for the U.S., these expatriates (and their spouses) perceive the leisure culture and opportunities as being very different from those at home. Thus, they happily embrace the possibilities that their host localities offer in this regard, from having a private pool and being members of a local sports club, to undertaking weekend trips to beaches and other leisure destinations.

Forms of attachment, thus, are tourist, temporary, and ephemeral, and forms of flexible belonging typically refer to their host localities as sites of "permanent vacation" (as several put it)—a paradoxical notion that already carries the semantic of dis-attachment with it. In this case, cosmopolitanism is practiced in the form of participating in the 'U.S.-American leisure culture' for a limited period of time.

Properties of Host Country Germany and German Host Localities

Finally, we now analyze the properties of Germany as a host country and of the German localities where expatriates from this subsample were posted, including the ways in which they use these properties for their space-making.[24]

The U.S. expatriates posted in Germany from our sample had been delegated to different areas and cities in Germany. None had been posted in Berlin, Frankfurt, or Hamburg, which are perhaps the only German cities that could be termed (second order) global cities. One expatriate had been delegated to a relatively larger city in Germany; the others were posted in more remote areas and small towns. In each of these host localities, however, smaller or larger U.S. expatriate communities were in place, not least because of the U.S. military personnel stationed in these respective areas.[25]

Images of 'Germany'

In the case of U.S.-American expatriates posted in Germany, we also witnessed a segmented image of their host country. This image, again, consisted of three different and partly contradictory segments.

First of all, interestingly, the majority of the expatriates posted in Germany pointed to its recent history when asked to give their reasons for this decision. They perceived Germany, and especially Berlin, to be *the* hotspot of direct clashing between the two world powers. German reunification was perceived to represent major historical shifts and changes. Mr. Fisher, for example, intimates to us,

> In the early '90s, when the former Soviet Union fell apart, yeah, I was working for an American MNC, and one of the reasons I came over to Germany at that time was because I was actually one of those people who said 'the wall's gonna fall,' (. . .) and back in 1989 I got a phone call from a gentleman who was looking to find American managers who wanted to work overseas, it's just being in the right place at the right time.

Hence, the image of Germany is one of a politically exciting place featuring a major historical and geopolitical shift.

Secondly, the U.S.-American expatriates perceive Germany as being just one part of Europe. Being stationed in Germany meant also being able to visit other European countries, and, thus, experience 'good old Europe' as a whole. Searching for 'difference' in a tourist manner as the main mode of attachment, thus, also applies to the U.S.-American expatriates posted in Germany. The Carters, for example, tell us that they want to make use of their stint to visit and experience as many tourist features and destinations as possible. For the them, Italy, Salzburg, Vienna, and Prague can all be reached within a few hours by car. The family had already visited all of these cities for sightseeing tours, and, as they told us, they were planning to visit more. For Mr. Carter, all of Europe is right at his doorstep. The Carters add that these trips represent a very important and unforgettable experience for the children, too.

In the case of Germany, as part of 'old Europe,' the U.S.-American expatriates perceive the main difference to their home country to be the historic features, with ancient cities dating back to the Medieval Ages, such as Prague, with Paris as the place of the French Revolution, and with Berlin as a hotspot where German and even post-war European history can be studied in a nutshell, and they experience this difference in weekend and holiday trips to these European hotspots dripping with history.

And finally, on their stints, the U.S.-American expatriates develop the image of a very calm, nice, and secure place to stay—as nothing special. The Carters, for example, tell us that in Germany people prefer to walk short distances instead of taking the car. Mr. Carter walks the children to school and kindergarten. Their daughter, already a school-aged, can even go on her own to visit friends in the neighborhood. They have also gotten to know the balance bike, something they had never come across back in the U.S. They think it is a brilliant invention, because it allows the family to undertake longer walks without the children getting tired. They anticipate not being able to practice this kind of short distance mobility and leisure practice back in the U.S., and they find this very regrettable. They say that it is much more necessary to look after the children in the U.S., whereas they perceive Germany to be an extremely secure country. Some activities are completely unusual there—such as riding the bike—or are even impossible to practice, such as letting the children go visit their friends on their own. Thus, they construct an 'ordinary everyday German space' that is perceived as being calm and secure and also generally working in slow motion.

The biggest challenge confronting U.S.-American expatriates with Germany as host country is the language barrier. Most of the expatriates posted there, however, had a very good command of German so that the language barrier represented an obstacle mainly for the trailing spouses (see Chapter 6). Beside this, the U.S.-American expatriates did not report any challenges or adventurous traits attached to their host country, such as the expatriates posted in China did.

In the next subchapter, we will investigate how these images interfere with social and material properties of Germany as a host country and how the specific localities where the expatriates from our sample are posted shape expatriates' cosmopolitan practices.

Material-Symbolic Properties

Focusing at first again on the dwelling spaces, we can observe that the U.S.-American expatriates from our sample posted in Germany were living in neither gated communities or compounds nor in elite subdivisions, but instead lived in *ordinary German upper-class or middle-class neighborhoods*. Most of the expatriates of our sample—due to their specific (impatriate or 'local hire') contracts—do not dispose over a comprehensive expatriate package. Thus, they do not have extra benefits that would lift them up class-wise in terms of income, housing standards, and consumption opportunities, as is the case for their counterparts posted in the U.S. or in China. Hence, they do not have the budget to choose luxurious housing. Host country Germany also does not offer compounds or mansions in gated communities or subdivisions, as China and the U.S. do. Whereas German cities certainly also feature socially differentiated and segregated urban districts, these are not as secluded and isolated from one another as is the case for compounds in China and in the subdivisions of the U.S. where the expatriate managers of our sample were living. Entry gates, for example, are completely missing.

The Carters, already introduced in detail in Chapter 6, are a good case example. The family lives in an ordinary single-family house in a typical German residential area. The urban district is situated on the fringes of one of the largest German cities; there is a church, there are middle-class houses, and it has an altogether calm atmosphere. There are a number of sports clubs, like the tennis club where the Carter children take tennis lessons, several kindergartens, and a primary school. Most of their neighbors are German, and the Carters fit into this area very well class-wise. Hence, drawing upon the relatively leveled social and spatial structure of German cities, the expatriates construct 'ordinary integrated dwelling spaces.'

Expatriates with children have been sending them to local schools. And again, other than in the case of the German expatriates in the U.S., these are not elite private schools but are instead *ordinary public schools.*

With regard to their consumption spaces, the same that has been said for the German expatriates in the U.S. applies to U.S.-American expatriates posted in Germany: They also obtained their everyday supplies from local shops and supermarkets and did not report any difficulties in finding what they wanted. This is here, hence, also a Global North consumption space.

With regard to working spaces, we did not observe any strategies and practices to make the workplace like in the home country—as we did in China. Instead, same as with the German expatriates in the U.S., the U.S.-American expatriates smoothly integrated themselves into their host working spaces that were perceived as representing 'Western' or 'Global North' standards.

In the next subchapter, we investigate the consequences of these findings for the kinds of Others chosen by expatriates to populate their spaces.

Social Structure and Its Spatial Arrangement

As was the case for the German expatriates in the U.S., we also witness that the sociabilities of the U.S.-American expatriates in Germany, their spatial integration into the host localities notwithstanding, only selectively and in a more or less ephemeral way include host country nationals. Instead, in this case, too, their sociabilities rely strongly on home country nationals and also, to some extent, third country nationals—i.e., they take place within an international community.

First, one major reason why expatriates orientate themselves toward their own national peers is the language barrier. The Carters are an example in case. Whereas Mrs. Carter has a very good command of German, she is not able to engage very much in making acquaintances because her management job is very demanding and keeps her in the office until late in the evening and also requires her to frequently go on business trips to the U.S. Additionally, Mr. Carter does not speak German. Even though he takes online courses, he has not succeeded in acquiring a sufficient command of German, which would allow him to participate in chats and gatherings with the German people he meets at his children's school and kindergarten or in the neighborhood. Thus, his primary networks and spaces of interaction are with a Hungarian woman, who speaks English and has been very helpful to him; his local church, which is headed by an U.S.-American pastor; and a couple of U.S.-American families who are also members of the church.

All of the localities where expatriates from this subsample were posted are home to larger expatriate communities or groups of home country nationals, either because their employer MNCs had several U.S.-American expatriates on-site, or because the locality hosted U.S. military, or because the host locality was a major economic hub hosting a larger number of MNCs and, therefore, numerous expatriates. Hence, findings are the same as for the German expatriates posted in the U.S.: Even though the spaces constructed by the expatriates embrace host country nationals, the latter are positioned at arms-length distance and are only very selectively and ephemerally included into the sociabilities of these expatriates.

Space Making and Practicing Cosmopolitanism in Germany

As we have seen, the properties of Germany as a host country and the German localities where expatriates were posted support firm spatial and social integration into the host society. Dwelling and leisure spaces are not—as has been witnessed for China—segregated from the host population and are also not segregated class-wise to the same degree as witnessed in the U.S. The images expatriates have of their host country and localities are also quite positive, and—like in the case of the U.S.—do not support hierarchical distancing. Therefore, sociabilities including host country nationals are supported. On the other hand, language is an important barrier to such kinds of sociabilities. Even though English is taught in all German schools as the first foreign language and, thus, all Germans dispose over at least a basic command of English, this does not suffice for establishing close friendships and often also does not even allow for managing daily problems like visiting the doctor or attending consultation hours at the children's school. Consequently, spatial and social integration into the host society notwithstanding, the U.S.-American expatriates from our sample have established sociabilities that only selectively include host country nationals. Contacts to German colleagues and neighbors remained ephemeral, and the expatriates strongly relied on peer expatriates from their own home country.

Even though the U.S.-American expatriates posted in Germany experienced their host country (and wider Europe) in a tourist manner, due to their spatial and social integration into the ordinary German everyday life, most of them still embraced and adopted some practices they had gotten to know on their assignments that they identified as 'typically German.' Yet other than observed in the U.S., these elements are not embraced for the purpose of being detached from ordinary everyday life on a temporary basis, like a vacation, but are instead seen as elements of a different ordinary life, elements that could be permanently integrated into one's own everyday life, even after returning home. The Carters, for example, very much liked to bike ride or to walk short distances instead of taking the car, and they would like to integrate these practices into their everyday life when they are back in the U.S. They also want their children to take German classes back in the U.S. in order to sustain the very good command of German they developed on the stint. Hence, they have multiple attachments and flexible forms of belonging. Cosmopolitanism, thus, is practiced in the form of a 'hybrid everyday life,' i.e., integrating one's own usual/common (home country) practices, such as celebrating Thanksgiving and cooking Mexican food, with those practices identified as being 'German,' such as bike riding or walking short distances.

Conclusion

In this chapter, we have comparatively reconstructed the imaginative, material-symbolic, and social-structural properties of the three host countries China, the U.S., and Germany and the respective host localities expatriates from our sample enacted in space-making processes. We have been able to show that these space-making practices differ for each host country in typical ways. We have also shown that these typical differences in space-making result in different types of practiced cosmopolitanism by expatriates posted in the three different host countries.

Comparing the ways in which expatriates in the three host countries experience and attach themselves to their host localities, we can conclude that all of them enjoy and make use of that which they perceive as being 'different' to their home countries and towns: China is perceived as being the most different host country compared to Germany or the U.S.; in some respects, it is positively evaluated as being exotic, exciting, and challenging. In other respects, however, it is devalued as being backward, uncivilized, and unbearable. The U.S. and Germany, on the other hand, are perceived as being different enough to make new experiences possible but similar enough to not represent a major challenge. Both of these host countries are perceived in terms of stereotyped images that have been shaped for decades by movies and narratives distributed by the media and are, therefore, familiar and not at all 'exotic' or 'alien.' The expatriates here also enact images of the respective host countries as tourist places. However, this image in the case of the U.S., in contrast to China, refers to a young, modern, and mainly leisure and fun-oriented culture, reflected in sightseeing destinations like Las Vegas and beaches. Germany as a host country, for one, is perceived as part of Europe as a whole and equated with a medieval and renaissance history, reflected in sightseeing destinations like Prague, Vienna, and Paris. Additionally, it is also perceived as a hotspot of contemporary history with regard to the fall of the 'iron curtain' and the restructuring of the world political geography in the aftermath of this event.

Besides these different images, the three host countries and the respective host localities also feature very different material-symbolic and social-structural properties, which, in turn, are enacted by expatriates in processes of space-making. And the different types of spaces enacted by the expatriates posted in the three different host countries not only support different *degrees*, but different *types* of practiced cosmopolitanisms.

Social segregation in the U.S. and Germany is not as extensive and all-encompassing as it is in China, for example. Most of the expatriates in the U.S. and in Germany had at least *some* contacts with host country nationals, be it practicing sports together with local peers or frequently talking to neighbors, even though their main reference group was still expatriates of their same nationality. These frequent and selective contacts are not only possible because of the missing spatial segregation but also because language is not a barrier to the same extent as it is in China. Secondly, and most importantly, social segregation was not based on neocolonial images of the Others. This is also reflected in their evaluations of local work and management practices (see Chapter 8). Whereas most of the expatriates in China devalued Chinese practices at the workplace, German expatriates in the U.S. as well as U.S.-American expatriates in Germany noted differences in the work practices and management styles, but did not, however, devalue them to the same extend as expatriates posted in China, and did not first and foremost conceive of them in national-cultural terms (as in China), but instead in organizational terms—i.e., differentiating between a headquarters culture and a subsidiary culture. Interactions with local colleagues at the workplace, thus, were not characterized by neocolonial positionings (see Chapter 8).

For expatriates posted in China, forms of multiple attachments and flexible belonging can only be observed with regard to the glamour zones of the global cities seen as 'not being China.' The properties of host country China and Chinese host localities generally strongly support the realization of an expatriate 'bubble' life.' Where practiced cosmopolitanism can be observed, it typically does not draw on properties perceived as Chinese, but instead draws on exactly those properties of the global cities that are perceived as not being China, but as global. Hence, China as a host country and the Chinese host localities suggest a specific type of cosmopolitanism: a *disembedded urban cosmopolitanism* that is practiced within the non-Chinese global spaces of global cities and could equally as well be practiced in global cities elsewhere in the world.

Attachments to the U.S. and Germany as host countries, however, build on the perception of the host localities as ordinary places to live among the local population. This applies, however, more to Germany than to the U.S. Local shops, restaurants, bars, transportation services, etc. are used without hesitation and are smoothly integrated into everyday life on the stint. Several traits of everyday life in the host countries Germany and the U.S. are welcomed and embraced.

The U.S. and Germany and the respective host localities, however, support two clearly different types of practiced cosmopolitanisms: In the U.S., practiced *cosmopolitanism* typically *builds on orientations and practices* related to *leisure*, and is *structured sequentially*—i.e., life at home and life on the stint are perceived as two different and separate phases. The perception of the stint as a "permanent vacation" stresses that the expatriates will be returning to their ordinary lives back home in Germany after their stints.

On the contrary, practiced cosmopolitanism in Germany refers to permanently integrating practices from home with practices learned on the stint. This type of cosmopolitanism can be termed *integrated* or *hybrid cosmopolitanism*.

To sum up, our comparative reconstruction of the properties of the three host countries enacted in space-making processes has revealed three different country-specific types of practiced cosmopolitanism shaped by these spaces and the properties incorporated within them. However, with regard to space-making practices and impacts on practicing cosmopolitanism, our findings indicate that the differences between localities in China and localities in the other two host countries are much more important than those between localities in Germany and the U.S. It is important to note here that accentuated in theoretical terms, our sample with expatriates posted in *three* different host countries only represent *two different configurations*: (1) expatriates from the Global North posted in a host country in the Global South and (2) expatriates from the Global North posted in a host country equally being part of the Global North. In this chapter, we have shown that imaginative, material-symbolic, and social-structural properties typically in place in countries of the Global South tend to prompt 'bubble' life' practices (at least with Western expatriates) more than cosmopolitan ones. And those traits of cosmopolitanism that can still be observed here are either performed in tourist or in global spaces. Both of these spaces, however, are *disembedded* and secluded from the spaces of ordinary life of the host population. Contrastingly, imaginative, material-symbolic, and social-structural properties in place in countries of the Global North support types of cosmopolitan practices that are performed in spaces shared with (a specific strata of) the host population and based on eye-level encounters with the Other.

Notes

1 Sometimes, the construction of the sample simply necessitates including expatriates from different home countries or in different host countries because the sample would otherwise be too small. An example in case is the study of Petison and Johri (2008) who conducted seven case studies with international automobile manufacturers in Thailand. The aim of their study was "to analyze the role of expatriate managers in the growth of subsidiaries located in Thailand—a developing country with a relatively recent experience in modern industrial development" (745). "The multiple cases method was used to get rich information via replication, in order to reveal common patterns across the multiple cases" (745). Note that a comparative design does not underlie this study. See also Peterson (2003), Nowicka (Nowicka 2006); Fechter (2007), and Lauring and Selmer (2009). See also Meier's summary of the literature with regard to assessing impacts of specific host localities (2016, 487).

2 Peterson, Napier, and Won Shul-Shim (2000), for example, observe "at least three fairly distinct models of expatriate management and corporate-foreign-subsidiary control"—an Anglo-American, a Japanese, and a German variation (Peterson, Napier, and Shul-Shim 2000, 145). And the study of Beaverstock (2004) investigating expatriation strategies of London-headquartered

professional service legal firms that were expatriating to the financial centers in North America, Europe, and East Asia revealed that in East Asia, "expatriation followed a 'Multinational' typology, characterized by one-way knowledge diffusion from London and a demarcation of labour where expatriates manage offices, departments and teams. In contrast, expatriation in Europe and North America reflected a 'Transnational' typology, where knowledge was developed and diffused in a network of relationships" (ibid., 157).

3 Meier (2016) asserts that there is a "dearth of research which analyses the specific effects of locality" (487).

4 For a critical account of the so-called container-model of space, see Löw (2001); Nowicka (2006); Schroer (2009).

5 All cited authors draw upon Giddens's theory of structuration here, and point to the duality of structure and also of space. See Löw (2013, 725): "Spatial structures must, like all structures, be realized through action whilst at the time structuring that action. The duality of action and structure can thus also be expressed as the *duality of space*. This means that spatial structures bring about a form of action that, in the constitution of space, reproduces precisely those spatial structures" (emphasis in original).

6 Meier, in his study (2015) reconstructs the contrasting images of London as "a confusing and 'gigantic behemoth' of a city where they must come to terms with an identity-related feeling of a permanent danger of interpersonal boundary transgressions" (64) and of Singapore as "a safe 'city of social harmony'" (66), or of London as an old empire and "center of the (financial) world" versus Singapore as an outpost with colonial past.

7 See Chapter 8 on dealing with difference at work.

8 Without expatriates originating from Hong Kong, Macao, and Taiwan.

9 See http://china.org.cn/top10/2011-06/10/content_22756927.htm: "A total of 593,832 foreigners were living and working on the Chinese mainland by November 1, 2010, according to the sixth national census data released by the National Bureau of Statistics of China (NBS) late in April"; 14,446 of them originated from Germany (rank 9) and 71,493 from the U.S. (rank 2; Korea = rank 1).

10 As can be explicitly or implicitly identified in the statements of the expatriates from our sample, these images are derived from the media, from specific expatriate sites on the internet (see, for example, the HSBC 2015 survey elaborating on expatriates' complaints regarding the deterioration of their quality of life on their stints in China (http://ig.ft.com/sites/2015/special-reports/shanghai/)).

11 Mr. Pätzold, for example, who has been delegated to the U.S. and would never consider going to China, says about the location of his company's Chinese subsidiary that it "is a ten million people city, but like all of them are. It is so dirty, and people's behavior is even worse than in Beijing. And the quality of life is zero, really zero." He asserts that he does not know anybody who likes to live in China and that all expatriates who accept to go there do it because of career expectations. He terms a stint in China "a sour drop" that people agree to eat in order to get promoted afterward.

12 This aligns with a new strand in urban sociology, the so-called intrinsic logic of cities (Eigenlogik von Städten) approach (Löw 2012): Löw stresses that the "city can hence be considered an important context for sociation alongside global and national frames of reference" (Löw 2012, 304)—i.e., they "offer a form of sociation basically distinct from that of the nation state" (ibid.). Within this approach, cities are considered "entities of meaning" (Löw 2012, 304). Löw posits that "the ascendance and reproduction of practices and structures are specific to their city" (ibid., 308).

13 This is very clearly exemplified by Mr. Winkelmann, who commented, "And now we are leaving China," when we drove into the compound where he and his family were living (see Chapter 5).

14 See Meier (2015), who states the same for Singapore as being an important precondition for the residential decisions and practices of expatriates.

15 For these two features also see Meier (2015, 2016)

16 Note, however, that in our era of globalization, there is no such thing as a purely 'national' pattern of consumption; product ranges and services even in the home countries of the Global North are 'globalized' (see the notion of "Mcdonaldization" (Ritzer 1993).

17 See the case of the Winkelmanns, who participated in one such international congregation (see Chapter 5).

18 Another case example of trying to establish transnational sociabilities including host country nationals are the Kellys, as elaborated in Chapter 5. The Kellys have shown a strong willingness to immerse into the host society and to expose themselves and their children to the local Others. However, their children had severe problems in the Chinese school and they had to let them change to the International school. They also did not succeed in making friends within their Chinese neighborhood—due to a lacking command of Chinese and class distance (see Chapter 5).

19 See www.internations.org/usa-expats/guide/16555-introduction-key-facts/demo graphics-of-the-us-16552: "Temporary workers and their families made up 5.7% of nonimmigrant admissions to the US in 2012, amounting to a total of some 3 million people. Another 144,000 people were granted employment-based preference (i.e., permanent residency). Diplomatic staff accounted for some 365,000 entries. Obviously, the earlier figures cannot account for the number of expatriates already in the country at any given time. However, it is safe to say that no matter where your expat assignment might take you, you will be able to find established expat circles in your vicinity."

20 An expression that Mrs. Schwartz has used when differentiating the subdivision where she and her family reside against other neighborhoods of the city.

21 Although the cities where the expatriates from this subsample were posted were predominantly African American with regard to their proportion of the whole population, the expatriates were living in exclusively 'white' neighborhoods. Some commented on this by expressing that racial segregation is a quite strange phenomenon to them, but has to be accepted as a property of the U.S.-American society.

22 For the differentiation of societal effects, globalization effects, and organizational effects see Mueller (1994)

23 See Meier (2015) who describes the same strategies for expatriates' dwelling practices in London.

24 Before we continue, we have to point to the fact that our subsample of U.S.-American expatriate managers posted in Germany is partly characterized by features that differentiate it from the other subsamples: Most of the managers in this subsample are not expatriates in the narrow sense that they have been assigned to a German subsidiary of their U.S.-American employer for a limited period of time. Instead, two of these expatriates are 'impatriates'—i.e., they are employed at the U.S.-American subsidiary of a German MNC and have been assigned to the German headquarters for a limited period of time in order to work in projects related to their home organization. Another expatriate is a so-called 'local hire', i.e., he had already lived in Germany before his current employment with a German medium-sized company, and—as he is married to a German wife and raising his children in Germany—has been looking for a job on the German job market. However, he had been working for an U.S.-American MNC at an earlier stage of his career and was previously assigned to the German subsidiary of this MNC. Only two of the expatriate managers from this subsample are expatriates in the sense that they are employed at an U.S.-American MNC and have been assigned to the German subsidiary of their employer. However, both

of these managers have strong relations to their host country: One is married to a German wife and raising his children in Germany, the other originates from a family with very international outlook and has been living in Germany before his actual assignment. Note that neither 'local hires' or localized expatriates nor 'impatriates' dispose over an expatriate package as rich and comprehensive as expatriates in the narrow sense do. This considerably influences the ways that these 'expatriates' live in and attach themselves to their host localities.

25 All in all, in the year 2015, 251,000 U.S.-American citizens were registered as living in Germany.

Bibliography

Beaverstock, Jonathan. 2004. "'Managing Across Borders': Knowledge Management and Expatriation in Professional Service Legal Firms." *Journal of Economic Geography* 4 (2): 157–79. doi:10.1093/jeg/4.2.157.

Boyacigiller, Nakiye. 1990. "The Role of Expatriates in the Management of Interdependence, Complexity and Risk in Multinational Corporations." *Journal of International Business Studies* 21 (3): 357. doi:10.1057/palgrave.jibs.8490825

Dörrenbächer, Christoph, and Mike Geppert. 2006. "Micro-Politics and Conflicts in Multinational Corporations: Current Debates, Re-Framing, and Contributions of this Special Issue." *Journal of International Management* 12 (3): 251–65. doi:10.1016/j.intman.2006.07.001.

Fechter, Anne-Meike. 2007. *Transnational Lives: Expatriates in Indonesia*. Aldershot and Burlington: Ashgate.

Geppert, Mike, Dirk Matten, and Peter Walgenbach. 2006. "Transnational Institution Building and the Multinational Corporation: An Emerging Field of Research." *Human Relations* 59 (11): 1451–65. doi:10.1177/0018726706072888.

Glasze, Georg, and Abdallah Alkhayyal. 2002. "Gated Housing Estates in the Arab World: Case Studies in Lebanon and Riyadh, Saudi Arabia." *Environment and Planning B: Planning and Design* 29: 321–36. doi:10.1068/b12825t

Hannerz, Ulf. 1990. "Cosmopolitans and Locals in World Culture." *Theory, Culture & Society* 7 (2): 237–51. doi:10.1177/026327690007002014.

Hannerz, Ulf. 2011. "Kosmopolitismus." In *Lexikon der Globalisierung*, edited by Fernand Kreff, Eva-Maria Knoll, and Andre Gingrich, 197–201. Bielefeld: Transcript.

Harzing, Anne-Wil. 2001. "Who's in Charge? An Empirical Study of Executive Staffing Practices in Foreign Subsidiaries." *Human Resource Management* 40 (2): 139–58.

Lauring, Jakob, and Jan Selmer. 2009. "Expatriate Compound Living: An Ethnographic Field Study." *The International Journal of Human Resource Management* 20 (7): 1451–67. doi:10.1080/09585190902983215.

Löw, Martina. 2001. *Raumsoziologie*. Frankfurt/Main: Suhrkamp.

Löw, Martina. 2012. "The Intrinsic Logic of Cities: Towards a New Theory on Urbanism." *Urban Research & Practice* 5 (3): 303–15. doi:10.1080/17535069.2012.727545.

Löw, Martina. 2013. "The Emergence of Space Through the Interplay of Action and Structures." In *D.A: A Transdisciplinary Handbook of Design Anthropology*, edited by Yana Milev, 714–27. Frankfurt/Main: Peter Lang.

Maurice, Marc. 1991. "Methodologische Aspekte internationaler Vergleiche: Zum Ansatz des gesellschaftlichen Effekts." In *International vergleichende Organisationsforschung: Fragestellungen, Methoden und Ergebnisse ausgewählter Untersuchungen*, edited by Martin Heidenreich and Gert Schmidt, 82–90. Opladen, Wiesbaden: Westdeutscher Verlag.

Meier, Lars. 2015. "Learning the City by Experiences and Images: German Finance Managers' Encounters in London and Singapore." In *Migrant Professionals in the City: Local Encounters, Identities and Inequalities*, edited by Lars Meier, 59–74. New York: Routledge.

Meier, Lars. 2016. "Dwelling in Different Localities: Identity Performances of a White Transnational Professional Elite in the City of London and the Central Business District of Singapore." *Cultural Studies* 30 (3): 483–505. doi:10.1080/0 9502386.2015.1113636.

Mueller, F. 1994. "Societal Effect, Organizational Effect and Globalization." *Organization Studies* 15 (3): 407–28. doi:10.1177/017084069401500305.

Nowicka, Magdalena. 2006. *Transnational Professionals and Their Cosmopolitan Universes*. Frankfurt/Main and New York: Campus.

Peterson, Richard B. 2003. "The Use of Expatriates and Inpatriates in Central and Eastern Europe Since the Wall Came Down." *Journal of World Business* 38 (1): 55–69. doi:10.1016/S1090-9516(02)00109-8

Peterson, Richard B., Nancy K. Napier, and Won Shul-Shim. 2000. "Expatriate Management: Comparison of MNCs Across Four Parent Countries." *Thunderbird International Business Review* 42 (2): 145–66. doi:10.1002/1520-6874(200003/04) 42:23.0.CO;2-N

Petison, Phallapa, and Lalit Johri. 2008. "Managing Local Employees: Expatriate Roles in a Subsidiary." *Management Decision* 46 (5): 743–60. doi:10.1108/ 00251740810873743.

Ritzer, George. 1993. *The McDonaldization of Society: An Investigation into the Changing Character of Contemporary Social Life*. Thousand Oaks: Pine Forge Press.

Sassen, Saskia. 2001. "Global City: Einführung in ein Konzept und seine Geschichte." *Peripherie* 81/82: 10–31.

Schroer, Markus. 2009. *Räume, Orte, Grenzen: Auf dem Weg zu einer Soziologie des Raums*. Frankfurt/Main: Suhrkamp.

Sorge, A. 1991. "Strategic Fit and the Societal Effect: Interpreting Cross-National Comparisons of Technology, Organization and Human Resources." *Organization Studies* 12 (2): 161–90. doi:10.1177/017084069101200201.

Stadlbauer, Johanna. 2016. "Privilegierte Migration und Geschlechterverhältnisse: Expatriate Spouses in Österreich." In *Migration und Integration – wissenschaftliche Perspektiven aus Österreich*, edited by Jennifer Carvill Schellenbacher, Julia Dahlvik, Heinz Fassmann, and Christoph Reinprecht, 167–82. Vienna: Vienna University Press.

Tungli, Zsuzsanna, and Maury Peiperl. 2009. "Expatriate Practices in German, Japanese, U.K., and U.S. Multinational Companies: A Comparative

Survey of Changes." *Human Resource Management* 48 (1): 153–71. doi:10.1002/hrm.20271.

van Bochove, Marianne, and Godfried Engbersen. 2013. "Beyond Cosmopolitanism and Expat Bubbles: Challenging Dominant Representations of Knowledge Workers and Trailing Spouses." *Population, Space and Place* 1 (4): 295–309. doi:10.1002/psp.1839.

Whitley, Richard. 1999. *Divergent Capitalisms: The Social Structuring and Change of Business Systems*. Oxford and New York: Oxford University Press.

10 Conclusion

The Paradoxes of Practiced Elite Cosmopolitanism

Anna Spiegel

With this book, we endeavored to understand and to further theorize the practiced cosmopolitanism (Nowicka and Rovisco 2009a) of corporate expatriates. We put the social figure of *the expatriate manager* center stage, as the expatriate manager is a core protagonist in economic globalization and the management of MNCs and represents a specific form of global mobility—namely, a privileged and organized mobility. The book is, thus, situated within the ongoing scholarly debate about the relationship between mobility and cosmopolitanism (Amit 2015; Amit and Barber 2015), both considered key characteristics of the second modernity (Beck 2006; Urry 2007; Beck 2009; Elliott and Urry 2010).

Classical sociology already assumed a direct relationship between mobility, the experience of being a stranger, and the emergence of objectivity and cosmopolitan reflexivity (Schütz 1944; Simmel 1950). Additionally, contemporary scholars have conceived of cosmopolitanism as a direct consequence of increased mobility and global connectivity (Szerszynski and Urry 2002, 2006; Beck 2009). However, doubts about this relationship are increasing. Specifically research from the field of migration and identity studies pleads that this connection should not be taken for granted and encourages instead a theoretical deconstruction of "teleological connections among mobility, transnational networks and cosmopolitanism" (Glick Schiller, Darieva, and Gruner-Domic 2011, 414). This question has particularly gained relevance in the context of economic and cultural globalization and increased transnational mobility of managers and cross-border careers, but is also subject to significant dispute, as elaborated on in Chapter 2. Scholars in mainstream management literature had argued that a new global business elite with cosmopolitan mindsets and homogeneous lifestyles emerged (Kanter 1995; Sklair 2001), whereas scholars from anthropology and sociology had highlighted the disconnection of those elites from their local surroundings, the 'bubble-like' everyday life within national expatriate communities, and their focus on maintaining social and symbolical boundaries to local 'Others.' Thus, the question of whether today's mobile professionals can be described as interculturally open and competent cosmopolitans or as pronounced anti-cosmopolitans represented a research gap, with a lack of empirical studies on the everyday junctures and disjunctures of mobility and cosmopolitanism.

This book addressed this question by building on intensive ethnographic case studies of expatriate managers, most of them high-ranking executives assigned to foreign subsidiaries to perform demanding coordination tasks within their MNCs. The ethnographic case studies of German and U.S.-American corporate expatriates show that the ways in which they deal with difference are far too complex to be subsumed under the polar opposites of being either cosmopolitans or anti-cosmopolitans. Everyday life—both inside and outside their work spaces—turned out to be highly ambivalent with highly self-contradictory ways of relating to cultural 'Others,' from openness to distantiation and repulsion. Our findings confirm that mobility does not automatically lead to cosmopolitan sociabilities (Glick Schiller, Darieva, and Gruner-Domic 2011, 404), but paradoxically, also leads to new "stoppages and fixities" (Beck 2009, 33). What became clear is that both closure and openness were related to the mobile lives of the corporate expatriates and their families. Our data thus strengthens the argument that empathy and reflexivity are not the only outcomes of mobility and diversity (Radice 2014; see Amit and Barber 2015). Based on such a conception of cosmopolitanism as one possible answer among others to the reshaping of everyday sociabilities and identities brought about by increased mobility, our research on the different contexts in which such specific answers are cultivated—professional and nonprofessional spheres, host countries in the Global North and the Global South, and different gender constellations—generated innovative empirical and theoretical contributions. These will be synthesized in the following.

Corporate Expatriates: Strangers or Autochthons?

Corporate expatriates differ from the figure of the classical stranger[1] in significant ways. They are caught in the paradoxical situation of simultaneously being strangers and autochthons. In classical sociology, the stranger was conceived of as someone who had left his country and who now "tries to be permanently accepted or at least tolerated by the group which he approaches" (Schütz 1944, 499). In this situation, objectivity and cosmopolitan reflexivity emerge out of the stranger's necessity to engage in interactions with the locals. The stranger is forced to engage in such a process of seeking an understanding of the group's cultural patterns because he does not possess a valid social position within the group he approaches and would otherwise stay socially isolated. This process of engagement, which his marginal position forces him to do, however, fundamentally calls into question the stranger's taken-for-granted knowledge of the world. The stranger's 'thinking as usual' that he applied at home in order to understand others' actions and to guide his own actions proves to be no longer valid in the new context. Also, he experiences that his knowledge *about* the Other is not compatible with the knowledge he needs in order to successfully interact *with* the 'Other.' His situation is characterized by an existential uncertainty and the unsettling experience of being "no longer permitted to consider himself as the center of his social environment" (ibid., 504). He moves in a social space with completely different rules and practices, in which he has to find a social position, which is meaningful for the locals as well as for himself. This crisis of being 'decentered' and socially dislocated, however, is the ground for the stranger's objectivity and cosmopolitan reflexivity. Within comparative interactions (Spiegel 2010, 291, 303–10) between one's own and alien cultural patterns he is able to reflect on the incoherence, inconsistency, and ambiguity of both interpretive frames which are hidden for the usual group members (Ossewaarde 2007, 370). The classical stranger was confronted with the impossible task of assimilating. He was confronted with the power of the locals to define the basic rules of social life. He was exposed to the disciplining actions of the locals and the nation state. He did not possess local knowledge and did not share the valid knowledge repertoires with the locals. The classical stranger was thus caught in a state of existential insecurity of not knowing what to do or how to act (Bauman 1991, 75). However, the expatriate managers in transitionally integrated MNCs researched in this book differ from classical sociology's image of the cosmopolitan stranger in significant ways.

First, corporate expatriates' mobility is characterized by a specific *temporality* that differs significantly from the one of the traditional stranger. They are not the 'men who come today and stay tomorrow' (Simmel 1950). They are not the men who leave tomorrow either. They are the men who come today, stay tomorrow, and leave maybe the day after tomorrow. Most of the managers in our sample did not aspire to settle down in the host locality, seeing it rather as a temporary and transient stay. These temporal patterns of the corporate managers are part of the general transformation of spatial and temporal patterns of sociabilities in the past decades. Liquidity (Bauman 2000, 2005), flexibility (Sennett 1999; Ong 2000), transience (Adler and Adler 1999), and mobility (Urry 2007; Elliott and Urry 2010) have been identified as key characteristics of postmodern life. Today, mobility and transience are no longer only associated with the marginalized and socially excluded, such as tramps, hobos, or nomads (Adler and Adler 1999), but, on the contrary, have become intrinsic modes of distinction and capital accumulation of the highly skilled postmodern workforce (Boltanski and Chiapello 2007). For many contemporary mobile people, mobility does not "entail a learning of how to be 'local' but how to be a particular kind of visitor" (Amit 2015, 564). This specific pattern of transience has, however, significant consequences for how the expatriate managers engage with local spaces. It reduces the necessity to engage with locals and to fully understand local cultural patterns and practices, be it inside or outside the workplace. Instead of engaging in a long lasting and potentially difficult learning process *with* the local Other in order to achieve and to understand local knowledge, they use networks with other expatriates within their national communities as a short cut for getting necessary information about the locality. As discussed in Chapter 6, these nationalized and gendered net-works were central for getting information about practical issues regarding the organization of the mobile families' everyday life, such as consumption, health, and schooling, and for, as suggested in Chapter 8, understanding unknown practices at the new workplace. The eminent role of other mobile conationals in the process of acquiring knowledge, however, significantly reconfigures their position in the host country. The shift from knowledge *about* the Other to knowledge acquired in interaction *with* the Other, which laid the ground for the evolvement of a cosmopolitan reflexivity, did not take place in the same way for the mobile managers as for the strangers imagined by Schütz.

Second, in the professional sphere, the corporate expatriates' *member-ship in transnational social spaces of MNCs* reconfigures and limits their position of being strangers. Modern corporate expatriates do not make the constitutive experience of existential uncertainty and of no longer being the center of their world to the same extent as the classic strangers. One could even go so far as to say they no longer occupy the position of a stranger at all. The situation of corporate expatriates from globally oper-ating MNCs cannot be adequately described with Schütz's vocabulary of moving between two opposed social or national worlds, their own and the local one. Their movement does not just take place between two nationally defined cultural spaces but is embedded into the transnational social space of their employing MNC. Although they move physically, they do not arrive at a social world totally different from. This dramatically changes the situ-ation, however. In the transnational social space of the MNC, expatriate managers do not act from a marginal, undefined or "border-case" (Schütz 1944, 504) position. In the subsidiary, they enjoy high status and usually occupy higher hierarchical positions than most of their local colleagues. Although confronted with different working practices, their professional taken-for-granted knowledge about how things *should* be done is not put into question in the same way as in the case of Schütz's stranger. They know how things *should* be done in order to be in accordance with the corporate world and culture. The practices familiar to them are, at least on a nor-mative level, the rules and practices that should also be adhered to at the spatially distant subsidiary. They are not confronted with existential uncer-tainty and the experience of being decentered, which was the basis for the cosmopolitan reflexivity of Schütz's strangers. Their position as a stranger is thus systematically reconfigured. However, as has been elaborated on in Chapter 7 and 9, the way their position as a stranger is reconfigured differed significantly between host countries located in the Global North and host countries located in the Global South. In the constellation where both headquarters and subsidiaries were located in the Global North, as in the cases of German corporate expatriates in the U.S. or U.S.-American corporate expatriates in Germany, the corporate expatriates' status as a stranger is limited, because at least initially, they conceived of themselves and the locals as belonging to the same cultural world. Expatriate managers initially constructed themselves *and* the local coworkers/subordinates as equally autochthon in the transnational social space of the MNC and did not expect pronounced differences. During the course of their assignment, however, when they realized there were conflicting work practices, they partially constructed themselves as autochthons of their corporate world and positioned the locals as strangers. Additionally, they were also confronted with locals who clearly positioned them as strangers. Yet their modes of dealing with these 'fellow autochthons who turned into strangers' were still inspired by collegial attitudes among equals. In the constellation containing a host country located in the Global South, as in the case for German and U.S.-American managers in China, the reconfiguration of the corporate expatriates' position was most radical, as the social positions of the autochthon and the stranger here were swapped. Expatriate executives, being representatives of the corporate culture, from the beginning constructed themselves as autochthonous to the company space and the locals as strangers and newcomers. Locals were thus put on marginal and inferior—real and symbolic—positions in a neocolonial manner and were even constructed as a threat to the quality of the transnational social space of the MNC. The many practices of avoiding, controlling, transforming, and displacing locals from the office space, as elaborated on in Chapter 8, are manifestations of this swap of positions.

Both of these reconfigurations of the corporate expatriates' status as stranger have far-reaching consequences for how expatriate managers relate to the local 'Other.' Because they do not automatically see themselves as being in the position of the stranger who ought to adapt, it is the task of the locals as strangers to adapt to the cultural patterns of the company space. In the modern MNC, the status of strangeness of the executives, despite their physical mobility, is partially eliminated. Other international organizations such as the UN have been described as enhancing cosmopolitan orientations and practices. As their very existence is based on the cosmopolitan idea, the cultural identity of the organization is not associated with just one nationality, and the work environment in which mobile professionals work is not limited to the opposition of 'home' and 'host' country nationals, but is rather constituted by multinational teams (Nowicka 2006; Nowicka and Kaweh 2009). The setup of a modern MNC in the global economy is significantly different. Despite the growing trend of taking up concepts like 'diversity' and 'cosmopolitanism' in management training, all of the MNCs in our sample had clear national identities, and the opposition at the workplace between home and host country nationals—of autochthons and strangers—and their working styles was striking. The cultural identities of the MNCs in which the corporate expatriates of our sample worked were not fully open to flexible interpretation. Our empirical research on expatriate managers of globally operating MNCs has suggested that MNCs do not provide their members a space for inclusive cosmopolitan sociability, as the inbuilt knowledge hierarchies between the headquarters and the subsidiary prevent such an egalitarian sociability.

Third, corporate expatriates' position as strangers in the private sphere is limited by their *membership in transitional expatriate communities*. Within the local space, they are indeed strangers, and in principle, they would have to approach the locality from Schütz's sense of learning. However, the experience of strangeness and of being socially and culturally dislocated in the private sphere is also limited. MNCs' mobility policies and the benefits they grant, as discussed in Chapter 4, play an essential role in this process of limiting the degree of strangeness for their corporate mobile workforce. Our findings indicate that the social positions of expatriate managers on their stints are shaped most significantly by the *global mobility policies* of MNCs. These *global mobility policies* allow MNCs to dispatch expatriates in large numbers to their numerous subsidiaries all over the world by *standardizing* and *routinizing* the assignment and relocation processes and by *homogenizing* their working and living conditions in the globally dispersed localities where they maintain operations. Our empirically based reconstructions of the lifeworlds and lifestyles of corporate expatriates have revealed that these lifestyles are indeed extensively privileged, affluent, and globally homogenous. All expatriate managers in our sample were much better off in terms of income, housing, and services at their disposal than before their assignments. They developed a leisure-oriented lifestyle and spent much more time on sports activities, traveling, and attending cultural events than at home. Moreover, this affluent lifestyle is largely homogenous for corporate expatriates, even in different localities and from different home countries, as the *global mobility policies* of MNCs, the management of expatriate compounds, and the global presence of the large European and U.S.-American retail chains work together to standardize income, housing, and consumption practices for expatriates and establish globalized "glamour zones" (Sassen 1998). These mobility policies must be interpreted as an attempt to limit the position of strangeness of corporate expatriates and to avoid extensive integration into the host country. The so-called home country approach is an obvious example of this attempt, as it explicitly aims at making the living conditions in the host country as similar as possible to those expatriate managers are familiar with from their home country. Thus, in their private life, mobile executives are never fully put into the position of the classic stranger; they always belong to their employing organization, and their everyday lives are shaped by this belonging to the organization, which equips them with resources and privileges setting them apart from the locals. In addition to the entanglement of work and private spheres through *global mobility policies*, also the infrastructure and specific institutions created by the host countries—in order to attract this specific segment of the highly qualified globally mobile workforce—such as segregated residential areas with a Western appearance in the case of China—limit their position of strangeness. In fact, the creation of such intermediary zones and enclaves turns the categories of strangers and autochthons upside down (see Chapter 9). Within such zones, expatriate executives attain the status of being autochthonous, whereas the local population is put into the marginal position of strangers. The perception of the residential compound as being located outside China, as elaborated on in Chapter 5, illustrates this changed position of corporate expatriates in a very vivid way. Such zones tend, however, to minimize hermeneutic problems of mobile people (Bauman 1991, 57) and reduce the potential for evolving cosmopolitan reflexivity. Additionally, the fact that corporate expatriates are part of transnational expatriate communities and do not live in isolation from conationals and other expatriates reduces the strangeness of expatriate executives and fosters the construction of the local 'Others' as strangers. The existence of expatriate communities with specific practices, spaces, and institutions overturns the situation of social isolation.

The above discussed shifts reconfigure the potential of the mobile situation for developing cosmopolitan reflexivity significantly. However, these reconfigurations are not complete, but only partial, and highly paradoxical. And they depend, as the comparative perspectives of Chapter 6 and 9 have shown, on gendered constellations of division of labor within the expatriate couples and on different host country contexts. Expatriate managers are not transformed into full-fledged anti-cosmopolitans but rather into inconsistent cosmopolitans. For example, although they represent the autochthons in the transnational space of the MNC, corporate expatriates do not hold the same position as the locals in the classic constellation of the local versus the stranger, as Schütz described it. Within the setting of the imagined community of the nation state, the kind of in-group Schütz had in mind, the autochthons did not need the stranger. However, in the transnational space of the MNC, expatriate managers are connected with their local, yet 'strange' coworkers and colleagues in multiple nets of micropolitical interdependencies. As shown in Chapters 7 and 8, they are "managers of local orders" (ibid., 14)—in the everyday sense of managing—and as such are involved in problem solving. They try to eliminate ambivalence— by modifying, controlling, and displacing it from the workplace—but are at the same time producing new ambivalences. In addition, global mobility policies of MNCs significantly shape but do not *determine* specific lifestyles and consumption patterns of expatriate managers. Institutional and material resources are only one component in the process of elite (re)production (Salverda and Abbink 2013, 4). They have to be seen as resources that are taken up by social actors who have specific agency. They are, thus, subject to creative and ongoing processes of negotiation and transformation.

We have argued so far that corporate expatriates and other mobile corporate professionals are very different from the classical strangers. Within the transnational professional space of the MNC, with its inbuilt cultural and organizational tensions, their status as strangers is significantly limited or even annihilated. Within the private sphere, their position of strangeness is significantly reduced, because their social position is not only shaped by local dynamics but also by different transnational spaces. Expatriate executives' social position in the local space is reconfigured both by the expansion of the MNC's transnational space into the private sphere through mobility policies as well as by their embeddedness in transnational expatriate communities. The particular situation of expatriate managers is characterized by their simultaneous embeddedness into both local and transnational spaces (Glick Schiller, Darieva, and Gruner-Domic 2011, 403) and, thus, into two different frames of belonging and identity—one that is transnational and professional and another that is territorial and national-cultural. It is never totally unambiguous as to what kind of expatriate manager they are, whether they are interested observers and learners in intercultural encounters acknowledging diversity and ambivalence or whether they manage problems and thus need to eliminate ambivalence (Bauman 1991). Defining a paradox as characterized by a "simultaneous presence of incongruent and contradictory patterns" (Quinn and Cameron 1988, 2), the simultaneous positioning of being both strangers and autochthons constitutes a highly paradoxical situation for corporate expatriates.[2]

Paradoxical Cosmopolitanisms

The paradox of simultaneously being a stranger and an autochthon fundamentally reconfigures expatriate managers' position toward cultural difference and their potential for evolving cosmopolitan reflexivity. And it has led to the emergence of paradoxical cosmopolitanisms. What came to light throughout the chapters is the fact that to conceive of corporate expatriates only in terms of either cosmopolitans or anti-cosmopolitans does not reflect the complexity of their everyday lives.

The data made visible a multiplicity of varying and contradictory modes of dealing with difference with varying degrees of exposure to and immersion with the Other going way beyond the dichotomy of cosmopolitan versus anti-cosmopolitan. Theoretically, this also raises the question whether cosmopolitanism can be conceived as a coherent disposition that social actors either hold or do not hold. Kendall, Woodward, and Skrbiš have pointed to the problems of understanding cosmopolitanism as a disposition, as "dispositions are consistent and homological structures—they are 'whole' in that they are structured and patterned in consistent ways, and relatively *inflexible*" (2009, 106, emphasis in original). We support their criticism, given that the idea of a consistent disposition does not take into account that the enactment of cosmopolitanism through located social practices shapes, transforms, or even corrodes cosmopolitanism itself. In the following, we first theorize empirically grounded modes of dealing with difference going beyond the dualistic opposition of cosmopolitan versus anti-cosmopolitan. In a second step, we theorize various paradoxes of corporate expatriates' practiced cosmopolitanisms.

Corporate expatriates' ways of dealing with difference display a significant amount of *diversity*. On the one hand, our ethnographic data made visible everyday practices deployed by the expatriate managers and their families that could be clearly identified as *anti-cosmopolitan*, as they actively devalued the Other and created symbolic and spatial boundaries to the Other. The corporate expatriates *avoided difference* altogether by retreating back to spatially segregated comfort zones of segregated residential spaces and national expatriate communities. They sent their children to national enclave schools and tried to keep their homes unpolluted by local objects and references. Or, when they could not avoid difference altogether—as at the workplace—they tried to *displace* and *control* difference by, for instance, delegitimizing local work practices and eliminating them from the office space either by *displacing employees* who were perceived as 'too local' or by *displacing local practices and aesthetics* from the office space. They hierarchized local working practices and their own working practices and used 'national culture' as a source of legitimation for the superiority of their own working practices and the enforcement thereof. They defined hierarchical cultural domains with nonnegotiable rules according to how they were defined by the global organizational culture of the MNCs. For them the cultural identity of their MNC's transnational social space was that of the company headquarters. Thus, they delegated the task of intercultural translation and of self-transformation to the local employees. They self-confidently assumed positions where the power of defining a situation laid with them. They clearly emphasized that only one practice was legitimate, whereas the other was not. This practice of displacing and delegitimizing different local practices is associated with closure rather than with cosmopolitan openness.

On the other hand, the ethnographic data also made visible practices that can be easily identified as being close to what had been defined as *cosmopolitan openness* to difference regarding dimensions of sociability, spatiality, and belonging. The expatriate managers in our study deployed everyday practices of *performing normality and undoing elite status* as well as of *deconstructing social distance* to cultural 'Others.' These corporate expatriates tried to *maximize spatial proximity and social proximity* to local nonelite groups and international expatriate groups with their choice of residence, modes of transportation in the urban space, and schools, as well as by consciously establishing networks crossing cultural boundaries at work and beyond. They actively worked on positioning themselves 'in the middle of China' or at least outside their national expatriate communities (Chapter 5). At their workplace, they countered their position as an autochthon of the transnational social space of the MNC and worked hard to perform their loyalty to the subsidiary and distance to the headquarters. They rejected *authoritarian modi of enforcing* their own practices on their local employees and instead put themselves into positions of learners, acknowledging their own knowledge gaps, which had the consequence of *transforming their own work practices* (Chapter 7). Additionally, they developed dialogic and nonhierarchical relations with their local coworkers, instead of just controlling and transforming the local practices. They integrated the cultural Other into the symbolic management and thereby created multi-referential office spaces (Chapter 5). They also undermined the culturalist interpretive scheme by denationalizing difference and employing various other interpretive schemes for explaining the differences between their local coworkers and themselves and conflicts between local management and the headquarters (Chapter 8). And last but not least, there were practices that simultaneously entailed both cosmopolitan and anti-cosmopolitan elements, such as engaging with local employees in a teacher-pupil relationship—which was the basis for intense interactions but at the same time in fact implied an inbuilt knowledge asymmetry (Chapter 7). Ethnographically exploring the everyday life of corporate expatriates has revealed the inadequacy of the dichotomy of cosmopolitan versus anti-cosmopolitan by making visible a *diversity* of modes of dealing with difference in everyday spatiality and sociability. The varying degrees of exposure to and immersion with the Other ask for a more differentiated analysis of the everyday lives of not only corporate expatriates but also other types of globally mobile professionals.

In very few of our cases, these opposed practices did assemble into coherent types of cosmopolitan or anti-cosmopolitan corporate expatriates, as the binary and rather simplistic images of mobile professionals in large parts of the existing literature suggest. However, most of the expatriate managers in our study—and this is the most interesting result of our research—*employed these very contradictory modes of dealing with the Other simultaneously.* This resulted in self-contradictory everyday practices that simultaneously revealed orientations of openness *and* distance to difference. The managers oscillated between immersion *and* closure and simultaneously made use of contradicting approaches to cultural difference. Whereas subscribing to the cultural superiority of the West, on the one hand, they championed cultural diversity and cosmopolitanism on the other. Sometimes they demanded that local employees be cosmopolitan translators whereas they themselves refused to assume such a position themselves. And finally, they were simultaneously using nationalizing and de-nationalizing interpretive schemes. In the following, we summarize and theorize the main paradoxes of practiced cosmopolitanisms found in the sociability and spatiality patterns of the corporate expatriates.

First, the ethnographic data revealed a *paradoxical entanglement of the professional and the private sphere.* All of the corporate expatriates in our sample emphasized their curiosity to experience something new and different and intended to be open to the local Other to at least some extent. However, they limited this curiosity for the Other to the private sphere of trying new food, using different modes of transportation, visiting touristic places, etc. But most interestingly, only very few of them translated this inclusive stance toward the Other into their own repertoire of practices in the professional sphere. We found that especially for the corporate expatriates in China, the professional sphere was not envisaged as a space for cosmopolitan encounters, but as a space where the Local needed to be controlled, transformed, and displaced. In the private sphere, many expatriate managers displayed a much higher degree of cosmopolitan openness and curiosity. Although the private sphere was shaped by the mobility regimes as elaborated earlier, this entanglement was highly complex. Expatriate managers had more room for maneuver outside the transnational social space of the MNC for negotiating cosmopolitan encounters with 'Others.' Thus, our findings clearly contradict the image of expatriate managers as moving in locally *embedded* professional spheres and locally *disembedded* private spheres, as is usually put forth in the expatriate literature. For instance, Beaverstock argued that corporate offices have a cosmopolitan character as "embedded workspaces," where expatriates interact with local colleagues, whereas locals were completely absent from the "disembedded home spaces" (2002, 536). In his study on expatriates in the financial sector in Singapore, he argued that "the expatriates' knowledge accumulation and dissemination is deeply embedded within their global—local corporate knowledge networks, cultural practices and spaces in their host country because of the interaction with 'Western educated/experienced' Singaporeans and clients alike" (ibid.). Our ethnographic approach, however, enabled us to draw a more complex and accurate picture. Because we did not rely solely on corporate expatriates' self-representations from interviews but instead observed them in their daily routines and were involved in less controllable, more ad-hoc conversations, we were able to go beyond the analysis of the mere physical presence of locals in the office space. We could not only see *whether* corporate expatriates interacted with locals but also *how* they did so. Our analysis of both networks and place making practices at the workplace revealed the anti-local and anti-cosmopolitan orientations and practices of expatriate managers at the workplace, as elaborated on in Chapter 8. Our ethnographic data also countered polarized and undifferentiated images of corporate expatriates as boundary spanners and of local employees as being confined to their locality. Especially the expatriate managers assigned to China actively tried to diminish their own boundary spanning work across language and cultural boundaries. We found two modes of how corporate expatriates in China limited their potentially risky and insecure boundary spanning position. They either delegated the actual work of boundary spanning to other local subordinates, mostly to those who were internationally experienced, or, if they were powerful enough, they even influenced the staffing policies of the local subsidiary in such a way that they created work environments for themselves where they could work primarily with other expatriates (of the same nationality), who then had to engage in boundary spanning work with local subordinates. In both cases, the existential insecurity resulting from the confrontation with unknown practices, as typical for Schütz's stranger, was decidedly curtailed. But even for the corporate executives assigned to the U.S., is was also the ethnographic perspective that revealed the limitations of an approach mainly focusing on the national composition of corporate expatriates' networks to grasp the intricacies of practiced cosmopolitanism in the work sphere. Although they were indeed embedded into dense networks with both local and expatriate superiors, coworkers, and subordinates, they made use of these networks in a way that created desynchronizations between formal and informal hierarchies and knowledge flows within the MNC (see Chapter 7). They were able to capitalize on their informal networks based on the shared national expatriate status which led to tensions with both higher ranking local and non-German expatriate managers, because they felt sidelined in important decision-making processes. Hence, our findings contribute a more differentiated view of expatriates as boundary spanners and shed light on the important role of other sorts of organizational actors at the subsidiaries (such as bilingual secretaries and local subordinates) in this respect.

Second, the corporate expatriates' practiced cosmopolitanism was paradoxical, because of a gendered inconsistency between the actual *practices of enabling, shaping, and stabilizing mobility* within expatriate couples, such as mobility work, local attachment work, and translocal attachment work, and the *practices of creating cosmopolitan sociabilities* (see Chapter 6). Comparing two differently gendered expatriate constellations, namely, *male expatriate managers* and their *accompanying wives*, and *female expatriate managers* and their *accompanying husbands*, our research clearly confirmed the existence of gender-specific "systems of responsibility" (Stadlbauer 2016, 171) regarding the stabilization of mobility. Women, be it as accompanying wives or female corporate expatriates, took over a significant amount of the mobility work, local attachment work, and most of the translocal attachment work. However, this mostly female local attachment work created sociabilities that were in most cases indeed rather anti-cosmopolitan and contributed to the stabilization of a national expatriate 'bubble.' As their families' mobility managers, accompanying wives focused not so much on the integration into the host country school system, but mainly on the reintegration into their home country. As their families' local networkers, they did not approach locals in order to acquire practical knowledge about the everyday life at the host locality, but instead primarily looked to others of their kind, who had gone through the same experiences, for advice. As their families' transnational networkers, they limited hospitality to friends and family from home, whereas hospitality to local 'Others' was rather neglected. In this constellation, female mobility work contributed both to the creation of a position of the autochthon within the transnational space of their national expatriate community and at the same time to the creation of the transient visitor position within the local space. In contrast, the sociabilities of the couples with a female manager and an accompanying husband reflect a higher, however still limited degree of openness. Accompanying husbands remained strangers in the predominantly female expatriate community and also, due to a lack of language knowledge, strangers in the social non-expatriate spaces around them. Surprisingly, these families had a dense network of friends transcending at least their own national 'bubble' and cultivated sociabilities including mainly other international expatriates and also to some extent, locals. This relatively greater openness was achieved either by friendships from the female manager's work context or by spaces such as the church group, where both partners were involved in networking. Thus, female managers' participation in establishing family friendships played a significant role. It was the less polarized gender-specific systems of responsibility (Stadlbauer 2016) with regard to mobility work and local and translocal attachment that apparently led to more open sociabilities.

Third, the type of *selective cosmopolitanism* that emerged from the ethnographic data is paradoxical in the sense that it combines the openness to cultural difference within international expatriate communities—characterized by a joint professional and religious culture—with the distance to difference with respect to the territorially defined culture of the host country. This inconsistency, created by the ambivalent situation of corporate expatriates and their dual frames of belonging, is based on the hierarchical distinction between different sorts of cultural 'Others' by the expatriate managers. This mode of managing meaning (Hannerz 1990) is characterized by a general cosmopolitan openness in the private sphere, but as a result of being part of an international expatriate community, the territorial culture of the host locality is excluded from the initial openness to difference. This specific form of inconsistency leads to a locally detached and selective cosmopolitanism based on a hierarchization of different cultural 'Others.' Our research thus supports the notion of "varying degrees and multitudes of cosmopolitanisms in everyday places" (Datta 2009, 353). Already Datta has pointed to the fact that, based on national, ethnic, and racial identity constructions, migrants differentiate between different categories of 'Others' and display contradictory orientations and practices toward these groups. In addition, Mulholland and Ryan (2015) have discussed such processes of distinction among certain segments of highly skilled French migrants in London who clearly did not want to belong to the national enclave 'bubble.' The contribution of our research lies in showing that such antinational practices and usages of place do not necessarily lead to a greater social immersion into the host country. Antinational aspirations can, however, be realized through another type of "encapsulated community" framed by a professional or religious identity.[3] Hannerz had spoken of the paradoxical interplay of mastery and surrender and of cosmopolitanism as a practice of voluntaristically selecting pieces from a variety of different cultures (Hannerz 2000, 103). Our data suggests that a general definition of cosmopolitanism as "openness to difference" in a Hannerz-like way, without taking into account the social and cultural location of the Other, is too vague, and the process of selecting goes much further than picking various parts from different cultures. The selecting is driven by longstanding ideas about the relative prestige of different national cultures.

The expatriate managers in our sample select some elements of specific cultures to be included into their cosmopolitan universe whereas rejecting others. They establish hierarchies of cultural 'Others' whereby those at the top are the ones who conform to their own professional experiences and belief systems. Cosmopolitan openness is thus constructed by closures toward other types of difference and groups of 'Others' (Jansen 2009). Typically, cosmopolitan openness and inclusiveness emerges in spaces where national difference is superseded by other nonnational identities, such as 'Christian believers' (see Chapter 5), or 'art lovers' (see Chapter 6). Such "communities based not on geography but on shared interests or 'affect' " contributed to the formation of cosmopolitan sociabilities (Szerszynski and Urry 2002, 474). Cosmopolitan sociabilities did not emerge predominantly through a widening of the spatial reach of one's identity from local to global, but through decentering the spatial, national dimension altogether. Cosmopolitan sociabilities were not based on the identity shift from 'national citizen' to 'world citizen,' but on the shift from 'national citizen' to several forms of intermediary identities. Without those spaces, no such inclusive identities as "citizen of the world" was available, and thus, corporate expatriates and the locals remained unrelated (ibid., 472).

Fourth, *unaccomplished cosmopolitanism* is characterized by inconsistencies between cosmopolitan ambitions and the way they are realized within specific local contexts. Many of our interview partners were well aware of the negative images of the ethnocentric, interculturally insensitive, and inappropriately privileged expatriate. Their narratives were full of descriptions of those 'other' expatriates, who behaved like 'King Kong' or 'military generals' without any respect for local employees (see Chapter 7) and who lived like tourists in 'holiday resorts' without any local social attachment (see Chapter 5). They were eager to differentiate themselves from those 'defective' corporate expatriates. In order to do so, they developed everyday practices of performing normality and undoing elite status as well as of deconstructing social distance to cultural 'Others.' As argued in Chapter 5, expatriate managers and their families pursued spatial proximity to local nonelite groups and international expatriate groups (for German expatriates in Singapore see Meier 2015, 70), and pursued social proximity to these groups by consciously establishing networks that crossed cultural boundaries. They sought to normalize luxury housing through alternative use of the house structure and used nonelite local means of transportation. They tried to translate their cosmopolitan orientation and aspiration into social and spatial practices. However, most of them failed. Possibilities for emphasizing their position as strangers and working against the institutional modification of their social and symbolical dislocation were limited. Despite their effort, they did not succeed in minimizing the social distance and building up sociabilities with the local population. Thus, frustrations and disappointments about the fact that they did not have local friends and that their everyday sociabilities were in fact not cosmopolitan formed a significant part of their narratives. However, the question as to why this spatial practice of self-distancing from the national or Western expatriate 'bubble' did not translate into cosmopolitan sociabilities remained unanswered. In previous studies, this discrepancy between aspirations and practices was discussed as having been the result of pragmatic choices by mobile professionals themselves. For example, in their study on highly skilled French migrants in London, Mulholland and Ryan (2015) explained the contradictions between cosmopolitan ambitions and practiced sociabilities with the local Other as the result of pragmatic decisions, such as sending their children to national enclave schools. In the context of non-privileged migration, the discrepancy between orientations and practices was explained by the lack of specific cultural capital such as language skills (Datta 2009). These are very valid arguments. However, our research indicates that there is more to it. One important factor mentioned by the managers interviewed for this book was that they were not able to smoothly 'blend in' into the local social context because of exclusionary practices of the locals themselves. In the U.S., expatriates felt they were being perceived as a kind of 'parvenu' by the local elite, in China they reported being perceived as different and even 'weird' by some locals they encountered. In both cases, the managers were confronted with practices of Othering and distancing by the local population (Walsh 2015). Our research therefore suggests that when taking the notion of "cosmopolitanism in practice" (Nowicka and Rovisco 2009b) seriously, it is necessary to investigate cosmopolitanism as a relational practice that is negotiated in specific encounters in specific spaces. This must, however, entail including not just one side of this relation into the analysis—in our case the expatriate managers—but also including the other/local side participating in this encounter, be it employees, colleagues, or neighbors. Thus, practiced cosmopolitanism understood as an encounter is always shaped by the agency of the Other, even for such powerful and privileged groups as corporate expatriates. The question of whether a cosmopolitan orientation can produce cosmopolitan sociabilities is a relational problem. It is embedded in mutual power relations and depends on how willing locals are to include corporate expatriates into their networks (Mao and Shen 2015, 1541). As Amit and Barber have pointedly formulated, "my cosmopolitan aspirations are dependent on finding or persuading other willing partners to join me in working out a set of measures for enacting that engagement" (2015, 546). Given that cosmopolitanism is an aspiration that depends on other people to be realized, Amit and Barber continue that it is "always liable to the possibility of being supported or being defeated by that dependence" (ibid., 548). Our ethnographic data about the 'unaccomplished cosmopolitans' made visible the uncertain relationship between cosmopolitan ambitions and their realization within the specific local contexts.

Fifth, the type of *conditional cosmopolitanism* displayed by the managers in our sample is paradoxical in so far as their general openness to the Other is at the same time accompanied by an attempt to control and reduce the amount of difference by only including local actors who themselves exhibit a certain distance from the local culture (see Chapters 5 and 10). Expatriate managers in our sample did indeed look to immerse themselves into the locality, but, at the same time, they tried to control this immersion as much as they could. They were intrigued by the Otherness of the locality as a sensory adventure, one that could be eaten, smelled, and consumed. The attractiveness of consuming the Other (Thompson and Tambyah 1999; Germann Molz 2007) lies in the fact that the place, time, and degree of exposure to the Other could easily be controlled by the expatriates themselves. At the same time, they were rather hesitant to include local 'Others' into their sociabilities. If they maintained friendships with local colleagues, they included only those who spoke their language and who had international migration trajectories. They embraced working with local colleagues, but only with those who themselves had international educational trajectories. MNCs and their partly transnationally educated local workforce constituted certain kinds of intermediary spaces that enabled corporate expatriates to engage in sociabilities with local coworkers and colleagues. However, these sociabilities were highly conditional in the sense that these local 'Others' had to first prove distance to the local culture in order to be considered for social inclusion. Only those coworkers who possessed international experience and proved to be less strange were integrated into the expatriate managers' networks.

Our ethnographic exploration of the everyday spatiality and sociability of expatriate managers' professional and private spheres showed that ambivalences and contradictions were the constitutive features of the everyday lives of most of the managers and their families who participated in this study (Beaverstock 2002; Ley 2004; Datta 2009; Kendall, Woodward, and Skrbiš 2009; Dharwadker 2011; Glick Schiller, Darieva, and Gruner-Domic 2011; van Bochove and Engbersen 2013). This overwhelming presence of ambivalences and inconsistencies, however, makes it necessary to rethink the question of how to conceive of cosmopolitanism in times inherently characterized by ambivalences (Bauman 1991). Cosmopolitanism cannot continue to be conceived of as a consistent disposition extending to all domains of everyday life, as has been the case in many studies on corporate expatriates and other migrants. Instead, it has become clear that it is necessary to theoretically integrate the empirical ambivalences into the very concept of cosmopolitanism itself. Cosmopolitanism is flexible and contradictory as it is "performed in particular contexts and settings as required" (Kendall, Woodward, and Skrbiš 2009, 107). Due to their simultaneous embeddedness in local and transnational spaces and their being both strangers and autochthons, collective identities of corporate expatriates are at the same time both intensified and transgressed in a cosmopolitan sense (Glick Schiller, Darieva, and Gruner-Domic 2011, 403). Whereas the research on corporate expatriates has usually focused on paradoxical *experiences* of expatriates and their strategies to solve these perceived paradoxes (Osland 2000; Osland

and Osland 2005; Russell and Dickie 2007), the paradoxes described in this book are significantly different. Our research approach revealed self-contradictory and thus paradoxical *practices* of corporate managers. These are not paradoxes that can be solved by individual expatriate managers through more reflexive reasoning; these are paradoxes that are systematically related to their situation of simultaneously being a stranger and autochthon both in the transnational social space of their MNCs as well as the local space by virtue of their embeddedness in expatriate communities.

This book contributes to a further theorization of the flexibility and inconsistency of cosmopolitanism with sound empirical research. First, it showed that definitions of cosmopolitanism as openness to an undifferentiated and placeless cultural Other fall short, because empirically, actors use differentiated and hierarchically structured concepts of the Other. Second, it uncovered an incongruence between discursive and practiced cosmopolitanism. This incongruence arises because cosmopolitanism, as a practice, only unfolds in encounters with the materiality and sociability of the Other, thus giving the Other a significant amount of power in shaping and defining this encounter, even to such an extent that the cosmopolitan ambition of one of the parties involved (locals, expatriates) can be severely sabotaged and thus not be translated into a practiced cosmopolitanism. Third, the findings indicated that cosmopolitanism is related to practices of controlling difference and is more likely to be found in individually controllable spheres of the everyday life—such as consumption or housing practices—than in the more complex spheres of sociability.

Notes

1 In the following, we will use the male form to talk about the ideal type of the stranger. However, empirically, this includes both women and men.
2 For the paradox lifeworlds of another group of mobile professionals, see Silke Roth's book on expatriates in humanitarian aid and development (2015).
3 *Transnational Pentecostal churches* created ambivalent "cosmopolitan moments" (Krause 2011, 430), as they served as spaces for practicing sociabilities beyond national and even Western communities, but were totally detached from the local population.

Bibliography

Adler, Patricia A., and Peter Adler. 1999. "Transience and the Postmodern Self: The Geographic Mobiltiy of Resort Workers." *Sociological Quarterly* 40 (1): 31–58. doi:10.1111/j.1533-8525.1999.tb02357.x.
Amit, Vered. 2015. "Circumscribed Cosmopolitanism: Travel Aspirations and Experiences." *Identities* 22 (5): 551–68. doi:10.1080/1070289X.2014.975709.
Amit, Vered, and Pauline G. Barber. 2015. "Mobility and Cosmopolitanism: Complicating the Interaction Between Aspiration and Practice." *Identities* 22 (5): 543–50. doi:10.1080/1070289X.2014.975714.

Bauman, Zygmunt. 1991. *Modernity and Ambivalence*. Ithaca, N.Y: Cornell University Press.

Bauman, Zygmunt. 2000. *Liquid Modernity*. Cambridge: Polity Press

Bauman, Zygmunt. 2005. *Liquid Life*. Cambridge: Polity Press.

Beaverstock, Jonathan. 2002. "Transnational Elites in Global Cities: British Expatriates in Singapore's Financial District." *Geoforum* 33 (4): 525–38. doi:10.1016/S0016-7185(02)00036-2.

Beck, Ulrich. 2006. *The Cosmopolitan Vision*. Cambridge: Polity Press.

Beck, Ulrich. 2009. "Mobility and the Cosmopolitan Perspective." In *Tracing Mobilities: Towards a Cosmopolitan Perspective*, edited by Weert Canzler, Vincent Kaufmann, and Sven Kesselring, 25–35. Farnham, Burlington: Ashgate.

Boltanski, Luc, and Eve Chiapello. 2007. *The New Spirit of Capitalism*. London: Verso.

Datta, Ayona. 2009. "Places of Everyday Cosmopolitanisms: East European Construction Workers in London." *Environment and Planning A* 41 (2): 353–70. doi:10.1068/a40211.

Dharwadker, Vinay. 2011. "Diaspora and Cosmopolitanism." In *The Ashgate Research Companion to Cosmopolitanism*, edited by Maria Rovisco and Magdalena Nowicka, 125–44. Aldershot: Ashgate.

Elliott, Anthony, and John Urry. 2010. *Mobile Lives*. London and New York: Routledge.

Germann Molz, Jennie. 2007. "Eating Difference: The Cosmopolitan Mobilities of Culinary Tourism." *Space and Culture* 10 (1): 77–93. doi:10.1177/1206331206296383.

Glick Schiller, Nina, Tsypylma Darieva, and Sandra Gruner-Domic. 2011. "Defining Cosmopolitan Sociability in a Transnational Age: An Introduction." *Ethnic and Racial Studies* 34 (3): 399–418. doi:10.1080/01419870.2011.533781.

Hannerz, Ulf. 1990. "Cosmopolitans and Locals in World Culture." In *Global Culture: Nationalism, Globalization and Modernity. A Theory, Culture & Society Special Issue*, edited by Mike Featherstone, 237–51. London, Newbury Park, and New Delhi: Sage.

Hannerz, Ulf. 2000. *Transnational Connections: Culture, People, Places*. London and New York: Routledge.

Jansen, Stef. 2009. "Cosmopolitan Openings and Closures in Post-Yugoslav Antinationalism." In Nowicka and Rovisco 2009a, 75–92.

Kanter, Rosabeth M. 1995. *World Class: Thriving Locally in the Global Economy*. New York: Simon & Schuster.

Kendall, Gavin, Ian Woodward, and Zlatko Skrbiš. 2009. *The Sociology of Cosmopolitanism: Globalization, Identity, Culture and Government*. London: Palgrave Macmillan UK.

Krause, Kristine. 2011. "Cosmopolitan Charismatics? Transnational Ways of Belonging and Cosmopolitan Moments in the Religious Practice of New Mission Churches." *Ethnic and Racial Studies* 34 (3): 419–35. doi:10.1080/01419870.2011.537355.

Ley, David. 2004. "Transnational Spaces and Everyday Lives." *Transactions of the Institute of British Geographers* 29 (2): 151–64. doi:10.1111/j.0020-2754.2004.00122.x.

Mao, Jina, and Yan Shen. 2015. "Cultural Identity Change in Expatriates: A Social Network Perspective." *Human Relations* 68 (10): 1533–56. doi:10.1177/0018726714561699.

Meier, Lars. 2015. "Learning the City by Experiences and Images: German Finance Managers' Encounters in London and Singapore." In Meier 2015, 59–74.

Meier, Lars, ed. 2015. *Migrant Professionals in the City: Local Encounters, Identities and Inequalities*. New York: Routledge.

Mulholland, Jon, and Louise Ryan. 2015. " 'Londres Accueil': Mediations of Identity and Place Amongst the French Highly Skilled in London." In Meier 2015, 157–74.

Nowicka, Magdalena. 2006. *Transnational Professionals and Their Cosmopolitan Universes*. Frankfurt/Main, and New York: Campus.

Nowicka, Magdalena, and Ramin Kaweh. 2009. "Looking at the Practice of UN Professionals: Strategies for Managing Difference and the Emergence of a Cosmopolitan Identity." In Nowicka and Rovisco 2009a, 51–71.

Nowicka, Magdalena, and Maria Rovisco, eds. 2009a. *Cosmopolitanism in practice*. Aldershot, Burlington: Ashgate.

Nowicka, Magdalena, and Maria Rovisco. 2009b. "Introduction: Making Sense of Cosmopolitanism." In Nowicka and Rovisco 2009a, 1–16.

Ong, Aihwa. 2000. *Flexible Citizenship: The Cultural Logics of Transnationality*. Durham: Duke University Press.

Osland, Joyce. 2000. "The Journey Inward: Expatriate Hero Tales and Paradoxes." *Human Resource Management* 39 (2&3): 227–38. doi:10.1002/1099-050X (200022/23)39:2/3<227::AID-HRM11>3.0.CO;2-R

Osland, Joyce, and Asbjorn Osland. 2005. "Expatriate Paradoxes and Cultural Involvement." *International Studies of Management & Organization* 35 (4): 91–114.

Ossewaarde, Marinus. 2007. "Cosmopolitanism and the Society of Strangers." *Current Sociology* 55 (3): 367–88. doi:10.1177/0011392107076081.

Quinn, Robert E., and Kim S. Cameron. 1988. *Paradox and Transformation: Toward a Theory of Change in Organization and Management*. Cambridge: Ballinger Pub. Co.

Radice, Martha. 2014. "Micro-Cosmopolitanisms at the Urban Scale." *Identities* 22 (5): 588–602. doi:10.1080/1070289X.2014.975711.

Roth, Silke. 2015. *The Paradoxes of Aid Work: Passionate Professionals*. New York: Routledge.

Russell, Roger C., and Laurence Dickie. 2007. "Paradoxical Experiences of Expatriate Managers in Indonesia." *Journal of Diversity Management* 2 (2): 17–28. doi:10.19030/jdm.v2i1.5002

Salverda, Tijo, and Jon Abbink. 2013. "Introduction: An Anthropological Perspective on Elite Powers and the Cultural Politics of Elites." In *The Anthropology of Elites: Power, Culture, and the Complexities of Distinction*, edited by Jon Abbink and Tijo Salverda, 1–28. New York: Palgrave Macmillan.

Sassen, Saskia. 1998. *Globalization and Its Discontents*. New York: New Press.

Schütz, Alfred. 1944. "The Stranger: An Essay in Social Psychology." *American Journal of Sociology* 49 (6): 499–507. doi:10.1086/219472

Sennett, Richard. 1999. *The Corrosion of Character: The Personal Consequences of Work in the New Capitalism*. New York: Norton.

Simmel, Georg. 1950. "The Stranger." In *The Sociology of Georg Simmel*, edited by Kurt Wolff, 402–8. New York: Free Press.

Sklair, Leslie. 2001. *The Transnational Capitalist Class*. Oxford: Blackwell.

Spiegel, Anna. 2010. *Contested Public Spheres: Female Activism and Identity Politics in Malaysia*. Wiesbaden: VS Verlag für Sozialwissenschaften.

Stadlbauer, Johanna. 2016. "Privilegierte Migration und Geschlechterverhältnisse: Expatriate Spouses in Österreich." In *Migration und Integration – wissenschaftliche Perspektiven aus Österreich*, edited by Jennifer Carvill Schellenbacher, Julia Dahlvik, Heinz Fassmann, and Christoph Reinprecht, 167–82. Vienna: Vienna University Press.

Szerszynski, Bronislaw, and John Urry. 2002. "Cultures of Cosmopolitanism." *Sociological Review* 50 (4): 461–82. doi:10.1111/1467-954X.00394

Szerszynski, Bronislaw, and John Urry. 2006. "Visuality, Mobility and the Cosmopolitan: Inhabiting the World from Afar." *The British Journal of Sociology* 57 (1): 113–31. doi:10.1111/j.1468-4446.2006.00096.x.

Thompson, Craig J., and Siok K. Tambyah. 1999. "Trying to Be Cosmopolitan." *Journal of Consumer Research* 26 (3): 214–41. doi:10.1086/209560.

Urry, John. 2007. *Mobilities*. Cambridge: Polity Press.

van Bochove, Marianne, and Godfried Engbersen. 2015. "Beyond Cosmopolitanism and Expat Bubbles: Challenging Dominant Representations of Knowledge Workers and Trailing Spouses." *Population, Space and Place* 21 (4): 295–309. doi:10.1002/psp.1839

Walsh, Katie. 2015. "British Transnational (Be)longing: Emplacement in the Life of Skilled Migrants in Dubai." In Meier 2015. 232–250

Appendix
Overview Over Ethnographic Cases

Overall Sample

Home country	*Host country*	*Gender*	*Industry*
Germany: 16 U.S.: 13	China: 13 Germany: 6 U.S.: 10	Male: 25 Female: 4	Automotive: 18 Construction: 1 Communication Technology: 1 Producer Services: 3 Food: 1 Mechanical Engineering: 2 Medical Technology: 2 Transport: 1

Total number of cases: 29

German Managers in China

	Alias	*Age group*	*Marital and family status*	*Management level*
1	Mr. Dittrich	50–59	married with children	top
2	Mrs. Frank	40–49	married with children	lower
3	Mr. Hoffmann	25–29	single	middle
4	Mr. Schmidt	40–49	married with children	middle
5	Mr. Simon	50–59	married	top
6	Mr. Winkelmann	40–49	married with children	middle

German Managers in the U.S.

	Alias	Age group	Marital and family status	Management level
1	Mr. Gruber	40–49	married with children	middle
2	Mr. Jäger	40–49	married with children	middle
3	Mr. Klett	40–49	married with children	middle
4	Mr. Novak	40–49	married with children	middle
5	Mr. Pätzold	40–49	married with children	middle
6	Mr. Rossi	40–49	married with children	middle
7	Mr. Scheffer	30–39	single	middle
8	Mr. Schwarz	40–49	married with children	middle
9	Mr. Walter	50–59	single with children	middle
10	Mr. Weber	30–39	single	top

U.S.-American Managers in China

	Alias	Age group	Marital and family status	Management level
1	Mr. Barnett	40–49	in a relationship	middle
2	Mr. Foster	40–49	married with children	middle
3	Mr. Kelly	60–65	married with children	middle
4	Mrs. Kelly	60–65	married with children	middle
5	Mr. Phillips	40–49	married with children	middle
6	Mr. Schulz	40–49	married with children	middle
7	Mr. Zacher	50–59	married with children	top

U.S.-American Managers in Germany

	Alias	Age group	Marital and family status	Management level
1	Mrs. Carter	30–39	married with children	lower
2	Mr. Fisher	50–59	married with children	middle
3	Mr. Nolan	30–39	in a relationship	lower
4	Mr. Parker	30–39	single	lower
5	Mr. Smith	40–49	married with child	top
6	Mrs. Williams	40–49	married with children	top

Index

accompanying husbands 107, 111–14, 116, 121, 123, 126–8, 129, 226
accompanying wives 107, 117–20, 124–6, 226
agency 3, 5; boundary spanners 43, 50n9, 55–6; of expatriates 47–8, 73, 221; managers and 29; role of 182–3; social practices and 6–7; structured and structuring 41, 45
ambassador, role 43
anti-cosmopolitan: boundary makers 48; cosmopolitan or 87, 101, 160, 165, 175, 216, 222–6; elite 67–72; parochial 2–3, 68; rejection of 156
anti-cosmopolitanism 3, 68

bear, role 44
belonging 5, 8
boundary making 159
boundary roles: modes of making 138; *see also* controller and transfer agent role; coordinator and negotiator role, learner and information seeker role, ambassador, task coordinator, scout, bear, bumblebee, spider
boundary spanner 1, 48, 159; expatriate managers in MNCs 42–4; MNC as transnational social space 137; from role-taking to role-making 44–8
boundary spanning 41; concept 42, 50n8; controller and transfer agent role 137, 139–46; coordinator and negotiator role 137, 147–55; cosmopolitanism and 156–7; exerting influence 43–4, 46, 50n9; functions of 43–4; ideal-typical intraorganizational roles 137–9, 155–6; individual subsidiaries 43,

50n7; interests and orientations 46–7; personnel 49n5; processing information 43, 45–6, 50n9
boundary spanning modes: expatriate manager as chameleon 138, 151–5; expatriate manager as service provider 138, 148–51, 154–5; expatriate manager as start-up entrepreneur 138, 142–6; expatriate manager as teacher 138, 139–42, 145–6; modes of making controller and transfer agent role 145–6; modes of making coordinator and negotiator role 154–5
'bubble' thesis *see* expatriate 'bubble' thesis
bumblebees, role 44

care work 111–12, 129
chameleon: expatriate manager as 138, 151–4; mode of making coordinator and negotiator role 154–5
China 9; cosmopolitanism of German manager in 169–74; cultural differences with Germany 161–5; dimension of difference in relating to culture 190–1; expatriate manager as teacher 139–42, 145–6; expatriate manager in 70–1; German managers in 235; German-shaped employees in 170–3; global mobility policies 191–2; as host country 181, 185–96, 207–9; housing 188–90; images of 185–8; leisure time in 190–1; material-symbolic properties of 188–92; national-cultural differences with Germany 165–9; properties as host country 185–96; social structure and spatial arrangement

192–5; space making and practicing cosmopolitanism in 195–6; U.S.-American managers in 236
church service: Christian congregation 190; Pentecostal Church 91–2, 102
conditional cosmopolitanism 97–100, 102, 229–30
contact zone, concept of 160, 176n1
contradictory environmental demands 27
controller and transfer agent role: boundary spanning 137, 139–46; expatriate manager as start-up entrepreneur 138, 142–5; expatriate manager as teacher 138, 139–42; two modes of making 145–6; *see also* boundary spanning
coordinator and negotiator role: boundary spanning in 137, 147–55; expatriate manager as chameleon 138, 151–4; expatriate manager as service provider 138, 148–51; two modes of making 154–5; *see also* boundary spanning
corporate expatriates: conditional cosmopolitanism 229–30; dealing with diversity 223; ethnographic approach to 7–9; membership in transitional expatriate communities 220–2; membership in transnational social spaces 218–20; position as strangers 220–1; practiced cosmopolitanism 226–7; selective cosmopolitanism 227–8; temporality 217–18; unaccomplished cosmopolitanism 228–9
corporate top management 25
cosmopolitan: characterizing 65, 75n16; expatriate manager as member of elite 61–7; global managers 17; openness 223; sociability 91
cosmopolitanism 2, 7, 64–5; asymmetrical 169–74; boundary spanning modes and 156–7; conditional 97–100, 102, 229–30; cultural diversity and 161–5; definition 4; demanding, while rejecting one's own 169–74; disembedded urban 208; everyday life beyond bubble and 86–92; gendered division of labor 105; mobility and 83, 215; mobility and connectivity 105; paradoxical

222–31; practiced 4–5, 85, 94, 159, 179; selective 87–92, 102, 227–8; theorizing corporate expatriate 3–4; unaccomplished 92–7, 102, 228–9
cost of living allowance (COLA) 57
country managers 24
creative actors, expatriate managers as 44–8, 49
cultural contact zone 135; concept of 160; cultural differences in 161–5; German-shaped employees 170–3
cultural diversity, cosmopolitanism and 161–5
cultural identity: asymmetrical cosmopolitanism 169–74; cultural standards 176n2; German-shaped employees 170–3; office space 159–60, 174–6

disembedded urban cosmopolitanism 195–6, 208
duality of space 210n5

elite 'bubble' 97–8
embeddedness: degree of, in local environment 34n5; of expatriates in non-work environment 55; multilayered societal 20, 25–7; simultaneous, in local and transnational spaces 230–1; in transnational communities 222
entrepreneur: expatriate manager as start-up 138, 142–5; mode of making controller and transfer agent role 145–6
ethnography: overview of cases 235–6; study of expatriates 7–9; *see also* focused ethnography; global ethnography; globography; go-alongs; multi-sited ethnography
everyday life: conditional cosmopolitanism 97–100; entanglement with professional sphere 224–6; expatriate bubble thesis 86–7; power of locality 92–7; relating to cultural Others 215–16; selective cosmopolitanism 87–92; sociality of 83, 85–6, 230–1; spatiality 83, 85–6, 97, 230–1; unaccomplished cosmopolitanism 92–7
expatriate 'bubble life' 102, 208
expatriate 'bubble' thesis 56; as member of parochial

anti-cosmopolitan elite 67–72; highlighting the hypernationalized 71; practices of dominance 69–71; self-exclusion from local spaces 68–9
expatriate cosmopolitanism 3–4
expatriate manager 1, 25; boundary role in multinational corporations (MNCs) 42–4; as creative actors 44–8; empirical analyses 10; global mobility policies of MNCs 56–61; as learner and information seeker 137; as member of cosmopolitan world class 61–7; multinational corporations (MNCs) 19–21; non-work sphere 10, 83; role in transnationally integrated MNCs 32–3; star role of 1; *see also* boundary spanning; everyday life

family mobility manager 108, 111–14, 116
female expatriate managers 105, 106, 129, 226; *see also* gendered mobility
focused ethnography 8
functional managers 24–5

gendered division of labor 105–7; mobility work 107–8
gendered mobility: accompanying husbands 105, 106, 129, 226; accompanying wives 105–6, 128–9, 226; female expatriates 105, 106, 129, 226; gender relations between couples 106; work 107–8, 129–31
German Ladies Regulars' Table (*Stammtisch*) 118
Germany 9; cosmopolitanism of manager in China 169–74; cultural differences with China 161–5; expatriate manager as chameleon 151–4; expatriate manager as service provider 148–51; expatriate manager as start-up entrepreneur 142–5; German-shaped employees in China 170–3; as host country 181, 202–7, 207–9; images of 202–4; material-symbolic properties 204–5; national-cultural differences with China 165–9; practiced cosmopolitanism 209; sample U.S.-American expatriate manager in 211–12n24; social structure and spatial arrangement 205–6; space making and practicing

cosmopolitanism in 206–7; U.S.-American managers in 236
Ghoshal, Sumantra 21
global business managers 24
global enterprise 22
global ethnography 11n8
global expatriate 'bubble' 90, 101
global industry 26
global integration 1, 20, 22, 29, 64, 165, 175
global managers 17, 159
global mobility policies of MNCs 55–6; corporate expatriates 220–2; mobility regimes 57; social positions of expatriate managers 56–61
Global North 185, 196, 198–9, 205, 209, 218
Global Relocation Trends Survey (2012) 49n2
Global South 182, 192, 196, 209, 218, 219
globography 8
go-alongs 8–9
Grounded Theory 11n8

home-country approach 57, 58–9, 74n7, 220
host countries: boundary spanning modes 145–6; China 185–96; comparing rates of expatriates 181–2; comparison of 182–5, 207–9; host country approach 5, 74n6; image of 184; material-symbolic properties 184; overview of cases 235–6; practicing cosmopolitanism 181, 182; social structure of 184–5; spacing modes 183–4; *see also* China; Germany; United States
house hunting, look-and-see trip 57, 108–9
housing allowance 57, 198
hypernationalized communities of transnationals 71, 72

impatriates 10n1, 211–12n24
incorporated wife, concept of 75n12, 131n1
information seeker *see* learner and information seeker role
institutional pulls, MNCs balancing contradicting 25–7
interests, MNCs balancing contradicting 27–9

International Business (IB) 1, 2, 20, 21,
   25, 48, 50n8, 55–6, 61, 181–2
international enterprise 21–2
International Human Resource
   Management (IHRM) 29, 33,
   41–2, 48–9, 55–8, 60, 75n11, 106,
   181–2
international schools 59, 93, 120, 123,
   190, 194, 198, 211n18
isomorphic pulls 26, 34n8

learner and information seeker, role;
   learning by doing 167–8
literature *see* International Business
   (IB); International Human Resource
   Management (IHRM)
local adaptation 165, 175
local attachment work 107, 117;
   gendered 116–17; in nontraditional
   gender constellation 120–3; in
   traditional gender constellation
   117–20
local elite 'bubble' 97–8
look-and-see trip 108–9

management models, expatriate
   209–10n2
mixed elite 'bubbles' 101
mobility regimes, concept of 57
mobility work: concept of 108;
   gendered 107–8; in nontraditional
   gender constellation 111–16; in
   traditional gender constellation
   108–11; policies for expatriates in
   China 191–2
multinational corporations (MNCs)
   1–3; balancing contradicting
   institutional pulls 25–7; balancing
   contradicting interests 27–9;
   balancing contradicting strategic
   goals in transnationally integrated
   21–5; co-constructing MNC as
   transnational social space 29–32;
   expatriate manager as boundary
   spanner in 42–4; expatriate
   managers in 19–21; global mobility
   policies of 55–6; role of expatriates
   in transnationally integrated 32–3;
   tensions and contradictions in 20,
   21; as transnational social spaces
   5–6, 20, 21, 175, 218–22
multinational enterprise 22, 23, 50n7
multi-sited ethnography 8

national 'bubble', 92
national expatriate 'bubbles' 102
networks: including Chinese culture
   194–5; nationally/ethnically
   homogeneous 193–4; transnational
   194
Newcomer Committees 118
New Institutionalism in Organizational
   Analysis 26
non-work sphere 10, 83

office space: cultural identity of
   159–60, 174–6; *see also*
   professional sphere
organizational field 28, 34n7–8, 57, 64
Others: conditional cosmopolitanism
   229–30; cosmopolitanism and
   5, 225–6; corporate expatriates
   interacting with 215–19; cultural
   4, 10n4, 65, 88–9, 223–4;
   deconstructing social distance to
   223; everyday life 215–16, 222–3;
   mobility allowing interactions with
   65; orientations of expatriations
   to 55, 61, 68; practiced
   cosmopolitanism 226–7; practices of
   Chinese 98–100, 102, 190; selective
   cosmopolitanism 87–9, 227–8; social
   segregation of 208; social structure
   in China 193–5, 211n18; types of
   cultural 88–9; spatial arrangement
   of Chinese 192–5; as strangers 221;
   unaccomplished cosmopolitanism
   228–9

parochial jet-setters 73, 85
practiced cosmopolitanism 4–5, 85, 94,
   159, 179; in China 195–6; corporate
   expatriates 226–7; in Germany
   206–7; host countries impacting
   mode of 181; in United States 201–2
product-division managers 24
professional sphere 10, 135, 159;
   defining negotiable and nonnegotiable
   cultural domains 161–5; demanding
   cosmopolitanism of others while
   rejecting own 169–74; differences
   in workplaces 174–6; entanglement
   with private sphere 224–6; life
   beyond cosmopolitanism 160–1;
   nationalizing and denationalizing
   difference 165–9; transnational
   space 175

scout, role 43, 129
selective cosmopolitanism 87–92, 102, 227–8
service provider: expatriate manager as 138, 148–51; mode of making coordinator and negotiator role 154–5
sociability 4, 8, 85–6; diversity in 102; expatriates 89–90, 94–5, 96, 99–100
social practice theories 6–7
social segregation, host country 208
social spaces 5; concept of 10–11n5; corporate expatriates in transnational 218–20
sociological role theory 41
space/spacing: definition of 183; host localities 183–4; housing in China 188–90; space making in China 195–6; space making in Germany 206–7; space making in U.S. 201–2
spatiality 4–5, 8, 85–6; of everyday life 101; of expatriates' everyday life 87–8, 93, 96, 97–8
spatially distancing 87
spider, role 44
start-up entrepreneur: expatriate manager as 138, 142–5; mode of making controller and transfer agent role 145–6
structural-functional role theory 44
structuration, Giddens' theory of 73, 210n5
subsidiaries: boundaries of individual 43, 50n7; embeddedness of 34n5

task coordinator, role 44
teacher: expatriate manager as 138, 139–42; mode of making controller and transfer agent role 145–6
theoretical generalization 9
tourist/tourism: China 186, 190; Germany 203; United States 197
trailing spouses 75n12, 90, 105, 122, 204; *see also* accompanying wives; gendered mobility
transfer coalitions, role of 35n11
transitory elite 74, 76n23
translocal attachment work 107; gendered 123–4; in nontraditional gender constellation 126–8; in traditional gender constellation 124–6

transnational capitalist class (TCC) 2, 61–2, 66–7
transnational elite: cosmopolitan orientations 62, 63–5; global managers 17; homogeneous lifestyles of 62–3; hypermobility of 65; luxurious consumption spaces 65; transnational networks 62, 63
transnational elite thesis 56; expatriate manager as member of cosmopolitan world class 61–7
transnational enterprise 22–4
transnationalism 30
transnationally integrated MNCs, role of expatriate managers in 32–3
transnational social space: co-constructing the MNC as 29–32; corporate expatriates membership in 218–20; definition 30; MNCs as 5–6, 20, 21, 175, 218–22

unaccomplished cosmopolitanism 92–7, 102, 228–9
United States 9; expatriate manager as chameleon 151–4; expatriate manager as service provider 148–51; expatriate manager as start-up entrepreneur 142–5; expatriate manager as teacher 139–42, 145–6; German managers in 236; as host country 181, 196–202, 207–9; housing 198; images of 196–8; leisure time 198–9; material-symbolic properties 198–9; practiced cosmopolitanism 208; social structure and spatial arrangement 199–201; space making and practicing cosmopolitanism in 201–2

Western dominance 70
Western expatriate 'bubble' 90, 96, 101
work *see* local attachment work; mobility work; translocal attachment work
workplaces *see* professional sphere
world class 2, 48, 61–6, 190
Worldwide Survey of International Assignment Policies and Practices (WIAPP) 58–9